HOMER

HOMER

The Poetry of the Past

ANDREW FORD

Cornell University Press

Ithaca and London

First published 1992 by Cornell University Press.

International Standard Book Number 0-8014-2700-2
Library of Congress Catalog Card Number 91-55543
Printed in the United States of America
Librarians: Library of Congress cataloging information
appears on the last page of the book.

patri optimo manibusque optimae matris

CONTENTS

vii

ACKNOWLEDGMENTS

Like Homer, I could not tell nor could I name all those from whom I have learned in the course of writing this book. For a peripatetic academic, acknowledgments must be an exercise in synecdoche. This work began with a version of its second chapter, which was presented at a symposium at Smith College honoring George E. Dimock, Jr., on the occasion of his retirement in 1985. It is a pleasure to reiterate my thanks to George for many hours of generous and learned conversation on Homer, and to the members of the Classics Department at Smith, who, along with friends in many departments, afforded an ongoing interdisciplinary discussion that was ideal fare for a new Ph.D. I am also grateful to the Andrew Mellon Foundation for its helpful program of postdoctoral fellowships which allowed me to carry on work at Cornell University in 1984–1986. There Pietro Pucci, both in his seminar on the *Odyssey* and as chair of a welcoming department, orchestrated a reception for a former student that was lavish in every respect. Audiences at Brown University and the University of Virginia helped sharpen some of my conclusions, and I thank Michael Putnam and Jenny Strauss Clay for invitations in behalf of those departments. Finally, I doubt that I could have completed the manuscript and incorporated the suggestions of Greg Thalmann for Cornell University Press without the support and encouragement of my Classics colleagues at Princeton University.

A. F.

AUTHOR'S NOTE

Inasmuch as my inquiry depends on appreciating Homer's ideas in his own terms, I have transliterated some Greek words and phrases. I have generally Latinized the consonants (e.g., *chi* becomes *ch*), and used *ê* and *ô* to signal Greek *eta* and *omega* respectively. I have omitted accents where the form is unambiguous. But I have not been consistent where the literature on a word uses predominantly its Greek form (e.g., *kleos*). I have primarily sought readability, with the idea that the Greekless reader would be able to continue with less distraction (even perceiving English cognates more clearly) and the classicist would divine the form in question with little discomfort. The same applies to the transliteration of Greek names, where I have often preferred the more familiar Latin spellings.

All translations are my own and are designed simply as an aid to the reader. It will be quickly seen that any resemblance between my translations and verse is purely illusory. Eloquence had to be sacrificed to an attempt to repeat in English significant words that the Greek repeats and sometimes to reflect the order of words in the line. It is my hope that interested readers will want to check my interpretations against the Greek or better translations; thus I have tried as far as possible to make the lines of my translation correspond to the lines of the original, even at times reproducing in

English the word order of the Greek line, especially in Chapter 1 where such order is often significant.

I have used Allen's (1946) text in citing Homer and the Homeric hymns, and followed West (1966, 1978) and Merkelbach and West (1967) for Hesiod. For other poets I have indicated the edition used with abbreviations (listed alphabetically in the Bibliography); it should be noted that "Page" refers to his *Poetae melici Graeci* (1962); fragments from his *Supplementum lyricis Graecis* (1974) are indicated by *SLG*.

HOMER

INTRODUCTION

He was their servant (some say he was blind),
Who moved among their faces and their things:
Their feelings gathered in him like a wind
And sang. They cried "It is a god that sings."
—W. H. Auden, *Sonnets from China*

After reading the Homeric poems, and indeed after reading interpretations of them, I cannot help asking about Homer and
wondering what he thought he was doing. For to the extent that
the poems themselves or interpretations of them persuade me that
they are aesthetic objects, that they are cunningly wrought artifacts
with a coherent literary meaning governed by a command of rhetorical effects (that is, that they are like what academic criticism
since the nineteenth century has taken poetry to be), I am troubled
by what we know of the history and origin of these texts. Though
much is cloudy, it is now generally acknowledged that our *Iliad* and
Odyssey represent only the final outcome, a fixing by writing, of a
long-standing art of oral performance and composition. For centuries before this transcription took place (and we are not sure
whether it was in the eighth century or the sixth, or whether a
master poet wrote it himself or dictated it or stood in line to give
his contribution before some tyrant's art committee), the sum and
substance of these poems and of all their antecedents, variants,
and sequels, were only a series of changing oral performances by
many singers in many parts of Greece. It is not difficult to conceive
that the very idea of poetry may have been profoundly different in
a milieu where stable texts were never the primary and definitive
form of a song and where each performer presented himself only

as the spokesman of a tradition and not as an artistically gifted individual.

Along such lines Eric Havelock and Albert Lord have powerfully claimed that we misread our Homer as a literary text when it was originally nothing of the sort. Their work has been controversial in some respects, but it is at least certain that we cannot assume a priori that such an art, answering the needs of such a different society and formed in what was to some extent a different medium, should have intuited the same values and aspired to the same effects as we see or seek in poetry now. Hence, calling Homer for the moment the one poet, or the two poets, through whom, speaking or writing, rough but recognizable approximations of the *Iliad* and *Odyssey* first came into being, I cannot help wondering what on earth he was about and whether "poetry" meant for him and his audiences what it has meant for us.

Provoked by Homer, the reader of poetry then turns historian of the idea of poetry and returns to the poems to ask what it was to be a singer of songs in that world. But of course Homer is hardly to be found: beyond the notorious historical problems of his identity and even existence, there are major theoretical difficulties in looking for the poet behind the poem. New Criticism has long forbidden us to consult the putative author for the meaning of a text; structuralism has added that we can never emerge from the labyrinth of words to reach our author; and deconstruction warns us that if we got there nobody would be home. Yet if we must forgo trying to find the flesh-and-blood bard who, in any of the dozen or so Ionian cities that claimed him in antiquity, once sang these songs, it is possible to derive from these texts a good deal of information about the nature and function of poetry in that time and place. In fact, the Homeric "view" or "idea" or "conception" of poetry, as it must be cautiously named, is by now a well-established subfield in Homeric studies and in histories of criticism.

Once the question about Homer becomes a question about the view of poetry found in the poems, we are able to follow many philologists, historians, and students of comparative epic who have secured from these nearly anonymous poems an inventory of important statements about poetry and its place in society. The best of these studies manage to interpret these passages without imposing anachronistic literary categories on them, keeping the discussion in terms derived from the epics themselves or at least in terms not obviously inappropriate to an oral poet's milieu. This caution is necessary because our own ideas of what poetry is have been deeply influenced by nineteenth-century romantic idealism and eighteenth-century aesthetics. And if we seek a critical perspective closer in time to the epics, we can get no further back than the fifth century B.C.E., a time when the oral culture of Greece was waning and its earlier productions were being reseen through new sciences of language such as rhetoric and philosophy.[1] But if we are willing to question our most fundamental literary categories as we proceed, a vigilant reading of these poems in their archaic context can yield the Homeric chapter in what Robert Curtius called the "history of the theory of poetry"; on the basis of a close study of the terms for "poetry," its kinds and parts, we can follow Curtius and study Homer's theory of poetry, his "concept of the nature and function of the poet and of poetry, in distinction from poetics which has to do with the technique of poetical composition."[2]

Valuable as work on Homeric and archaic Greek poetics has been, I cannot agree with a colleague who has charmingly remarked, "Most of what can be said about the significance of Demodocus and Phemius, the so-called bards, and Odysseus, bard manqué, has been said by now, some of it thoughtfully."[3] For I have found that what has been said suffers from incompleteness: too often it focuses exclusively on those words and statements in Homer that look like criticism to us and views them apart from the entire world of epic in which they are fully defined. But to extract from the poems obiter dicta about art and poetry as we define them is to limit our evidence in advance and to beg the central question of what belongs in a theory of poetry. Moreover, such ideas of poetry as Homer implies in his poems are inextricable from the entire imaginative world of epic; they must be read in relation to it.

What I am saying is that the idea of poetry is itself finally a poetic

[1]This is one of the significant implications of Havelock (1963). For the eighteenth- and nineteenth-century foundations of modern criticism, see Eagleton (1990) and Abrams (1989).
[2]Curtius (1953) 468.
[3]Martin (1989) 9.

idea, because it was at first an idea of poets. For this conception I take support from Wallace Stevens, a poet closer to us in time. "One of the functions of the poet at any time," he claimed, "is to discover by his own thought and feeling what seems to him to be poetry at that time. Ordinarily he will disclose what he finds by way of the poetry itself. He exercises this function most often without being conscious of it, so that the disclosures in his poetry, while they define what seems to him to be poetry, are disclosures of poetry, not disclosures of the definitions of poetry."[4] When Stevens came to collect his quasi-critical essays in *The Necessary Angel*, he prefaced them with a warning that he had already been writing about poetry in his poems, though not exactly writing definitions of poetry. And he quietly insisted that any poet at any time must do as much, must have first discovered—in part logically and in part aesthetically—what poetry should be. Thinking of Homer, we may be inclined to dismiss Stevens as too romantic in his belief that the idea of poetry needs to be continually recreated and in projecting onto all poets his own concern with poetry as an expression of the idea of poetry. Such demands may seem not to apply to a poet like Homer, whose vocation was evidently to receive and preserve a heroic tradition the unquestioned value of which would have freed him from the need to work out for himself some new approach to beauty and truth and also from the rather sophisticated project of presenting such abstractions to his warrior audiences. But this is just where Stevens's reminder that the idea of poetry is not an unchanging Platonic essence becomes indispensable: it is all too clear that poetry is at best a sum of what many different poets in different times and places have decided to do with their different languages. If we realize that there is no universal and eternal definition of poetry, we see that even the sturdiest poetic tradition depends on a series of poets who must each embrace, and perhaps reinterpret, this collective idea. Furthermore, if this idea of poetry was originally and for a long time remained an idea of poets, it cannot fail to be embodied in the poems, consciously or not. It is indeed part of the function of the poet *at any time* to take up or make up an idea of poetry and to communicate it along with what-

[4]Stevens (1942) vii.

ever else he or she tells the audience. The necessary angel, after all, proves to be another godchild of the Muse, and I think Homer gives his audiences (including us) an idea of poetry and its ambitions in more ways than are commonly realized.

If Homer's idea of poetry is inevitably a poetic idea, I have tried to set what we know about the terminological and technical aspects of his art in the wider context of the world he represents. Guided by the words and phrases repeatedly used in connection with poetry, I have been especially concerned to bring to bear other passages that have not been read in this connection. I do so not in the expectation that all poetry is about poetry—a tiresome allegorization that reduces all texts to a single monotonous message; rather, I think that any poetry must give or renew for its audience an idea of what it is, if only as a way of telling them how to receive it. But it is also clear that the "idea of poetry in Homer" will be not a doctrine, an illiterate's notes toward Aristotle's *Poetics*, but a way for a working poet to explain to his society, and perhaps to himself, what he was doing and what it was for. Accordingly, I have tried to listen to the authors speak but also have kept in mind what they leave open and what they might be evading or disguising. In addition, I have interpreted such passages as seem to bear on the singer's art not solely in relation to the texts but also as statements made in the concrete context of an epic poet performing or composing in the eighth century. Homer's ideas of poetry must first be read in relation to his fictional cosmos and then reread in relation to the world in which he performed. Only on this fuller view will we get a sense of how Homer represented poetry in relation to all other forms of human endeavor and how such a view worked and made sense to the poet and his audiences.

Thus the fact that the idea of poetry is always changing and the fact that all poets must take up one such idea and in some way embody it in their work combine to make it necessary for us to consider Homeric epic on its own terms, to make clear what basis, purposes, and methods this art claimed for itself in its time and place. If we want a sense of that poetry as it was, we must look behind the fertile but now aging modern consensus of poetry as the fashioning of aesthetic artifacts. My formulation—the poetry of the past—is intended to encapsulate the two central claims that this poetry made for itself and by which it established, dialectically, its special place and function.

First, epic is poetry of the *past* in the obvious but significant sense that it defines itself by its heroic subject matter. Indeed, it is noteworthy that epic prefers defining its subject matter to defining any other aspect of itself. This sustained and nearly exclusive emphasis on the tales at the expense of the telling has the effect of bestowing a prestige and reality on a past which the poetry pretends merely to disclose. Thereby questions about the rhetorical form and literary structure of epic poetry are evaded, for form and structure are not located in the account of the past but are projected onto the heroic deeds as their real, natural, and permanent articulations. Epic thus resists rhetorical analysis by collapsing the form and content of heroic poems into a notion of past actions as the substance on which poetry offers us a transparent window: the poetry of the *past* is constituted as a genre whose laws and forms pretend to have been written by heroes on the indelible surface of divine memory.

Second, however, epic is *poetry* of the past; although it pretends to be a mere unrhetorical rendering of ancient deeds, it does claim to give a unique access to those events and to bring them especially close to us. This claim—lodged with the Muses—distinguishes epic from all other discourse about the past: only the version they sponsor is "poetic" and can bring the past fully before us. To reduce this promise of closeness to a claim for historical accuracy would be anachronistic and feeble. The poets' tales are of course presumed true—after all the past is real—but the Muses are less an archive than divinities presiding at a performance, a presentation of deeds as they happened and still happen under their divine purview. Yet it would be equally anachronistic to translate poetry into a purely aesthetic activity, seeing it, for example, as an artistic representation of painful deeds that makes them pleasurable through the imposition of order and meaning. In a mysterious way, the Muses do make the experience of poetry so wholly persuasive and absorbing that it becomes an emotional transport, but this experience is less like aesthetic contemplation than like presence at a divine epiphany or a necromancy.

In grounding itself in magic and enchantment rather than rhetoric or history, epic again forecloses certain aesthetic and rhetorical questions. In particular, the relationship between the audience and the work of art is transformed into a relationship between the present and an invisible past evoked. Accordingly, questions we as critics may wish to raise about how poetry works and what makes it unique must be answered in psychological terms, such as memory and forgetting, combined with phenomenological ones, the seen and the unseen. By connecting itself with these ideas, epic manages not only to efface poetry as a set of linguistic effects but even to efface the importance of poetic performance as a confrontation between poet and audience, song and psyche, text and reader.

Since we know that poets lie, it is easy for us to diagnose the dialectic playing here to shore up this idea of epic. The poetry of the past first of all pretends that it is only an emanation from a prior, distant but potent world and then claims to be the sole way for that world to become fully apparent to us. Like other language we may call fictive, epic assumes a power by creating a reality that it pretends only to disclose. But these are our concerns because we want to know why epic will not finally declare its allegiance to either history or rhetoric. For their rapt audiences and for their successful poets, as long as the dialectic remained unraveled, epic could remain a speech without rhetoric and a history without distance from the past. The poetry of the past fulfilled its design as long as audiences forgot the performing poet, and themselves, and everything but the vivid and painless presence of heroic action of old. The idea of such a poetry was satisfying and intelligible long before the rise of technically skilled rhetorical critics and historians in the fifth century B.C.E.; but from the first it was not achieved and sustained without what Curtius calls "tensions," the conceptual contradictions and compromises required so that any such thing as poetry can be postulated. I have made these tensions the focus of each of my individual chapters, which treat the genre of epic, the status of the poem, the role of the poet, the nature of the text, and the idea of poetry itself. I begin by examining the tensions inherent in defining the genre of poetry, which involves laying down an always-disputed border between poetry and nonpoetry. If the poet grounds this central distinction in the Muses, who supervise the realm of poetry and keep its borders intact, another tension may thereupon arise between the idea of an individual poem and the supraindividual tradition on which it depends and against which it must claim some sort of autonomy. Similar difficulties may face the poet in an agonistic culture as he attempts to define himself as an individual against other poets, who are, at least in theory, equally favored by the Muses. And for later poets at least, there may be a conflict between the songs they sing and the texts made out of them. Finally, these fruitful compromises can be resumed in the tensions that inhere in the very word Homer uses for his poetry.

To approach the Homeric conception of poetry it is first necessary to define as far as possible the form in which Homer was working, for it was within or against such a view that he was a poet. Accordingly, in my first chapter I have set out to give the traditional definition of *epic*. Here it is necessary to synthesize earlier scholarship that has looked at the terms for poetry, its kinds and functions in Homer and other early hexameter verse. On this basis I ask how what we call epic was defined in relation to other poetry, including a larger class of unmelodic verse to be defined as *epos,* and also in relation to nonpoetic speech. From this I go on to articulate, as far as possible in the poets' own terms, a common "poetics" of oral epic—a basic view of the poet, his role, and his activity to which Homer, his peers, and his audiences would have generally assented.

The definitions of epic and the larger category of poetic epos lead me in the second chapter to reflect more deeply on the greatest abstraction we use when speaking about Homeric poetry, tradition. To ask of Homer what precisely is involved in making a poetry out of phrases and legends that one's society has developed for centuries is to ask about his relation to his Muses. Yet this personification is far from simple, and glossing the Muses as "memory" or "tradition" can be a way of settling all too easily the problematic attachment of modern criticism to literary "property" (as the common metaphors for tradition as a "storehouse" or "treasury" attest). A writerly accounting of tradition might assign to the poet as "his own" any language in his poem that has not been recorded as another's elsewhere; but in an oral tradition such bookkeeping is not possible, and not every view of language and poetry would value most highly the speaker who is the original enunciator of a given idea. We will see that the Muses' function is more complex than to be the repository of themes and language for the poet.

Whatever uses the fiction of the Muses had for Homer, it falsified the way poets actually learned and taught, and my concern in Chapter 3 is to redress this balance by asking about the poet's relationship to other poets. The symbolic use of the Muses for "the tradition" must be set against the actual workings of transmission, the reconstructible processes by which Greek epic was disseminated and handed down from generation to generation. If all poets serve the same Olympian goddesses, how does one differentiate himself (as excellent, worth rewarding, worth protecting) from another poet, perhaps his peer, rival, or even teacher? For this distinction I turn to the so-called bards whom Homer has placed in his heroic world. Though Phemius of Ithaca, Demodocus of Phaecia, and the handful of other poets glimpsed but not named must be regarded as fictional characters no less than Achilles or Agamemnon, we can learn much about Homer's sense of his own role from their ostensible place and function in the world. Balancing these portraits against what we can divine from comparative and historical evidence about the relations among poets in archaic Greece, we can explore how the poet reconciled two of his most imposing obligations: the imperative to establish himself as a superior singer and the expectation that the good singer presents the past without idiosyncrasy, only in the Muses' impersonal view. If these singers are not to be completely identified with actual working bards, their portraits can be interpreted for what they say about an ideal relation of the poet to his society and to his material, to the past.

The fourth chapter takes as its starting point the simple fact of the existence of the epic texts. Whether Homer himself wrote or dictated to a scribe, his songs passed across what we think of as a great gulf into literature, to become objects that last through time. Even if we assume the two great poems were crystallized early as oral "texts" and then handed down by memorizing bards until writing became available, there is already in this process of crystallization (or "monumental composition") an attempt to fix a song permanently which is not far from writing. The question then

arises about the poet's relation to his poem as a fixed and lasting
structure of his own words. A wholly oral poet may view singing
as something he does, but one who produces a text or who causes
a text to be produced may consider his art as *making* something,
perhaps something that he owns or can sell. In Homer the best
way to approach this question is through his one reference to writing, which he calls "signs" (*sêmata*). Setting these signs in the context of the poems' many other signs, we can discuss in his terms
the question of what is the right device to preserve fame. In particular, funeral markers, also called *sêmata*, will be seen to have a
function analogous to that of the epic song, to preserve the name
and memory of a great hero through time. If we can get some idea
of the poet's notion of signs, we may supply something of his
views on the poem as artifact and the possibility of its survival as
text into posterity. The relationship of song to sign, *aoidê* to *sêma*,
may describe the relationship of singing to text, bard to poet, performance to posterity. Though Homer may well never have been so
self-consciously troubled about these matters as we in this great
century of language, yet words were his work too, and evidently
work in the world.

The final chapter resumes these matters and asks what poetry
meant for Homer and his contemporaries. There I take a close look
at the traditional word for what a poet does, "singing," *aoidê*.
"Singing" may seem so natural an expression for this art as to be
hardly significant, but the etymology of *aoidê*, supported by a
number of texts, leads me to explore its relation to a word for the
human voice, *audê*. The trope of singing as voicing suggests tensions between reducing poetry to substance, the timbre and volume of the oral poet's voice as his instrument, and allowing it to
dematerialize into meaning, voice as an expression of thought. The
epithet common to the poet's singing and voice, *thespis*, "god-
spoken," will resume these and the other problems raised in the
near contradiction of an art of "a god-spoken human voicing."

My outline may indicate that I have not forborne to press questions of importance to me and to any historically minded reader,
even though the poet's interest in them may have been oblique or
even unconscious; and it may seem to some that I at times interrogate the witness too harshly, twisting his replies or forcing him to

speak when he has nothing to say. Yet he does volunteer some information, and I at least hope that I have not put words in his mouth. If it be asked who exactly do I think held these views, to which of the many Homers are they to be ascribed, the answer must be the same weak answer to any question tracking Homeric origins. At the most, to the extent that we arrive at a general and coherent account of poetry, it may be assigned to that "hypothesis" Homer, the last bard through whose mouth or pen these texts passed and presumably passed muster; at the least, they can be assigned to the one who made by uttering the passage in question. Some ideas, as in the first and final chapters, I have adduced as general views, embodied in traditional language and tropes that extend across poems. Other readings, like that of great invocation to the Muses in Chapter 2 or of the Phaeacian games in Chapter 3, can at the least be assigned to the poet composing the passage in question, or to the one who gave it final form. My own view, as I make clear in Chapter 4, is that even as the poems took their last form, the oldest problems of poetry were alive for that shaper and provide a resonant undertext to the monumental compositions we now have.

I conclude with a word on the purpose and intended audience of this book. I have tried to recreate a sense of Homer's view of poetry not so that we might set down an alternative, antiformalist aesthetic that would tell us how we must read his poems. For my part, I find that a sense of the historical context of a work enriches reading and indeed that poetry (even of the most revolutionary posture) is never made out of thin air but out of earlier poems; but criticism will always have to follow the questions that interest it, and no text demonstrates better than Homer's that each age will wrench its inheritance into a form it can use and respond to. For classicists and for any who enjoy thinking of poetry in terms of its past, I have hoped to offer something more than thin and bloodless Homeric "conceptions" of poetry, not a kitbag of bizarre and archaic superstitions combined with crude rules of art but a sense of how Homer and his peers persisted in and were rewarded for that peculiar and enduring activity. This is the final sense of my title, which orients this book: Homer and all the authors of classical literature are part of the poetry of our past, and the ways that they defined what poetry could be had a fundamental influence on Western poetry and criticism. Twenty-five centuries of reading and rereading Homer have made this centrality an inescapable historical fact, though its workings have not always been wholly benign for readers or critics, as some recent criticism has suggested. It seems that some today would like a poetry without a past, or at least without the past of the Greeks. I hope that such readers might wish to consider a Homer who did not yet think of himself as the father of Western literature, who was a poet contending with difficulties in defining poetry that are in many ways like our own and in some cases ancestral to them. Other readers would readily embrace the classics as the unsurpassed best in art, but in finding "real" poetry only in what can be pronounced definitive because it is past, they may lose the life these classics once had, seeing them as distant and isolated in their achieved success. The very centrality and canonicity of classical works can be unfair to works felt to be outside that tradition; it can also be confining to the classical works themselves: for a too assured reader, poetry may become recognizable only when it is in the past, when it is canonized and understood within a canonical tradition of interpretation. It would be very unfortunate if the classics should have the effect of weakening instead of vitalizing our sense of this ancient and persistent human behavior. This book finally aims to aid the work of the poets and readers among us who must discover once more what poetry is in our time.

CHAPTER 1

THE GENRE
Traditional Definitions of Epic

Defining an Oral Art

Ideally we should not speak of "poetry" in connection with Homer at all, for it may be prejudicial to ask Homer what "poetry" is when that good Greek word is not attested before the fifth century; it seems that it was only in that enlightened critical culture that sophists and other philosophers of language began calling what Homer and his fellows did "making" (*poiêsis*) and the performer a "maker" (*poiêtês*).[1] Such terms imply a quite different activity from that in the word "singer" (*aoidos*), which Homer would seem to have used for himself. Asking the question in our terms, then, may be misdirected. Instead, let us leave the categories "poet" and "poetry" open for the time being and ask the same question less categorically: What makes a poet or "singer"? What is it exactly that he does? After we have an account of what is involved in epic "singing," we may move on to more abstract questions such as how does the singer of themes we call "epic" differ from other singers, and indeed from nonsingers? In this way we

---

[1]The difference between an *aoidos* and a *poiêtês* was already noted by Wolf in 1795 (1963) chap. xii, p. xlii n. 9 (English ed., 72). The fifth-century context of "poet" has been discussed by Diehl (1940) 83 and Durante (1960); cf. Lanata (1963) 229–230.

may construct from Homer's terms the "genre," or special kind of speaking, to which epic belonged.

It is surely a delicate, even paradoxical business to define a genre of poetry that stands on the verge of orality and literacy, for closely attached to any literary description are notions of texts, forms, and authors that may well be irrelevant to the "song culture" of archaic Greece: at a time when few, if any, people would read poetry, the text of a song was a rare thing, and always of less importance than the vivid but fleeting and variable performance.[2] In such a context "genres" will be defined not by rules of art but by the protocols of socially constructed occasions. Such occasions may indeed prescribe aspects of the performance that we would assign to the "literary": in burial songs (thrênoi), for example, singers would be expected to strike certain themes and to interact with their audience in certain ways. Hence it is possible to think of distinct, defined, and named kinds of singing in a song culture provided that we remember that such kinds were not constructed from the rules of an autonomous art of poetry but belonged to the entire organization of social life.[3]

When texts are made out of such performances, the words gain permanence and may be subjected to precise formal analysis and classification, but at the price of being severed from the contexts that gave them their fullest form and meaning. The words we read, when spoken in performance, belonged to a larger context that vitally depended on the mood of the audience, the persona of the poet, even the day of the year. We would like to know just when and how the Homeric poems passed from the oral performances out of which they grew into the monumental texts we now have, but we are pitifully in the dark; it may have been as late as the sixth century or as early as a manuscript or dictation by Homer himself.[4] But it is clear that as they made this crucial passage they retained marks of their oral heritage in many features of so-called oral style

[2]For the "song culture" of archaic Greece, see Herington (1985) chap. 1. On the importance of context in oral performance generally, see Finnegan (1977) 28–29, 121–126.

[3]Alexiou (1974) is a study of the traditional forms of the Greek lament. Martin (1989) 43–88 uses anthropological and comparative material to elicit a number of "heroic genres of speaking" from the poems.

[4]The question will be taken up in Chapter 4.

and structure and also in the way they present themselves as poetry. I think they did so in part because a text-based conception of
poetry and critical terminology did not spring up overnight, and,
perhaps more important, because it would have been foolish to
dispense with what was familiar, proved by long use, and perhaps
even considered the ritually "right" way to go about things. Hence
the writer who wrote down the *Iliad* began "Sing, goddess," and
the entire Homeric corpus refers to epic poems basically as *aoidê*,
"singing," an action noun, a word that names poetry not as text or
aesthetic object but as activity and performance.[5] What singing
had been before Homer and what it remained to some extent for
performers like him and their audiences may have been very different from what it was for the scholars and bibliophiles from whose
hands we have received the texts and so much of our basic literary
terminology. Indeed, Albert Lord has suggested that our very conception of poetry as literature is completely alien to Homer's milieu: *"The traditional oral epic singer is not an artist:* he is a seer. The
patterns of thought that he has inherited came into being to serve
not *art* but religion in its most basic sense. His balance, his antith-
eses, his similes and metaphors, his repetitions, and his sometimes
seemingly willful playing with words, with morphology, and with
phonology were not intended to be devices and conventions of
Parnassus, but were techniques for emphasis of the potent symbol.
Art appropriated the forms of oral narrative."[6] I think Lord makes
a fundamental and valid point: what we have in Homer need not
be an idea of poetry fundamentally like our own once it has been
stripped of its religious and other nonliterary aspects; we should
allow for the possibility that Homer had a completely non- or pre-
literary way of defining that activity. Nevertheless, one would not
want to speak of Homer as a naïf in the nineteenth-century sense,
and it should not be thought that archaic oral epic was wild, un-
sponsored, and free or so "naive, strange and earlier than any

[5]The excellent article in *LfrgE* s.v. *aoidê* 2 defines it: "*Song* as activity . . . its
character as an action noun always persists (not 'work')" ("Gesang als Tätigkeit,
wobei . . . der Charakter des nom. act. jedoch immer gewahrt bleibt (nicht
'Werk')"). See the fine analysis of *aoidê* in Homer by Walsh (1984) chap. 1, esp. 12–
14.
[6]Lord (1960) 220–221. For an extensive consideration of Lord's most important
work, see Foley (1981).

rules of art" that it had no conception of itself as one among other forms of song.[7] The tradition of poetry that matures in Greece with Homer had by his time developed, if not a theory of art, at least a steady and sure way of going about its business and, moreover, had evolved ways of referring to itself and presenting itself to its society. Long before Homer, in fact reaching back to his Indo-European ancestors and the ancient cultures of the Near East, poets had set apart some forms of speech that we now call poetry and had spoken about its nature, its way of proceeding, and even its structure and organization.[8] Hence, while I recognize with Lord that our ideas of literary art may well be inappropriate to oral epic (and even that they are a sort of detritus of these incantations), I cannot accept his wholesale reduction of the poet to the seer, for the Greek poet at least had his own title, *aoidos*. An *aoidos*, literally, a "singer," is not just any singer but only a professional.[9] Anybody can "sing" (*aeidein*)—goddesses on earth or on Olympus (*Od.* 10.254; *Il.* 1.604), men at arms, a boy in the fields (*Il.* 1.473, 18.570), or a reveler after too much wine (*Od.* 14.464); Achilles can even sing the "fames of men of old" to a lyre, just as Homer does (*Il.* 9.189). But none of these singers is ever called an *aoidos*.[10] In addition, the singer was set apart by having his own patron deities, the Muses, and a special range of themes. We can therefore legitimately attempt to define the singer's activity in terms of genre, as a kind of speaking that is somehow set apart from that of seers and other nonpoets; and we may ask generally what is the "art" of a poetry so defined.

[7]Cf. Egger (1886) 4: "une poésie naïve, étrangère et antérieure aux règles de l'art."

[8]Indo-European and Near Eastern influences on the poetry of archaic Greece are explored in the works of Durante, Nagy, Schmitt, and Burkert. I should note at this point that I do not propose to treat the pre-Homeric history of many of the ideas of this book; instead, I mean to give a synchronic description of their significance within archaic Greek poetry.

[9]*LfrgE* s.v. *aoidos* B.1: "*Gesang* als Fertigkeit oder Tätigkeit des Sängers (s. *aoidos*), . . . kaum Gesang vom Laien" ("*Song* as the ability or activity of the singer (*aoidos*) . . . hardly ever of nonprofessional song").

[10]The telling exception to the restriction of *aoidos* to professional singers is in Hesiod's fable of the Hawk and the Nightingale: here the nightingale (*aêdôn*) stands for the singer and is addressed as an *aoidos* (*Works and Days* 208). In fact, even the verb "to sing" (*aeidein*) is used in an extended sense here, for it is only rarely used of animals in epic, and then only as a figure of speech. So in *Od.* 19.519 the nightingale that "sings" is the metamorphosed daughter of Panadareus; cf. *LfrgE* s.v. *aoidos* B.2.

Evidently, to recover the ideas of what singing was and was not we must turn to the texts with a cold eye toward too-familiar literary categories. In defining the genre of epic, for example, it is necessary to avoid the reductions of formalism and its appealingly "objective" way of defining genres in terms of meter, diction, figures of speech, and so on. There is little warrant in Homer for making formal considerations so significant in defining kinds of poetry. It is more fruitful to be attentive, as the first Greek critics were, to the "ethos," or persona, presented by the poet as a way of announcing and constituting his genre. This will help us place epic in relation to a larger category of hexameter poetry I will call *epos*, defining this term somewhat more narrowly than is now common. Epos may refer to "speech" of many kinds, and Homer's project is that subclass of epos that offers a Muse-sponsored presentation of the past. I define his work not metrically (though most epos was in hexameters) or musically (though epos was normally not sung); rather it was a combination of a certain subject matter, the past, presented with a certain ethos.

After I have assembled the poem's descriptions of itself as a kind of epos, it will be necessary, before attempting to translate these statements into our terms, to bear in mind the ubiquitous danger of anachronism, assuming that certain concepts now fundamental in the Western critical tradition are universally valid and significant when of course they have a history of their own (and usually one that goes back no further than the fifth century B.C.E.). It is of course impossible to have no preconceptions; so I have sought mine in the negative poetics of Lord, Havelock, and Walter Ong, that is, the constant challenge they offer to certain fundamental ideas we may wish to thrust onto the text. I take them, together with the reservations expressed by Ruth Finnegan, not as dogma to be applied a priori but as salutary warnings that this poetry may work differently from how we expect.

The conclusions that such a vigilant reading leads me to in this chapter are in the first instance negative, for it is necessary to clear away persistent but inappropriate readings of many key passages. We cannot continue to describe Homer's idea of the poetic art in rhetorical terms, that is, as an art of form and content; on Homer's account, poetry is not a rhetorical effect, since the past is valued for itself, not for the way it is told, and the poet presents himself not as a proprietor or craftsman of words but first and foremost as a performer and enchanter. Nor can we convert this "unrhetorical" poetry into a kind of history, for its declared aim is always and only pleasure. This pleasure needs special definition, for to convert it into aesthetic contemplation would be as anachronistic as the other views rejected here. Understanding this pleasure permits us to define epic as the *presentation* of the past, without moralizing; it was a pleasure simply to represent the past "as it was" and still is for the Muses, without pointing to the presence of the performance. Lord seems to be right in saying that Homer has no art of poetry in our sense; at least on the traditional view, the "art" of poetry is to be inspired by the Muses and a poet is a poet not because he is skilled or truthful or improving but because he is sacrosanct.

We can approach Homer's idea of his singing in three ways: the first is to consider how the texts present themselves to us, especially how in their openings they announce what they are and indicate their structure and aims; the second way is through the poet's terms for poetry and related concepts, including a few highly suggestive metaphorical expressions for poetry and its processes and even some words that must have served as terms of the singer's trade; the third way is by considering the depictions of poets within the poems, comparing them with Homer's own self-presentation and with representations of nonpoets to see what sustains the special place of the epic singer. The place to begin must be the beginning of the poems we have.

Beginnings: Invocations and Ethos

The beginning of a work of art must also in a sense be its definition, since it acts like a frame to set that work apart from others and to enclose it as a single thing in itself. As Edward Said observes in his book *Beginnings*, "A beginning immediately establishes relationships with works already existing, relationships of either continuity or antagonism or some mixture of both."[11] To understand what the archaic poet set out to do is to put to him the same questions as Said puts to himself when he begins: "What is a beginning? What must one do in order to begin? What is special about beginning as an activity or a moment or a place? Can one begin wherever one pleases? What kind of attitude, or frame of mind is necessary for beginning? Historically, is there one sort of moment most propitious for beginning, one sort of individual for whom beginning is the most important of activities?"[12] These questions are all the more worth putting to Homer because for the Greeks the beginning of anything, from song to sacrifice, was a sacred moment not to be casually passed by. Accordingly, we are not surprised to find that by the time of the composition of the Homeric poems there was what Hermann Fränkel has called "an established art of beginning and beginning anew."[13] A comparison of Homer, Hesiod, and other early hexameter poetry has revealed firmly established traditional ways to organize the beginnings, middles, and ends of these performances; in addition, certain expressions and ways of phrasing, including a number of repeated formulas, were found useful again and again to signal such moments.[14] These epic beginnings are also among the most traditional parts of the texts: the repetition of phrases and patterns in poems so widely dispersed in time and place is a sign that they are derived from the period of wholly oral composition and performance that preceded our texts. Hence, insofar as these patterns imply something about the nature and structure of the poetry, they express the aspects of the poetry as it was traditionally conceived.

Though Homer is praised for plunging in medias res, he must, like any poet, take a few lines to establish a relationship between himself and his expectant audience, and the traditional form for doing this we call an invocation. Susceptible of variations, the invocation is essentially a prayer to the Muse to tell a story: for-

[11]Said (1975) 3.
[12]Said (1975) ix.
[13]Fränkel (1973) 14, in an excellent chapter.
[14]By formulas I mean specifically words that are repeated in the same place in the line with the same function in context.

mally, it is initiated by an imperative ("sing," "tell," or "hymn") and a vocative to the Muse (or Muses or goddess). So begin the *Iliad* and *Odyssey* and, among the later epics, the *Thebais* and the *Persica*.[15] But the invocation is more than this; in fact, invocations are prayers, and they are formally based on prayers and hymns, reworked to identify and initiate a story instead of naming and evoking a god.[16] Partly as a result of this heritage, certain elements of the invocation and their relative order were fixed within the limits of an oral art as the standard way of opening any particular epic song. First in the line comes an emblematic "title," meter permitting, signaled by its stereotyped form: most often it is a noun as the object of the imperative with a qualifier in the same line making it more specific: "the wrath . . . of Achilles"; "the man . . . with many turns" (though the genitive, the "of" case, is more common). This form for identifying the story to be sung is recurrent enough to be called the "titling" syntax, though such "titles" hardly imply that the story to follow was rigidly fixed in its details.[17] The rest of the invocation fleshes out the story in a hymnlike series of relative clauses depending from the title-phrase. Sometimes these are read as a kind of table of contents, but the *Odyssey*'s opening does not provide a very good index of what is to follow, and announcing in advance a fixed plan might not always be a good idea for an oral poet who had to vary his song according to his audience's interests and endurance.[18] Rather, the function of these clauses seems to be to reassure the audience that the qualities typically expected of such songs will be forthcoming, for they regularly refer to the great scope of the action, its pathetic quality, the nations involved, and the role of the gods in all of it. The mention of the divine will (especially Zeus's plan) is a signal that the invocation is beginning to conclude, and at this point the poet specifies where the tale is to begin. Hence the "wrath of Peleus's son

[15]Of archaic epics, only the *Little Iliad* opens differently; see note 28 herein.

[16]See Meyer (1933) 19–22 and Norden (1913) 168–176.

[17]Aelian *Var. Hist.* 13.14 gives a rich list of epic "titles" in this form. For the classical ways of referring to parts of the Homeric poems, see Pfeiffer (1968) 115–116, and on the titles of archaic "books" generally, see Van Groningen (1958) 65–66.

[18]On proems as tables of contents, see Van Groningen (1946), Pagliaro (1956), and Pucci (1982). The analyses of the *Odyssey* proem by Redfield (1979) and Rüter (1969) 28–52 are also valuable, though they read it ex post facto as a full table of contents.

Achilles," which caused "many woes" for the Achaeans and was accomplished through the plans of Zeus, is to be sung "from the time when the son of Atreus and Achilles first stood apart in contention" (1.7–8);[19] the *Odyssey*'s theme is the rather more meandering "Man of Many-turns" who saw and suffered "many, many" things while he returned from Troy and Helius took away the return of his companions; out of this rich store, "of these things," the poet asks the Muse, "starting from some point at least, tell us now" (1.1–10). The opening of the *Thebais* neatly manages to compress the "title," imperative, vocative, epithet, and relative clause into a single line: "Argos, sing, Goddess, the thirsty, whence the leaders" (1 D, K).

To draw attention to this recurrent structure in the Greek I will capitalize these typical elements in translation. Thus we can observe that when Homer depicts bards within his poems, they employ the same conventions: an invocation is recognizable behind the line and a half describing the Ithacan bard Phemius: "and he Sang the Return of the Achaeans / the Grievous one, Which Pallas Athena accomplished From Troy" (*Od.* 1.326–327). On Phaeacia, the poet Demodocus appears to use the same format when he sings:

> the Quarrel of Odysseus and Achilles, son of Peleus,
> How once upon a time they quarreled at the rich feast of the gods.
>
> . . . . .
>
> For then the Beginning of Suffering was cresting
> for the Trojans and the Danaans through the Plans of great Zeus.
>
> [8.75–76, 81–82]

Again, there is a recognizable invocation in line 75, where the noun and dependent genitives are followed by a relative clause that expands to sketch out the action (76–81). The paraphrase concludes with the mention that this was the beginning of something, some-

---

[19]*Il.* 1.6 clearly indicates a starting point for the story, even if one takes *ex hou dê* in 6 with the previous line, i.e., "the will of Zeus was accomplished / from that point when [their strife began]," as does Redfield (1979) 96. Yet I prefer it with the imperative of line 1, "Sing . . . from that point": the imperative may still be felt since locative phrases that conclude other invocations often depend on imperatives repeated from the opening (e.g., *Od.* 1.10; Hesiod *Theog.* 114–115).

thing that involved massive human pain (cresting like a wave, *kulindeto*, in 81), and finally that all of this was the plan of Zeus.

The ideal full form of the invocation is very clear, as is the kind of poetry it announces. It is a heroic story involving suffering, and the gods take a part in it. It is itself a massive and complex action and yet also part of a larger story. In this much at least Homer's definition of his art coincides with our definition of epic according to "content"—a long, traditional heroic story. But more can be understood if we look at the invocation in terms of the persona or, in Greek, the ethos adopted by the poet.

The earliest Greek critics classify poetry, and indeed all imitative art, not only according to its form (e.g., meter and music) and content (the "objects" of imitation), but also by ethos. In the *Republic*, Plato analyzes the tales of poets and "mythologues" by looking first at *what* they say and then at *how* they say it (392C). The "how" turns out to be a matter not of diction or arrangement but of the way the poet's persona or character (*ethos*) appears in the poems. Ethos divides poetry into three classes (392D). In pure narrative a poet simply recounts or "goes through" a story in his own person (*diêgêsis*). In drama the poet impersonates his characters and speaks speeches as if he were Agamemnon or Calchas; here he "conceals" his own identity (393C) and tries to "turn the audience's attention away" from what they see (*dianoian allose trepein* [392D]). Finally in poetry such as epic "simple recounting" is mixed with speeches. Aristotle follows Plato in considering "*how* one imitates" as marking poetic genres in a separate way from how formal properties such as music or rhythm might do so (*Poetics* 1448a19–29). This classical Greek analysis, I think, describes what would have been a real and significant aspect of oral poetic practice, for projecting a certain persona would have been an important way for an oral performer to establish the terms of his relationship to the audience and to constitute his own special authority. But the epic poet's ethos also implies a great deal about what each kind of poetry is and can do, so that examining the ethos presented by Homer will help us both to define his genre as distinct from other forms of poetry that may treat the same matter and to understand the role of the poet in the poem, or the poet's place in performance.

The distinctive ethos of epic is epitomized in the imperatives that set the invocation proper apart from the rest of the poem: the first eight lines of the *Iliad* and the first ten of the *Odyssey* are not narratives presented to the audience but prayers addressed by the singer to a god, overheard by the audience. This orientation extends to a repeated imperative or question directed to the god at the invocation's end, whereupon a character comes on and the ancient action commences. The poet is present in the *Iliad*'s invocation as the one with the right to utter the command, and in the *Odyssey*'s "tell *me*," but by the end his presence has modulated into the impersonal voice of the omniscient epic narrator. This epic voice, the voice of no particular bard, continues, alternating objective narrative and speeches, in a long, unbroken strain until the poet finds it is time to "begin anew."[20] The invocation promises an ethos that is well enough summed up by the old term "epic objectivity": once it is over, we will not expect to hear the voice of the poet as poet, only the voice of an omniscient narrator or the voices of his characters.[21]

Proems and Genre

By the fifth century B.C.E., *Mênin aeide thea*, "The wrath, sing, goddess," were already familiar as the first words of the *Iliad* and the archetype of how to begin an epic tale.[22] Yet, the beginning of an oral performance is likely to have been more elaborate than

[20]In Chapter 2 I consider passages in which the invocation is repeated in the text to focus on or make a transition to new themes: *Il.* 2.484, 2.761, 11.218, 14.508, 16.112; Hesiod *Theog.* 965, 1021, fr. 1.1–2 (M-W).

[21]On epic narration, see Edwards (1987) 29–41. It is true that the poet breaks this "objectivity" some seventeen times to apostrophize a hero or a god. Some have sought thematic motivations for these puzzling intrusions, as does Frontisi-Ducroux (1986) 21–27, but more interesting is Martin (1989) 234–236, who sees this as a performatory convention in which the poet identifies with his hero and addresses other characters from this perspective. In any case, such shifts in persona in fact bring us closer to the epic world being presented and further away from the poet as individual speaker.

[22]Protagoras (probably with tongue in cheek) censured the imperious imperative, and Aristotle praised Homer's directness, *Poetics* 19.1456b15–17; cf. *Rhetoric* 3.14.1415a14–18.

our Homeric texts indicate, so that even the beginnings have a context in which they must be read. This larger context is the proem, or introductory poem, which prefaced the invocation proper in performance. Our best surviving example is the proem of Hesiod's *Theogony,* which goes on for more than a hundred lines before Hesiod gets around to the invocatory imperatives. These first 104 lines are sometimes called the "Hymn to the Muses" but are better called by the classical term *prooimion,* or proem (Thucydides 3.104), inasmuch as one of the earliest and most important functions of proems was to introduce the kind of poetry Homer and Hesiod produced.[23] This purpose for proems emerges from a comparison with the so-called Homeric hymns, a miscellaneous collection of hexameter poems in epic language including some pieces of archaic poetry (that is, composed within a century or two of Homer) and others of much later date.[24] This mélange is nevertheless useful in reconstructing the archaic form of the proem since the hymns preserve much traditional language and are replete with traditional formulas.

The established word "hymn" misleadingly implies that the proem is some kind of separate genre defined by subject matter, a song in praise of gods, as distinct from epics treating heroes. And the longer Homeric hymns, approaching the length of a short epic book, seem to indicate that the proemic listing of a god's attributes could blossom into an independent narrative form.[25] But this categorization is alien to archaic Greek: early uses of *humnos* and the verb *humnein* can refer to any kind of song, to the Homeric hymns and to Homeric, Hesiodic, and lyric poetry as well.[26] The specific

[23]For the Homeric hymns as proems and epilogues to epic recitations, see Allen, Halliday, and Sikés (1936) lxxxiii–xcvi; Càssola (1975) xii–xxv; and in general, Lenz (1980). For an analysis of the opening of the *Theogony* as a proemic hymn, see Friedlander (1914) and, more generally, Van Groningen (1946) and Janko (1981).

[24]The longer hymns, to Apollo, Aphrodite, and Demeter, are generally agreed to represent archaic poetry. The date of the *Hymn to Hermes* is more controversial; I agree with Görgemanns (1976) that it is archly sophisticated and smacks of the fifth century. Of course, even very late hymns (e.g., 31, 32) can preserve valuable versions of ancient formulas, even if these are only perfunctory where they now stand.

[25]Informative hypotheses about the early historical connections between epics and proems are in Koller (1956) and Durante (1976) 46–50, though lack of evidence makes the question of priority a chicken-and-egg affair.

[26]See, e.g., *Od.* 8.429 (of Demodocus's heroic songs); Hesiod *Works and Days* 662

nature and function of the proem are best defined not by its divine subject matter or by its language and meter (which are the same as epic's) but by its ethos. This distinctive ethos is evident as Hesiod begins: "From the Muses of Helicon let us begin to sing, who once." The proem allows the poet to refer to himself, to begin by saying "I" (or a royal "we").[27] Such a liberty is not allowed in epic, which restricts itself to the less assertive "sing" or "tell me."[28] The difference between the "I will sing" of the proem and the "Sing, Muse" of the invocation summarizes a great difference in the way the poet is allowed to present himself in different stages of the performance. In fact, the function of the proem seems to have been to allow the poet to say "I" and to refer to himself as a particular poet about to perform on a particular occasion.[29]

Although the proem of the *Theogony* contains great praises of the Muses, to think of this section only as a hymn is to miss the equally important fact that it also allows Hesiod to name and praise himself.[30] When Hesiod tells of his election as poet and dilates on the value of poetry in society, he is present as poet and personalized to a far greater degree than he will be once the narrative proper begins. A similar self-referring ethos can be found in a proem used to link the two halves of *Hymn to Apollo* (166–178): the poet names himself and where he comes from (cryptically, as the blind man of

(of his own song); Pseudo-Hesiod fr. 357 (of Hesiod and Homer); *H. Ap.* 161 (of a choral lyric). The differentiation of hymns to gods from "encomia" for mortals is found first in Plato (*Republic* 10.607a etc.). See, generally, Càssola (1975) x–xii and Wünsch (1914) 141–142 for a speculative reconstruction of the change in sense.

[27]For "I" / "we" as the subject of "sing" / "shall sing" see *Hymn* 6, 10, 12, 15, 18, 23, 25, 27, 30.

[28]The only exception is the *Little Iliad* which begins "Ilion I sing" (1 D, K). Here I think the poet is borrowing from proemic style, for the first syllable of "I sing" is long (*âeidô*), whereas it is generally short in epic. (The one exception is the acephalous *Od.* 17.519). In proems, however, this odd scansion of "I sing" is common (*Hymn* 12.1, 18.1, 27.1, cf. 32.1) and exactly paralleled in Theognis's proem (4 *IEG*) and Apellicon's "ancient" opening to the *Iliad*, which I quote hereafter.

[29]Most of the Homeric hymns do not sound very personal now, and some of them begin with the more neutral invocation (*Hymn* 4, 5, 9, 14, 17, 19, 20, 31, 32, 33) or take the form of a general prayer (8, 21, 24, 29). But it is worth noting that the collection of Homeric hymns is a sort of anthology, and the usefulness of anthologies is to strip the exempla of any too particular references that would be difficult to adapt.

[30]On the poetic persona projected by Hesiod, see Griffith (1983) and Nagy (1982).

Chios) and boasts of the excellence of his singing and his hopes for eternal fame.[31] In addition, proems allow the singer to refer objectively to his performance and its structure: he can explicitly call attention to his "beginning" and "leaving off" (*lêgô* [*H. Ap.* 177]) or "moving along" to another song (*Hymn* 5.293); he can ask the gods' favor for *his* song, or at least for the song as performed by him. Like prayers, proems conclude with petitions, but these are very much a poet's petitions: the "grace" (24.5), wealth, or excellence (15.9, 20.8) that he prays may attend his singing are not simply indirect self-praise but requests for the things by which he sustains his livelihood (cf. 2.494, 30.18, 31.17). The poet's sense of himself as individual singer among other singers is never stronger than when he prays for "victory in this poetic contest" (6.20).[32] Finally, and most significant, proems sometimes use language that calls attention to a certain artistry in singing which is not found in the epic poems themselves: only in proems do we hear poets speak of "adorning" or "ordering" song (*kosmêsai* [7.59]) or describe a chorus as "knowing how to imitate" and their song as "finely fitted together" (*kalôs sunarêren* [*H. Ap.* 163–164]).

At the end of the proem this "I" is transformed into a "thou" and the individual poet is fading from view, so that by the end of the invocation the poet's individual personality is submerged. Like the invocation, then, the proem effects a crucial change in the speaker's stance, and the special function of the archaic proem seems to have been to situate the performance, the speaker, and the occasion. If the invocation gets the tale going, the proem makes the invocation possible.

Although Homer's epics have been transmitted to us without proems, he could not have failed to know a practice that was already well developed in Hesiod, and indeed he once refers indirectly to a proem, under its archaic formulation of "beginning from the god": Homer says that the poet Demodocus, embarking on a song about the fall of Troy, "was stirred and *took his beginning from the god* and he brought forth the song / taking it from that point when. . . ." (*Od.* 8.499–500). Uniquely here in Homer, we find the

---

[31]On the transitional passage in the *Hymn to Apollo*, see Miller (1986) 57–65.

[32]On the agonistic context of the hymnic passages, see Aly (1914) 246 and Svenbro (1976) 78–80.

expression *theou arkheto*, which, in the first person, is a common way to announce proems.[33] In addition, we hear that one "ancient" text of the *Iliad* had a "proem," whose quoted line quite well fits the form: "The Muses *I* sing and Apollo famed for his bow."[34]

It would hardly be surprising that any such proems that Homer or his circle may have used were not included when performance became text, for proems are essentially separable from any particular theme since they were focused on the occasion. Hence literate critics such as the Hellenistic Crates of Mallos could delete the proems to both Hesiodic works on grounds of irrelevance, and he may have condemned an Iliadic proem as well.[35] Already by the time Aristotle came to write his *Rhetoric*, *prooimion* could be used for the beginning of a show speech (those for display, the rhetorical equivalent of literature) in which the speaker indulges himself, saying "whatever he likes and then tacks it onto the main theme."[36] For text-based critics, the proem could appear to have

[33]For "I begin from" (*arkhomai* with the genitive) as a way to signal proems, cf. *H. Aphr.* 293; *Hymn* 25.1, 32.18; and Hesiod *Theog.* 1 with West's (1966) note. Some scholars would break up Homer's allusion by taking *theou* with *hormêtheis*, "stirred by the god, he began." This reading gives too little weight to the hymnic parallels and leaves *arkheto* hanging, for the finite forms of this verb usually require a nominal or verbal complement in epos; see Calhoun (1938); Stanford (1974); and Heubeck, West and Hainsworth (1981) on *Od.* 8.499. It is possible to take *theou* with both, as does Lenz (1980) 69 n. 1, but *hormêtheis* is commonly used absolutely, and here Demodocus may be "stirred into action" by Odysseus's preceding words rather than by the god.

[34]From the "Roman Life of Homer" (Wilamowitz-Moellendorff [1929] 32). See Wade-Gery (1952) 71–72 for a discussion. A highly literate development of this function of the proem can be found in the lines prefaced to the *Aeneid* in some ancient lives of Virgil. The poet begins by identifying himself and his origins ("ille ego qui quondam gracili modulatus avena / Carmen": "I am he who once played my song on a slender reed" [1–2]), sketches out his works, and then turns to his present theme: "at nunc horrentia Martis / Arma virumque cano" ("But now, Mars' bristling / Arms and the man I sing" [4–5]). With the transitional "but now" (*at nunc*), compare the "tell me now" (*espete nun moi*) in the "ancient" *Iliad* proem (line 2) and in Homeric transitional invocations (e.g., *Il.* 2. 484, 11.218; cf. Hesiod *Theog.* 965, fr. 1 M-W).

[35]See Pfeiffer (1968) 238–240 and West (1966) 150, (1978) 136–137.

[36]*Rhetoric* 3.14.1414b19–26 (Kassel [1976]). Aristotle compares the proems of flute players, who begin by playing "whatever they can execute skillfully and then attach it to the key note." Similar language can be found in Pseudo-Plutarch's discussion of kitharodic proems, apparently lyrical versions of the kind of proems we have in the Homeric hymns: the singers would dedicate themselves to the god "in any way

little connection with what followed, but what formal classification severs could be closely joined in performance, and we may regard the proems not as a genre distinct from epic but as a subgenre or part of its full performance.

Once proems are returned to the beginnings of Homer's epics the nature of that poetry becomes clearer. With their potential for self-reference, proems provided the way for a particular singer on a particular occasion to translate his speech into the eternal song of the Muses. The theme to be introduced, being pan-Hellenic in scope, would have aspired to the quality of the universal, and the proem puts this timeless tale of the Muses in its place.[37] Though one is obliged to describe ethos in formal terms, focusing on the poet's use of linguistic shifters, in performance it was not reducible only to such features. At a great festival with an international audience, the proem was an opportunity to lay claim to a large reputation; in less formal circumstances, it was the privileged moment for the poet to speak as "I" to that audience at that time and place. But once the Muses are called on to sing, the voice we hear will be divested of peculiarity and personality, and the proem, in my view, was the place for this divestiture. Short or long, it could allow these poets, whose pride, competitiveness, and self-assertiveness had made them Greek poets, to assert themselves and then sublimate themselves into the transcendental voice of the Muses. The proem carries the poet and audience from the personal to the

they pleased" in their proems and then proceed to the poetry of Homer or others (*On Music* 1132b).

[37]Perhaps the *Hymn to Hermes* plays on the proem's use of self-advertisement in its contrast of two different proems sung by Hermes. When the god first invents the lyre, he begins with "impromptu" snatches of verse, "the sort that youths bandy back and forth," and then proceeds to sing of Zeus and Maia, "naming in his proem his own renowned begetting" (59). Hermes later refines this "primitive" singing when he sings to Apollo what is in all respects a theogony (cf. 427–428). The proem to this Hesiodic theme is more correctly Hesiodic: "Mnêmosunê first of the gods he honored in his song / mother of the Muses" (429–430). Between the two performances poetry evolves from natural crudity to a well-defined form suitable for an Olympic audience, and self-reference is similarly refined. The progressive view of art implicit here is characteristic of enlightened fifth-century thought: see in general Democritus (68 B frr. 144, 154 D-K) and Aristotle *Poetics* 4.1448b4–27, where imitation arises "naturally" in children, and poetry evolves from "improvisations" to invective or hymns and encomia, according to the character of the singer.

traditional, from the local to the Panhellenic, from the present to the eternal.

In epic beginnings, then, we see a sequence from proem to invocation with a complex rhythm and function. By being mindful of the appropriate god on a given occasion, by "not forgetting," as they say, poets ensure the best hope of success. The conventions or "laws" operating here are clearly not of a purely literary nature, to be taken as tokens of genre. Rather, they have something of the force of ritual prescription and are repeated as a tried and secure way to start singing such themes. The careful management of ethos in these openings permits a more precise definition of epic as a genre than do purely formal properties, such as meter. And so it seems that the poets looked at things with a different set of distinctions from those formulated in W. G. Thalmann's 1984 survey of the forms of archaic Greek hexamater poetry. Thalmann grouped together the longer archaic hexameter poems as part of an extended argument for the case that "meter is not an artificial or arbitrary means of lumping together poems that might otherwise have few similarities" and that early Greek hexameter poetry has enough "homogeneity" to constitute a "poetic type."[38] This grouping proved fruitful for Thalmann's readings, but in consideration of ethos, I would place archaic epic in a narrower subclass. The most basic formal class of poetry that I can discern from the scanty early evidence is that of "sung poetry," what we call lyric and the Greeks called "speech and song" or simply "song," *melos*, in the sense of words and music.[39] Poetry that was not sung was negatively defined, essentially by never calling it *melos*, though it could be designated by the plural of *epos*: Homer uses *epea* for the substance of the poet's song (cf. *Od.* 8.91, 17.519), as do early elegiac poets (Solon 1.2; Theognis 20 *IEG*).[40] In defining epic as a subclass of unsung poetry, it seems that the metrical difference between, say, the hex-

---

[38]Thalmann (1984) xiii.

[39]Alcman 14.2 Page (*melos*), 39.1 (*epê . . . kai melos*); cf. Plato, *Republic* 398D.

[40]This broad use of the plural of *epos* for unsung poetry (and not only hexametric poetry) seems to have persisted into the classical period, for Herodotus 5.113.2; Xenophon *Mem.* 2.2.21; and Plato *Meno* 95D can use *epea* for elegiacs. This class of poems was the basis of the term "rhapsody." See Ford (1988). Koller's study of *epea* (1972) unnecessarily restricts the word to hexameters.

ameter and the elegiac couplet, was less significant for the archaic vocabulary than was the ethos epic presented. On this basis, though Hesiod's *Works and Days* is presented in "epic" hexameters, I would set it apart from Homeric epic, Hesiod's *Theogony* and *Catalogue of Women*, and other "Hesiodic" poetry that proceeded with epic objectivity (such as the *Shield of Heracles*). The *Works and Days* I would classify as parainetic epos, as (unsung) advice poetry.[41] My warrant in the text for this distinction is first of all the ethos of the *Works and Days:* its proem turns from the gods to an individual, Perses, and his individual circumstances; the rest of the poem continues to address itself to him or to a "you."[42] Second, it is hardly a connected story: though at times it relates bits of divine and heroic history (e.g., the story of Pandora), its fundamental "ethical" difference from epos is in its constant oscillation from sacred time back to its present auditor in order to draw lessons about the human place in the moral order of the world. This class of hexameter poetry, to which we should add other works attributed to Hesiod, such as the *Bird Divination, Astronomy,* and *Precepts of Cheiron,* was from an ethical point of view quite distinctive and later found heirs in the "philosophical" hexameters of Parmenides (frequently recurring to a "you") and Empedocles (addressed to a certain Pausanias).[43]

Thus Homer's epics and Hesiod's extended narratives belonged to a subclass of epos whose function was to present stories of the past impersonally and not for immediate application to their auditors' lives. This ethos, together with a difference in mode of presentation, also separated what I call the poetry of the past from the contemporaneous poetry we call lyric, for lyric could present mythic and legendary stories, but these were either personally

[41]Cf. Martin (1984), who also shows how parainetic poetry could be incorporated into the Homeric poems as a separate "genre of discourse" used by certain characters in certain situations.

[42]For the addressee in wisdom literature (cf. Theognis's Cyrnus), see West (1978) 33–40. The proem of the *Works and Days* is also the reverse of that in epos, proceeding from an invocation (1–2) to "*I* would tell" (10).

[43]The ethos of Parmenides' "On Truth," as it is called, is actually hybrid: though the words purport to be those addressed by goddesses to the neophyte philosopher (the "youth" of B 1.24 D-K), they are (over)heard by the audience as parainetic poetry, urging them to correct their false beliefs.

addressed to an individual or coterie (in the form we call monody) or closely attached to a ritual or social occasion and indeed defined by those moments (as in choral lyric). Although Alcman or Pindar may give fairly extensive stretches of mythic narrative, this past is always exited and one returns to the present, either via a moralizing gnome that draws a lesson from the tale or by a reference to the mythic act as founding or paralleling the present ceremony.[44] We may observe that tragedy, heir to both epic and choral lyric, uses the ethos of both: the heroic deeds are dramatized "objectively"— any reference to fifth-century Athenian concerns is only implicit— yet in many plays and trilogies the tragic action issues in the founding of a cult or civic institution that continues into the "present" day.

Epic keeps a chaste distance from the present of performance, though it is not absolute: similes playfully evoke, if not the present, at least the quotidian, and as we shall see in Chapter 3, the occasion of performance could sometimes be evoked and exploited for ironic effects. But on the whole, epic leaves the relationship between individual poet and particular audience wholly implicit; it pretends to be an impersonal tale, universally interesting, told for its own sake. After the proem, the circumstances in which it is performed are dismissed, and once we have entered on the epic tale we are presented with action, as it was before it became poetry. But if Homer is giving us a story beyond momentary interest, without idiosyncrasy, we may well wonder exactly what the poet's role is once the Muses begin to sing.

Art and the Muse

The appeal to the Muses is so conventional by now that we may forget that they are uniquely Greek. No other traditional heroic poetry gets its topics from similar transmitting deities. Germanic

---

[44]Some recent finds of Stesichorus suggest that a lyric in "epic" style, with sustained objective narrative, was sung at least in the sixth century; such an art form would have been a more ornamental rival for epic performance according to the suggestive reconstruction by Burkert (1987).

heroic poetry, for example, treats past glories under such introductions as "so it is said" or "the world has heard."[45] But Greek epic cannot dispense with the Muses; they ground the definition of epic. In fact, as we have seen, the simplest definition of *aoidê* in *epos* is that it is the particular singing of the *aoidos*. But who then merits the title of "singer," *aoidos*? The short answer is the one whom the Muses have favored; hence the epithet restricted to singers, their songs, and their voice is *thespis*, "speaking like a god" and one of their characteristic descriptions is *theios*, "godlike."[46] But it is not clear how the central role the Muses play here can be reconciled with all the poet's artistry evident in the poems—their smooth and flexible meter, their elevated and cosmopolitan diction, their cunning ways with a story. How is the art of poetry accounted for under the sway of the Muses? This question may also be put: How literally are we to take the invocatory imperatives? If it is not the Muse herself who sings, for we hear the poet, what is it that the poet does?

It is disagreeable to the romantic in us to see the poet as merely the "tool" or "passive instrument" of the Muses.[47] Accordingly, some have read a division of labor into "tell *me*, Muse," deducing that there is a human contribution too.[48] Since the poetry is demonstrably traditional in its stories, the special work of the poet has been thought to be in his style, the way he handles traditional matter: the Muse tells the poet, he performs some operation on what he is told, and we get his poem as distinct from what another would give us.[49] Often it is said that the Muse gives the poet the content and he puts the form on it.[50] Some go so far as to speak of the poet's "intellectual" relationship with the Muses,[51] since, after all, Homer's idea of inspiration does not imply being possessed or out of one's wits.[52] In support of such views a speech of Phemius is

[45]Cf. Bowra (1952) 40–41; Niles (1983) 51.

[46]E.g., *Od.* 17.385, 1.336. These terms will be discussed more fully in Chapter 5.

[47]Glosses, respectively, of Fälter (1934) 5 and Grube (1965) 2. See Lanata (1963) 1–2.

[48]For earlier views, see Lanata (1963) 9–10.

[49]Lanata (1963) 14.

[50]Marg (1957) 61–63; Dodds (1957) 80; Murray (1981) 90–91.

[51]Murray (1981) 96; Maehler (1963) 19; cf. Tiegerstedt (1970).

[52]Lanata (1963) 8–9; cf. Thalmann (1984) 127 with notes.

often quoted: defending himself to Odysseus, he boasts, "I am self-taught, and the Muse has made stories / of every kind grow in my heart" (*Od.* 22.347–348). In various ways it has been asserted that Phemius distinguishes his own "original" or artistic work from the contribution of the god.[53]

But it is anachronistic to foist upon this oral art form a clear and significant distinction between form and content.[54] To be sure, words (*epea*) are quite concrete entitles in the Homeric world: they may have "shape" and come forth fast and thick as winter snow (*Od.* 11.367; *Il.* 3.222), but it is not clear that Homer would think of different styles of speaking as much as simply different speeches. Certainly there is no sense in Homer that there are different versions of the "Wrath of Achilles" or the "Quarrel of Achilles and Odysseus." Such a distinction has very little use in what we know of other traditional oral poetry, where stability of theme is prior to and more important than stability of form.[55] The bards Lord studied did not claim to "compose" songs artfully; they actually repudiated originality and claimed (falsely of course) that they only reproduced them, the same way each time.[56] These claims are intelligible in practical terms: while the singer learns the songs and performs them, the story and the way it is told are united; there is no benefit or intellectual reward for separating them. George Walsh puts it well: "What a modern reader conceives to be 'knowledge of facts' or 'subject of song' . . . Homer simply calls 'song.' . . . the facts presumably speak for themselves. Thus there is no occasion for a specifically human verbal art to make facts into poetry."[57]

[53]Lanata (1963) 14 says this passage shows that skill and inspiration are "co-present"; cf. Murray (1981) 97. Schadewaldt (1965) 78–79 gives an avowedly Pindaric interpretation: the singer says that he has not merely "learned" his songs (like the lowly handworkers in his guild) but has adapted his art from the Muses. Fränkel (1973) 19–20 interprets it as boasting that the poet not only can repeat what he has heard but can produce songs on a proposed topic. Walsh (1984) 11 takes it as "equivocally a claim also for the artistry of a god" (further references at his 137 n. 24).

[54]Russo and Simon (1968) 493–497. Thalmann (1984) 230 n. 27 makes this point apropos of Hesiod.

[55]Finnegan (1977) 58–69; Ong (1982) 60–62.

[56]Lord (1960) 26–29, 101, (1954) esp. 240–241, 409–413; cf. Jensen (1980) 68 and Thalmann (1984) 128 and 171 n. 29.

[57]Walsh (1984) 10–11.

Thus the poet's conception of his art as an impersonal telling and the way the oral verse technique was learned would not have contributed to any distinction, fundamental though it is for our rhetoric, between form and content, the poet's polish and the Muse's memory. Invocations may be read simply as the poet's claim that he didn't simply make up the stories he is about to sing. Hence in Phemius's proclamation the two clauses are synonymous: an inspired poet gets his song from the Muses and so is self-taught in the sense that he gets them from no one else.[58]

We should not then let a romantic interest in the creative artist distort the absolute dominance given to the Muses, and we must agree with Fränkel that "Homeric epic arose under conditions under which one cannot speak of literary property in our sense."[59] Yet a different if equally fallacious romantic idea threatens if Homer's indifference to verbal artistry is embraced as his sensitivity to the primeval power of language, working autonomously merely by being uttered, like magic spells. On this view, this impersonal poetic would represent a stage of thought before the fatal fall of form away from content, when the poet is still less an artist than a medicine man.[60] It seems to be true that the origins of poets and seers lie close together, and Homer certainly has faith in magical language, such as the "incantations" that can heal (*Od.* 19.457). Yet, by Homer's time the poet's role and name have been growing apart from that of the seer or magician, and the word for incantation (*epaoidê*) can be distinguished from that for song (*aoidê*). Alternatively, one might posit that the notion of the self is still inchoate, so that the poet's minimal role in singing is explained by the early stage of a gradual evolution toward proud, self-conscious artistry, an evolution in which Hesiod's boastful proem marks the next step and lyric (romantically conceived as self-expression) the culmination.[61] But this kind of explanation mistakenly sees Homer as less self-reflexive than Hesiod just because his texts have no proem and hence none of the conventional self-advertisement. Finally, some

[58]The best recent discussion of these lines is Thalmann (1984) 126–127.

[59]Fränkel (1973) 7, and cf. 11, 15–16.

[60]Marg (1957) 11–12; Maehler (1963) 9–10. For "medicine man," see Schadewaldt (1965) 78–79.

[61]Kranz (1924) 67; Sperdutti (1950); Maehler (1963) 17; Lanata (1963) 21.

speak of epic poetry as "society's means of self-expression."[62] It is true that early Greek literature generally does not value self-expression per se, but this is not to say that epic poets were unconscious or paradisiacally unconcerned for themselves; this idea is hardly credible for Greeks, who at one time or another made competitions out of virtually every form of poetry from high tragedy to singing over wine. And it is hard to square with the praise given within the poems to poets as performers; with the names given them, Phemius ("man of fame"), for example, and Demodocus ("received by the people"); and with the obvious pride in themselves and what they do which poets display in the proems.

The point I would make is not that Homer is naïve about language or the self but, as Jesper Svenbro has shown in his study of early Greek poetics, that Homer goes out of his way to avoid speaking of the poet's activity in terms of "art" or "skill" or "craft."[63] Svenbro points out that Homer does have a stock of old, even Indo-European words from the arts and crafts which can be applied metaphorically to intellectual and verbal contriving. Indeed, such metaphors often describe that pervasive and highly valued cunning summed up in the word *mêtis*.[64] Homer speaks of "constructing" a clever trick (*mêtin . . . tektênaito* [*Il.* 17–19]), "fitting together a snare" (*dolon . . . êrtue* [*Od.* 13.439]), or "weaving" and "stitching together" evil plans (*Il.* 6.187, 18.637). But the masters of *verbal* cunning turn out not to include poets: it is Odysseus who "constructs a tale" (*epos . . . paretektênaito*) to get a robe from Eumaeus (*Od.* 14.131–132), beggars who "fit together lies" (*pseudea . . . artunontas* [*Od.* 11.363–366]), and councillors who "weave speeches" (*muthous . . . huphainein* [*Il.* 3.212]). As historians of archaic Greek thought, we might put the poet's skill in the category of *mêtis*, a not quite scientific but highly effective ability to combine "all kinds of elements" (*pantoios*), especially to make a snare or trick. But in trying to define Homer's conception or representation of the place of his art among human activities, we must

---

[62]E.g., Schadewaldt (1965) 75–79; Marg (1957) 12; the quoted formula is taken from Thalmann (1984) 113.

[63]Svenbro (1976) 193–212. This provocative and insightful book has been controversial on some points but this is not one of them. Cf. Ritoók (1989) 344–346.

[64]Detienne and Vernant (1974) offer a rich study of *mêtis*.

note that his vocabulary for his art and its "product" is centered not on matter, making, and artifact but on a special singing sanctioned by divinity—*thespis aoidê*. Conceptions of poetry as performance allied to magic and religion dominate his self-presentation. If Homer tells us anything about a bard's song beyond the mere fact that he was singing, he will tell us what the song is about; he may add that the song was pleasing or enchanting, but he takes little notice of concrete form or any other aspect of the text.

This is in part an argument from silence, but it gains force if we contrast for a moment a quite artistic description of the working poet from *Beowulf:*

> At times the king's thane
> a man with memory   for songs of praise
> who stored in his mind   a vast number
> of old stories,   found word after word
> bound in truth;   in his wisdom he began
> to sing in turn   of Beowulf's exploit
> and skillfully related   an apt tale,
> varying his words.[65]

We have here explicit recognition of various aspects of the poet's personal excellence—his memory, creativity ("finding"), wisdom, skill, sense of aptness—and even references to poetic techniques specific to the scop—alliteration (so 871a may be read) and variation (874a). Search as we may, we find no comparable material in Homer, though two passages are often adduced to support a recognition of the poet's ability as a kind of skill: Telemachus lists poets among the *dêmiourgoi*, "craftsmen" (*Od.* 17.382–385) and Odysseus is praised for telling his story like a singer, "skillfully" (*epistamenôs* [*Od.* 11.368; cf. *Works and Days* 107]). But the interpretation of each passage is strained. A "demiurge" in Homer is far from being the craftsman that he would become in Plato; as the passage itself makes clear, the word applies to anyone who offers a special service not to a single household but to the community, the *dêmos.*

---

[65]*Beowulf* 867–874a. Translation Niles (1983) 37, together with a discussion. Cf. *Beowulf* 2105–2114.

Inasmuch as the ranks of demiurges mentioned by Telemachus include the prophet and the healer as well as the woodcutter any conception of an art they have in common must be very broad indeed. To call a singer a demiurge, then, only places him in a social class united by mobility rather than analogous skills.[66] So too with *epistamenôs:* it is tendentious and anachronistic to translate this adverb as "skillfully" or "according to the rules of his art"[67] as if its root verb were already Aristotle's word for scientific knowledge and Homer had a notion of art as a set of abstract rules wholly separable from the individual practitioner.[68] In epic *epistamai* means "to know how" in the broadest sense, extending from special knowledge to a dancer's dexterity. Used of poetry, it need not imply deliberative skill any more than when it is used of a herald's penetrating call or of nimbly dancing feet; nothing more need be read into this line than that the singer sings "capably."[69]

Svenbro, then, is right to draw attention to Homer's reticence about his own artistry, but his explanation is along the lines of the primitivist. On his view, Homer shies away from descriptions of his own skills because such self-assertion would be an impiety; for the same reason, he rejects signing his work.[70] I would say, rather, that the idea of the poet as artist is not so much absent from Homer as sequestered from epic proper: it is not allowed in invocations or in representations of poets, but would have been welcome in a proem, as indeed the poet's "signature" would have been.[71] In fact, the one exception to Svenbro's case shows that the skill that "fashions" heroic stories can be seen in Homer, but transposed onto the gods.

In maintaining that the Homeric poet is too pious to claim the

[66]Noted by Stanford (1974) of *Od.* 17.383–385.

[67]Murray (1981) 98; Schadewaldt (1965) 71 ("kunstgerecht").

[68]For the Homeric idea of *technê,* see Kube (1969) 14–19.

[69]See Snell (1924) 81–96. Cf. Walsh (1984) 135 n. 5. My "capably" is taken from the shrewd discussion of Jensen (1980) 73.

[70]Svenbro (1976) 18–25.

[71]I would add to the proemic vocabulary for "crafting" poetry noted in the previous section Pseudo-Hesiod fr. 357 M-W. In a fictitious proem Hesiod says that he and Homer "stitched song into new hymns."

status of artist, Svenbro has to reckon with Agamemnon's words about Penelope in the underworld:

> the fame [*kleos*] will never die,
> of her excellence, and a song [*aoidê*] for men on earth
> the gods will fashion [*teuxousi*], one pleasing to prudent Penelope.
>
> [*Odyssey* 24.197–198]

Svenbro appeals to the lateness of book 24 and also tries to dilute the sense of *teuxousi* from "fashion" to a vaguer "furnish."[72] But I am trying to take the whole poems as we have them, and it is hard to wring out all sense of artistry from the verb. *Teukhein* is very often a word for building or crafting (e.g., *Il.* 6.314; *Od.* 12.347) and is especially associated with the paragon of craftsmen, Hephaestus (*Il.* 2.101; *Od.* 8.195, 276, 18.373). It seems indeed that Penelope's song has been shaped by art, just as another artist intervened decisively in the Trojan War: the man who built the fatal ship that brought Paris to Greece is "Famebearer, the son of the builder / Fitterson, who knew how to fashion [*teukhein*] all intricate things with his hands" (*Il.* 5.59–61). We cannot then deny that the singing about Penelope has been artfully contrived, but note that the contriving has been done by the gods, not by poets. The idea of epic plots as the product of divine artistry can also be found in Nestor's account of the Greek returns: Zeus first "planned" (*mêdeto*) a baleful return for the Achaeans and then "fitted evil [*kakon êrtue*] upon them" (*Od.* 3.132, 152). So Helen makes the gods the ultimate creators of the epic in which she and Paris will figure: "Zeus has made an evil fate for us, so that hereafter / we might be a subject of song for men to come" (*Il.* 6.357–358).[73] The thought must be that poets simply present stories of the past, which have been directed and shaped by greater powers. Epic, then, seems to have chosen to

---

[72]Svenbro (1976) 194, citing *Od.* 10.118, among other passages.

[73]With "make" (*thêke kakon moron*) cf. *Od.* 3.136: Athena "made strife" for the Atreidae on their return. One also thinks of *Il.* 1.2 where the Wrath of Achilles "made" countless woes for the Greeks through the plan of Zeus. For the use of the verb (cognate with Latin *feci*) in divine creation, cf. *Works and Days* 173d, with West's (1978) note.

divert ideas of verbal artistry from its singers and to have trans-
ferred them onto gods as the ultimate shapers of events.[74]

Thus Homer discounts and even denies the significance of the
poet in shaping and defining poetry. The work of the poet is not to
tell a story in a certain way but simply to tell a certain story, and the
figure of the *aoidos* is linked not with artisans but with itinerant
specialists who can do things most people cannot. Homer's depictions of poets present a poetry without rhetoric, a pure presentation of the tale without embellishment or distortion from the teller.
It seems that Homer would have the meter and dialect of his texts
pass unnoticed in our conception of his art, for the form of a story
is not of interest apart from the story. Genres of unsung poetry,
then, are demarcated significantly by their ethos, and the invocation and the representation of poets in epic are part of that genre
which advertised itself as a tale told without rhetoric. We need not
think that epic poets were purely selfless or that they yielded to
some larger social voice; nor need we strike a fine balance between
the "I" and "you" of invocations, primitivizing or historicizing the
poet's "I." What we have is a convention: we are not in some
period before the discovery of the self, but we are in a genre in
which it was expected that the poet would remove himself from
the text and speak not as an artisan of words but as transmitter of
stories.

These negative conclusions throw into more prominence those
tales that are presumably told without art. To know more about the
art of poetry, then, we should look more closely at these stories and
at how they are classified. Of particular interest is a system of
metaphors centrally important to the poet in organizing his tradition in his mind and in relating himself to that tradition. We will
find that just as Homer has projected poetic artistry onto the gods,
he has projected narrative structure onto the deeds themselves.

---

[74]A further parallel can be found in Hesiod fr. 273 M-W if one reads the manuscript's *edeiman,* used of house building (instead of *eneiman*): "Sweet it is to find out
all those things the gods have *erected* for mortals, as a clear mark distinguishing the
coward and the brave."

A Topical Poetic

Invocations tell us obvious things about epic tales—that they are large, that they are about sorrowful deeds of heroes, that the gods' plans work through them. But the very care and consistency with which these things are repeated is significant, for as stories are a primary and constant interest of the poet, they are the one element in this fluid, variable art of performance that is given stability, identity, and a name. In its regularized way of defining and announcing particular stories, this oral art comes closest to establishing fixed, essential elements of the singer's profession. To be sure, the "Wrath of Achilles" doesn't fix the story into a single, unalterable verbal form like a written, titled work, but identifies only a flexible constant behind the oral performance. Certainly it could not be told so that it contradicted major events of accepted heroic history, but beyond that, it was little more than a flexible plan of events to be presented as the occasion demanded.[75] Nor is the distinction between one theme and the next or between a theme and a subtheme rigid and easy to demarcate: stories belonging to the same general area of mythic history may be shaded into one another or isolated for individual treatment.[76] For example, in book 8 of the *Odyssey* Homer first calls what Demodocus sang the "Quarrel of Odysseus and Achilles, son of Peleus" (*Od.* 8.75); later Odysseus refers to this same song in more general terms as the "destruction of the Achaeans, / all that they did and suffered and wrought at Troy" (8.489–490); yet later, Alcinous seems to subsume this song and Demodocus's subsequent "Fashioning of the Wooden Horse" (*Od.* 8.500–501) under the larger title of the "Destruction of the Argive Danaans and of Ilion" (*Od.* 8.578). The focus on painful action is constant, as is the awareness of just who's getting the worst of it at each moment, but beyond that, the title gives no precise definition of the contents and limits of the story.

Yet it is fair to think of varying performances as centering on a

[75]See Lord (1960) 68, 96–97, 119–120, and cf. M. Parry's definition of "theme": "the groups of ideas regularly used in telling a tale in the formulaic style of traditional song" (Parry [1971]).
[76]Excellent remarks on this in Finnegan (1977) 107.

single, fixed story insofar as they recount determinate incidents that befell determinate heroes, and these in a determinate sequence. In addition, these individual stories are also more abstractly "fixed" together, for invocations tell us that each tale must take a starting point in a larger frame of memorable acts. The basis for this genre of singing, then, is the fiction that behind the telling of each story exists one divinely superintended tale, one connected whole that never alters, though parts of it may be performed in this or that time and place.

That Homer and Hesiod conceived of a larger realm of interconnected stories is clear from two technical terms or terms of the trade. One is the word for an individual theme, *oimê*, and the other the word for changing from one theme to another, *metabainô* (which occurs only once within epic, though is very well attested in proems). Taken together, these quasi-technical terms suggest what Walter Ong calls a "topical poetic," a poetic that identifies individual themes as having a determined place in relation to other themes along a road or path. The stability and continuity of individual stories are metaphorically expressed as paths, and the tradition is figured as the great tract in which these stories may be joined end to end. How the poets imagined this total structure of stories is significant for defining epic, for the metaphorical shape the poets give that matter is a map of poetic genres within epos. We will see that the final shape of these tracts of song is the entire world of the past, the "deeds of gods and men to which bards give *kleos*," including Homer's poetry but also Hesiod's theogonic poetry as well.

Both technical terms are found in Homer's longest sustained portrait of a bardic performance. Early in book 8 Homer describes an after-dinner performance by Demodocus:

> After they had put aside the desire for food and drink,
> the Muse then stirred up the singer to sing the fames of men [*klea andrôn*]
> from that path [*oimê*] whose fame at that time reached broad heaven,
> the Quarrel of Odysseus and Achilles, son of Peleus.
>
> [*Odyssey* 8.72–75]

The term here that has attracted most attention is the "fames of men," the *klea andrôn*. But I will reserve an analysis of that phrase for the next chapter and first look at its constituent parts. An *oimê* is an individual story within the heroic repertoire, which can in turn be conceived as a series of *oimai* (pl.): "The Muse has made *oimai* / of every kind grow in my heart" (*Od.* 22.347–348). To be a traditional poet is to "have learned" from the Muses (i.e., to know by inspiration) many *oimai*: "For among all men on earth singers / have a share in honor and respect, because the Muse has taught them / *oimai*, for she loves the race of singers" (*Od.* 8.479–481).

The way this word is used in early Greek indicates that it was a technical term for the individual themes of epic, and this sense of *oimê* is perhaps the source of the word "proem" (*pro-oimion*), meaning something like "the portion of the performance that comes before the main theme."[77] Apparently, *oimai* meant "paths" to the poet, so that the relative fixity and stability of themes was figured in Homeric language by describing them as if they were tracks cut into some landscape.[78] The process of singing was thus a progress, and Hesiod could sum up his election as poet by saying that the Heliconian Muses "made me walk upon [the path] of singing."[79] To proceed from one topic of heroic song to another was to "move

[77]So Chantraine (1977) defines *prooimion*, s.v. *oimê*: "That which is found before the development of the poem, prelude" ("ce qui se trouve avant le developpement du poème, prelude"). But an aspirated version of this word, *phroimion*, makes Frisk (1960–70) s.v. *oimê* judge this connection uncertain ("unklar"). See the next note.

[78]The etymology and original meaning of *oimê* are unclear, and it is not easily to be equated with *hoimos*, "path, road." But if it was a "technical" term adopted by singers (as both Frisk and Chantraine recognize), they may have distorted or not known its original sense. I take it as meaning "path" to Homer because the many spatial metaphors adduced here suggest that the poet has already assimilated it to the very similar sounding *(h)oimos aoidês*, "path of song," first attested in *Hymn to Hermes* 451; so Schadewaldt (1965) 74–75; Svenbro (1976) 36 n. 103. The "path of song" is an Indo-European metaphor (Durante [1958]), and is consonant with many well-established Homeric metaphors for the path or "way" of speech. Cf. Becker (1937) 36–37, 68–69. The same evidence, and the fact that archaic lyric rings so many happy changes on the metaphor, make it unwise to pronounce *oimê* a "dead metaphor" in Homer, meaning no more than "song," as does Harriott (1969) 65. Pagliaro (1951) 25–30, followed by Lanata (1963) 11–12 and others, has read the metaphor as "the thread of narrative," but his aim of distinguishing epic (as "connected story") from lyric is misplaced and anachronistic.

[79]*Works and Days* 659: *me . . . epebêsan aoidês*; cf. *H. Hermes* 464–465: "I do not begrudge you, Apollo, to walk upon [the path] of my art."

along" the paths of song, expressed in another apparently technical word, *metabainô*, to pass from one place to another. After Demodocus's "Quarrel of Odysseus and Achilles," Odysseus asks Demodocus for a different epic story:

> But come, move along [on the path of song] and sing the
>   Fashioning of the Horse,
> the wooden one that Epeius made together with Athena,
> which godlike Odysseus once brought to the acropolis as a trick
> filling it with men who sacked Ilion.
>
>   . . . . .
>   and he brought forth the song,
> taking it from that point when the Greeks embarked on their
>   well-benched
> ships and sailed away.
>
> [*Odyssey* 8.492–495, 499–501]

This is Homer's only use of *metabainô*, but it has the same sense it has in the conclusions of some hymns, where it signals their change of theme: "having begun with you I will move along to another hymn."[80] Like *oimê*, *metabainô* metaphorically conceives of song as spatially extended, and it belongs to the same quasi-technical language of early epos.[81] The choice of themes is therefore a choice of a place, as invocations choose where to start the story.

When a singer selects a particular theme, he is said to be stirred within his heart or mind (his *thumos* or *noos*) to go in a particular direction: "The Muse has given *aoidê* to the singer / to give pleasure, in whatever direction [*hoppêi*] his heart moves" (*Od.* 8.44–45); "why do you begrudge the noble singer / to give pleasure wherev-

---

[80]E.g., *Hymn* 5.293, 9.9. See Weber (1934) 445–448. This formula may even be used at the end of "longer" hymns. See Richardson (1974) on *H. Dem.* 495, against Böhme (1937) 76 n. 78.

[81]The same metaphor appears in lyric: Alcman 1.12 Page; cf. Pavese (1967). Xenophanes begins a song: "Now again I will enter on another story, and I will show the way" (*allon epeimi logon,* 7 IEG). A similar metaphor is in what Aristotle quotes as the first line of Choerilus of Samos's epic on the Persian War, but which is actually a transitional opening: *hêgeo allon logon,* "lead for me another story, how from the land of Asia / a great war came to Europe" (fr. 316 Ll-J–P). In prose similar metaphors mark a change of topic: Gorgias *Helen* 10, "Come now, I will move from one speech to another" (*pros allon ap' allou metastô logon*); cf. Herodotus 2.382, 6.39.1.

er his mind is stirred to go" (*Od.* 1.346–347).[82] The moving of the poet's mind is like a ranging over space; conversely, a god shooting speedily through space to Olympus "darts like the mind of a well-traveled man / whose mind [*noos*] flies . . . as he thinks, / 'I wish I were here, or there,' and he thinks of many places."[83] What we have here is a "topical poetic." This term from Ong's useful discussion (1977) nicely allies the identification of particular subject matter, particular "topics," with the figure of a theme as a particular place. The topics of epic are imagined as extending in space and their relation to each other is a matter of coming before or after. Within the "fames of men" the organization will appear to be genealogical-sequential: one tells a story straight through, the parent before the child, the first before the last, and so the Fashioning of the Horse before the Sack of Troy, but after Achilles' stories. But on the basis of this topical poetic we may also identify the special place for heroic song as a whole in relation to other songs with the same ethos, for the ends of our texts indicate that the tales of heroines and heroes have their place after but continuous with the stories of cosmogony and the rise of the gods.

Thalmann has shown particularly how the idea of "the poems and their larger unity" was more than an abstraction for poets, how it often resulted in individual "songs" being linked together when they were made into texts.[84] This process is most evident in the later-named "epic cycle," in which variously dated stories about the Trojan War were joined together to form a continuous history reaching from the origins of the war to its aftermath in the returns. But Thalmann notes too that the *Theogony* was linked (by Hesiod or another) with the *Catalogue of Women*, stories of gods'

---

[82]Cf. *H. Ap.* 20: "In every direction [*pantêi*] the range of your song extends, Phoebus." Perhaps we should also give locative rather than instrumental force to *pêi* in such phrases as "there is no way [i.e., direction] in which to remember song if I forget you," *Hymn* 1.17–18, cf. 7.58–59. The two adverbs are combined in Choerilus 317.4–5 Ll-J–P (= 1 K), discussed in Chapter 2.

[83]*Il.* 15.80–82. Apollo can fly off to Olympus "quick as thought" (*noêma* [*H. Ap.* 186]). For further examples, see Allen, Halliday, and Sikés (1936) on *H. Hermes* 43.

[84]Thalmann (1984) 75–77; on 77 he comes close to detaching, as I would, the *Works and Days* and its "sequel," the *Ornithomanteia* ("Bird Divination"), from his sense of epos. I would not follow him when he links this larger order to "the poem's structure, the paratactic linking of discrete passages that conform in shape to the traditional compositional patterns" (124).

pairing with mortal women and producing the great heroic lines. This seeming editorial violence was only realizing the vision such poetry had of itself, as can be seen from the *Theogony*'s proem, when the Muses sing such a continuous tale:

> Sending forth their immortal voice,
> the Gods' Revered Race they celebrate first in song
> from the beginning, whom Earth and broad Heaven begot,
> and the gods who arose from these, givers of good things,
> and next Zeus, the father of gods and men,
> as they begin and end their singing
> how he is mightiest of the gods and greatest in power,
> and next the Race of Men and of the Strong Giants
> they hymn, and they please the mind of Zeus on Olympus
> [*Theogony* 43–51]

The titling syntax draws attention to the various themes the Muses perform: their first song is devoted to the birth of gods and goddesses; then they sing a song devoted exclusively to Zeus; finally they proceed to tell of early generations of men. In this of course they anticipate the sequence of topics found in the *Theogony* and its sequel, the *Catalogue of Women*: gods from the beginning, Zeus's exploits, then mortal matters.[85]

Logically then, the *Iliad, Odyssey,* and all of what we call "epic" belonged further along on the same continuum. And so it appears if we gain a perspective outside of epic, from the *Hymn to Apollo*. It describes a Delian women's chorus who begin "from the gods" before moving on to heroic matters:

> When they first hymn Apollo
> and next Leto and Artemis who delights in arrows,
> calling to mind the men and women of old,
> they sing their hymn and enchant the tribes of mortals.
> [*Hymn to Apollo* 158–161]

The chorus's proem (n.b., "first," as in *Theogony* 44) acknowledges the presiding divinities on Delos; this proem may have included an

[85]Though the *Theogony* does not (now at any rate) give us the Muses' Giants, it is supplemented with the matings of gods and mortals as announced in 963–968 and 1019ff. (fr. 1 M-W). See West (1966) on *Theog.* 44.

extended narration of the birth of Apollo and Artemis, a favorite
theme of such poetry. When they turn from proem to heroic tale,
they are said to "call to mind" (*mnêsamenai*) the men and women of
old, that is, to invoke the Muses, daughters of Mnêmosunê.
Though proem and heroic tale are markedly distinct, they are also
continuous along the path of song and belong to a single "hymn-
ing." Pindar (*Nemean* 5.25ff.) represents the Muses obeying this
protocol even in those early times when gods were not yet set apart
from mortals: singing at the wedding of Peleus and Thetis, the
Muses' wedding song will perforce be a heroic song too, and needs
a divine preface: "They, after first / beginning with Zeus [*Dios
arkhomenai*], hymned Thetis / and Peleus, how Hippolyta wanted
to ensnare him."

The paths of song are very extensive, but they do not go on
forever: the continuum of stories pulls up at a time somewhat short
of the present. As both texts make clear (*Theog.* 100; *H. Ap.* 160),
klea andrôn are the "fames" only of men and women of old.[86] The
"epic" poet, then, is essentially a poet of the past, not a poet of
heroes or gods in particular. For his past he may turn, as Homer
does, to the noble heroes who fought beside gods at Troy, four
dark centuries before his day; or he may move further back in time,
to even earlier themes, to the women who, mating with gods,
founded the great royal lines, as Hesiod does, in a *Catalogue of
Women*.[87] What defines this "heroic" poetry is time: these mortals
are earlier and closer to the powerful origins of the world order.
Finally, the poet of the past may, without changing "genre," focus
on the affairs of the gods themselves, the earliest born of all, in a
theogony.

Just as in performance the gods must be acknowledged before
mortals, so in the abstract conception of the range of song any
heroic tale implicitly follows and continues the history of gods and
earlier heroes. Though for some kinds of (chiefly stylistic) analyses
it may be useful to distinguish Homer's poetry from Hesiod's as
epic from didactic, in the largest context the distinction between

[86]One might compare Bakhtin's notion of epic's "absolute past" in his "Epic and
Novel" (1981).

[87]I presume that "the hymn of ancient men and women" in *H. Ap.* 160 refers to
such poetry as the *Catalogue of Women* (cf. fr. 1.1 M-W).

them is not generic but topical. In his *Theogony* Hesiod no less than Homer is a poet of the past, and he calls his *Theogony* by the same name, *aoidê* (e.g., 22, 104). Each attributes the same repertoire to the *aoidos:* in Hesiod he "chants the fames of men of former times / and the blessed gods who hold Olympus" (*Theog.* 100–101); Homer's Phemius sings "the deeds of gods and men" (*Od.* 1.338), and Demodocus performs both Trojan saga and the affair of Ares and Aphrodite. Hence in the imagination of the "epic" genre, the *klea andrôn* as a whole are after but connected with stories of the birth and deeds of the gods. Epic is not a secular story about men as opposed to a divine story about gods but a later story in a continuous sacred history. Within this continuum one certainly knows the difference between tales purely about the gods and tales of heroic men and gods, but the "line" between them is not a generic line inscribed by literary considerations as much as one written across cosmic history. Within the poetry of the past Hesiod demands a special place by claiming that his is the first tale; Homer's poetry cannot claim that place but does announce that each tale is set under the same Olympian skies.

This whole is what I call the poetry of the past, a presentation of ancient but ever real and valid stories about gods and early mortals. The conventions of epic performance, the need for a *prooimion* before *oimê,* are not simply a matter of courtesy but define the place of epic in the order of things. This order, at once spatial and chronological, ritualistic and narratological, is the canon against which to define Homeric epic. Hence it is in a literary, religious, and cosmological sense that Homer's epic may be defined as poetry of the past.

The metaphors that establish the topical poetic have led us into the dark region of how poets imagine their art. It may seem natural to picture changing poetic themes as moving through space, but the idea as applied to epic seems to have a particular, if obscure, history. Karl Meuli has linked the poet's path of song to shamanistic ideas of journeying to hidden realms of knowledge.[88] The widespread but elusive figure of the shaman, who combined

[88]Meuli (1938) moots the shamanistic origins of epic on 164–176 and adduces the path of song on 172–173.

the roles of sacred singer, seer, healer, and visitor to the underworld, has more than once been adduced as the prototype of the
poet, and similarities between poets and these inspired seers could
be multiplied—as could differences. Such parallels are as tantaliz-
ing as our historical knowledge of Greek shamans is scanty, so that
to adduce them here would be to explain *obscurum per obscurius*.[89]
But it would be reductive to dismiss the magical notions near the
heart of the ancient idea of epic, and an inspired figure who knows
certain paths may be found closer to hand in the Homeric seer. It
has long been noted that Homer's description of Calchas's god-
given power to "know the things that are and will be and were" (*Il.*
1.70) is close to the Muses' gift to Hesiod to sing "what will be and
what was" (*Theog.* 32).[90] Indeed, Homer himself seems to suggest
the parallel between poet and prophet, for the first words Calchas
speaks in the poem are "Achilles, you bid me to tell / the Wrath of
Apollo, the far-darting lord" (*Il.* 1.74–75): the titling syntax in line
75 suggests that the Wrath of Apollo is a seer's account of events
that are later reincorporated into the poet's Wrath of Achilles.[91]
And we may further note that the proto-poet Calchas is also a
pathfinder: his gift of prophecy enables him not only to see deeply
into the present and future but also to lead the Achaean ships to
Troy (*Il.* 1.71–72). It does seem as if special ways of knowing are
also ways of navigating along seas whose measures can not be
taken by human skill.[92] Prophet and poet are seers of what is not
apparent, and both know paths we do not.

[89]For a cautious and informed assessment of Greek shamanism, see Burkert
(1972b) 162–165.

[90]Dodds (1957) 81, 100 n. 118; cf. Thalmann (1984) 225 n. 53 for discussion.

[91]We may note too that as Homer took up his tale in the ninth year of the war,
Calchas intervenes in the plague after nine days. Martin (1989) 40 says of Calchas's
use of "tell" (*muthêsasthai*) that it introduces a "discourse that has a formal nature,
often religious or legal; full detail is laid out for the audience, or is expected by the
interlocutor in the poem."

[92]So Teiresias will reveal to Odysseus "the road and the measures of the path"
toward home (*Od.* 4.389 = 10.539) and an Apolline oracle says it knows "the measures of the sea" (Herodotus 1.47.3). The poet Solon claims to know the "measure
of lovely wisdom" (13.52 *IEG*). Cf. Snell (1924) 7.

The Purpose of Poetry: Vividness

The final question to answer in defining the poetry of the past is what all this was for: Why rehearse the past? Why rehearse it in this impersonal way? The answer would seem to be simple: Homer and Hesiod speak constantly of the pleasure of poetry and its enchantment. But pleasure has rarely been seen as a sufficient justification for poetry in the history of criticism, and so a promise of the truth or instructive value of poetry has often been found in these texts. Here, the central dilemma of classical and neoclassical criticism threatens like Scylla and Charybdis: Is the purpose of poetry to instruct or to delight, to give us truth or pleasure? For on the one hand, to say that the purpose of poetry is only to stimulate aesthetic contemplation seems highly anachronistic and implausibly suggest that poetry was given and received as a recognized fiction and judged for the beauty and ingenuity of the artist's transformation of his material. Yet, on the other hand, it is not easy to attribute a strict ideal of historical truth to an age without documentation from the past, and to say that poetry provides us with moral instruction may be to read more into the texts than is there. Yet it is possible to avoid either of these impositions and take Homer and Hesiod at their words when they describe the purpose of poetry as pleasure; it is necessary, however, to understand such pleasure not as aesthetic appreciation but as an experience of what I will call *vividness*, a sense that the past is somehow present before us.

The only time epic mentions truth in connection with poetry is the notorious claim of Hesiod's Muses: "We know how to tell many lies that are like what is really so [*etumos*], and, when we will, to proclaim true things [*alêthea*]" (*Theog.* 27–28). Because Mnêmosunê, the mother of Hesiod's Muses, is interpreted as memory, and because Homer prays that the Muses may "remind" him, or "bring to mind" (*mnêsaiath'* [*Il.* 2.492]) the names of those at Troy, some scholars would find in epic a claim that the art and value of the poetry is to be "accurate," to convey "historical" truth.[93] Accord-

---

[93]The views, respectively, of Maehler (1963) 19 and Setti (1958) 144.

ingly, invocations are taken essentially as appeals for "information."[94] E. R. Dodds explains the reasoning behind such views:
"But in an age which possessed no written documents, where
should first-hand evidence be found? Just as the truth about the
future would be attained only if man were in touch with a knowledge wider than his own, so the truth about the past could be
preserved only on a like condition."[95] This is well observed, but
"truth" of course has a history all its own. Our best guide to what
the Muses mean when they claim to be able to say "true things"
may be A. T. Cole's important reconsideration of the concept of
truth denoted by *alêtheia* (1983). Cole notes that in the archaic period this word names a different kind of truth from historical accuracy (a sense better expressed by *etumos*). In Homer, *alêtheiê* and
its congates are used only of accounts by human speakers about
matters of which it is difficult to know the facts.[96] Hence, as an
evaluation of a speech, it is not a judgment on the reality of what is
told as much as on how it is told. Literally, "unforgetting," a "true"
speech was one that reported precisely and in detail, with scrupulous attention to what one has said before and the consequences
of what one is saying. Cole defines it in Homer as signaling "completeness, non-omission of any relevant detail, whether through
forgetting or ignorance."[97] This sense of truth is strikingly close to
the description an historian, M. I. Finley, has given of what he
found in Homer: "Yet, whatever else it may have been, the epic

[94]A very common view: Kranz (1924) 72; Minton (1960) 190; Lanata (1963) 13–14;
Maehler (1963) 16–19, 190; Murray (1981) 91, 96–97; Thalmann (1984) 224, and cf.
128.

[95]Dodds (1957) 81, who adds: "The gift, then, of the Muses, or one of their gifts,
is the power of true speech . . . it was detailed factual truth that Hesiod sought
from them."

[96]In fact, the only exception to this restricted use of *alêthea* in archaic epic is its use
(instead of *etumos*) of the Muses' divine discourse at *Theog.* 28, which Cole (1983) 21–
22 simply notices as "un-Homeric"; but perhaps the word is used there to suggest
that, for the human recipients of their song, its "truth" will still be of the human,
problematic sort. This interpretation may be implied in the rare verb used here for
"proclaim" (*gêruomai*), suggesting that the Muses are translating the truth for their
human public, as when Justice sits beside Zeus and "proclaims" his inscrutable
mind to mortals (*Works and Days* 260; but cf. *H. Herm.* 426).

[97]Cole (1983) 10; cf. Krischer (1965a) 167. Detienne (1967) offers an overview of the
evolving concepts of truth in archaic society.

was *not history*. It was narrative, detailed and precise, with minute descriptions of fighting and sailing, and feasting and burials and sacrifices, all very real and vivid; it may even contain, buried away, some kernels of historical fact—but it was not history."[98]

Looking for historical truth as the primary virtue Homer claimed for his poetry, then, may be anachronistic. Alternatively, the mention of the "hateful song" of Clytemnestra and the "pleasing song" of prudent Penelope in *Odyssey* 24.196–200 are cited for the belief that poetry provides moral instruction. If one adds Homer's Sirens, who promise Odysseus that if he listens to their song he will return "knowing more and taking pleasure" (*Od.* 12.188), one may read into Homer the neoclassical blend of *dulce* with *utile* and say that his poems contain both truth and delight.[99] Certainly there is nothing incongruous in taking pleasure from a true tale, as Thalmann notes, but it is a great inference to say with Walter Kraus that Homer's pleasure refers to the satisfaction of "the human desire to know."[100]

Homer certainly became the moral educator of the Greeks, but that is an entirely separate issue from whether Homer himself saw his poetry as instructive. The evidence suggests that it was specifically in the fifth century that, in James Redfield's words, the poet "lost the standing of a prophet and acquired the standing of a teacher,"[101] and there is a Socratic ring to such questions as What does the poet know? and What can he teach? I at least do not sense that these stories are presented to point to some "higher" truth, to reveal a moral or intellectual order underlying the appearance of things. Nevertheless, recent commentators have found Homer hinting at the moral uses of poetry and have even gone on to read into Odysseus's tears at the Trojan songs in book 8 of the *Odyssey*

[98]Finley (1975) 14–15. I think the Homeric phrase for such a style of narrative would be *kata kosmon*, which I will discuss in Chapter 3.

[99]Walsh (1984) 5–6, citing Maehler (1963) 33. Lanata (1963) 30 says, "If the end of poetry is delight its object is truth," but makes the point against her case that none of the names traditionally given to the Muses (e.g., "Enchanting-voice," "Radiance") evokes truth.

[100]Thalmann (1984) 129–130; Kraus (1955) 71.

[101]Redfield (1975) 42. Cf. Harriott (1969) 107 and Snell's (1953) tenth chapter, "Aristophanes and Aesthetic Criticism."

an essay on what makes the ideal poetic auditor.[102] But Kraus long
ago raised telling objections to this line of thought: poetry is consistently portrayed in epic as a passing enchantment or momentary
pleasure; its audience is rapt in silence. To interpret the tale for its
moral lesson would break the spell, and there is no mention of
anyone's doing so.[103] Just because Phoenix uses the heroic tale of
Meleager to instruct Achilles in *Iliad*, book 9, does not mean that
the singer presents his tales for the same reason. If we are compelled to allow that any poetry, whatever its claims for itself, cannot fail to teach us something, the truest and most profound teach-
ing that epic poetry may have done in its time would appear to
have been the very indirect and unconscious persuasion of its audiences to enjoy and admire a directly presented and unexplicated
image of heroic life.[104]

At least there is no doubt among commentators that the one goal
of poetry that Homer mentions, a dozen times at least, is pleasure
(*terpein*), even enchantment.[105] Our only insight into that emotion
is a much-discussed passage from Hesiod:[106]

> Happy is he whom the Muses love
> sweet flows the voice from his mouth.
> for if someone has pain and fresh grief in his soul
> and his heart is withered by anguish, when the poet,
> the servant of the Muses, chants the fames of men of former times
> and the blessed gods who hold Olympus,
> then straightaway he forgets his sad thoughts and thinks not of his
>   grief,
> but the gifts of the gods quickly turn him away from these.
>
> [*Theogony* 96–103]

[102]So Walsh (1984) chap. 1. Thalmann (1984) 147–148 on the *Theogony* draws a
distinction between the working of song and of anodyne drugs: "Poetry does work
forgetfulness of the pain and sorrow that are part of being mortal, but it does so by
turning its listeners toward a vision of ultimate truths that make their immediate
pains seem trivial by comparison." This sounds to me a better description of the
poetics of Parmenides.

[103]Kraus (1955) 69–70; cf. Walsh (1984) 13–14.

[104]On this deep level Vernant (1982) has credibly read a lesson to the citizen in the
epical image of the "beautiful death."

[105]References and discussion in Lanata (1963) 8–9. For enchantment, see *Od.*
1.337, 17.518–521; Hesiod fr. 27 M-W; cf. *Od.* 12.40, 44.

[106]See Nagy (1974) 257–258 and Pucci (1977) 16–21 and 200 n. 25 for bibliography.

Hesiod implies that it is at least in part because the songs are from the past—that is, not about ourselves—that they have their assuaging power. To put our minds on the deeds of others (especially when these deeds, as usual, entail great suffering) is to turn our minds away from our own griefs. The experience, then, which Plato called "turning the mind elsewhere" and which he confined to impersonation actually belongs to the whole of epos.[107] This is poetry that turns its listeners away from present cares to contemplate events of long ago: the happiness of the gods and the woe of other human beings are what turn us away from our own sorrows.

It is in this connection that we should appreciate the sacred nature of memory as Jean-Pierre Vernant has expounded it.[108] When Hesiod says the Muses are daughters of Memory, what *mnêmosunê* implies is less recollection or retrieval from storage than "mindfulness." The function of this memory is not simply preservation of the past but a psychological experience, to change the present frame of awareness.[109] As the passage from Hesiod puts it, when the poet sings, a man forgets sad thoughts and doesn't remember his grief (*oude . . . memnêtai*). Hence, when Hesiod describes the birth of the Muses from Zeus and Memory (*mnêmosunê*), he immediately riddles their name as "the forgetfulness [*lêsmosunê*] of woe and the cessation of worry" (*Theog.* 54–55). Vernant's insight is all the more comprehensible for a topical poetic in which time is space: sacred memory moves us not back in time but to another place, *au delà*, not "back" but elsewhere, along the tracks of memorable action.

Given this special power of memory, the audience is interested in epic song not because it happened but because it happened to others. The delight in the tale is not the satisfaction of accuracy or the communication of some higher truth but the pleasurableness of a convincingly full picture. From the poet's point of view we call this epic objectivity; but it has an equally important effect on the

---

[107]Pucci (1977) chap. 1 calls attention to Hesiod's metaphors for the ability of language to "deflect" the mind.

[108]Vernant (1959), discussed by Thalmann (1984) 147 and Detienne (1967) 9–20.

[109]*Mimnêskomai* is used of "being mindful of dinner" or "being mindful to defend your fellows"; cf. Snell (1964). Unlike Moran (1975), I would not separate from such uses a special "literary" sense of the verb for "remembering epic stories."

audience, something that we would not want to define as a purely aesthetic pleasure.[110] This effect has been variously named as a sense of "participation" or "Vergegenwärtigung," but I prefer to take a name out of Homer, via the Greek literary critics, *to enarges,* "vividness."[111]

In Homer the adjective *enargês* describes something or someone appearing convincingly and presently before one's eyes, especially a vision that others might not be able to see or that may not always be apparent to view. A dream may be vivid (*Od.* 4.841), but usually the word is used of the gods when they condescend to take on a form visible to men (*Od.* 3.420, 7.199–200, 16.161; *Il.* 22.131).[112] The Greek critics adopted this word to describe poetry that puts its incidents clearly before the audience's eyes.[113] Aristotle says the poet can achieve vividness by composing with his plot "placed squarely before his eyes," and he finds it especially keen in drama, even when read and not performed.[114] Longinus connects it with the poet's powers of visualization, *phantasia* (*On the Sublime* 15, 26). Again, I think that this is not pure theory on the part of these critics but the theorization of what was apparently a real psychological effect of epic performance, as can be seen in the testimony of Plato. His Socrates ventures that when a rhapsode performs Homer his soul is a little outside itself, and he "thinks that he is present at the events he is describing, whether they be in Ithaca or Troy or wherever" (*Ion* 535B). His interlocutor, a rhapsode, agrees with this "vivid point" and says that the audience "looks on me with awe and feels amazement together with me at what I say" (*Ion* 535E). The awe that the rhapsode provokes is

---

[110]As Setti (1958) 162 warns. Though I have profited much from Redfield's discussion of the "epic distance" I think he goes too far in saying (1975) 38: "The *kleos* of the song is the mark that, in it, history has been transformed into art. . . . A reversal then takes place. It seems that the event took place in order that a song could be made of it." Rösler's article (1980) reading a sense of "fictionality" into Hesiod's duplicitous Muses seems to me to fall into this mistake.

[111]Respectively Fränkel (1973) 15; Latte (1946) 159. Cf. Walsh (1984) 13 and Macleod (1983) 6–7 who adduces the later uses of *enargeia.*

[112]*LfrgE* s.v. *enargês* takes its association with epiphanies for its original meaning, translating "in splendor" ("'im Glanz,' sc. e Epiphanie").

[113]On "vividness" as a term in rhetorical criticism, see Ernesti (1962) 106 and Zanker (1981).

[114]*Poetics* 17.1455a22–26, 24.1462a16–17.

neither instruction (though learning comes from wonder) nor pure delight. It is the uncanny effect of the power of language to represent a hidden world merely by the accumulation of statements.[115]

I rehearse these passages because it is important to stress that the background of vividness is magical and epiphanic; we should not reduce it to an aesthetic notion, thinking of it, for example, as a compelling sensual impression as opposed to the clear and distinct ideas of logic. It is vividness as a feature of divine epiphanies that is involved in poetry's power to make the invisible past appear to its hearers. The first words of each poem effect this appearance by calling on the Muses: because we are granted their perspective, when the great speeches are given we seem to be on the edge of the assembly, and when the heroic actions are performed we seem to be present as onlookers.[116] Though epic is by definition poetry of the past, it is poetry that claims to transport us to an *au delà*, not a beyond buried in the vault of recollection but a place as present as our own, though elsewhere. According to Homeric eschatology, after death the heroes' bodies are destroyed in one way or another, and their souls fly off to Hades, the realm of the unseen.[117] The fundamental promise of his poetry is the paradox of restoring through mere voice these vanished heroes and rarely appearing gods to visibility. We may illustrate it simply by comparing again the power of Calchas with the power of the poet: Calchas reveals to the plague-stricken Greeks that what is really happening is that they have been beset by an angry Apollo; he can see and make known what they could not. But a similar skill also belongs to the poet himself, who in a few sublime lines has made Apollo, coming down from Olympus, appear to his audience, "with his bow, and the arrows clanged in his quiver as he went like night" (*Il.* 1.44–47).

The art of epic poetry which Homer inherited, then, was well

[115]Demetrius's prescriptions for achieving rhetorical vividness are interestingly close to the fullness of "true" epic style: it arises from "exact narrations, omitting nothing and abbreviating nothing . . . from everything that happens being said and nothing omitted" (*On Style* 209).

[116]Cf. Griffin (1980) 6: "The ancient commentators remark regularly on Homer's 'graphic' power, his skill at producing memorable scenes, and certainly this is a characteristic of Homeric writing that strikes the audience at once."

[117]The "helmet of Hades," which bestows invisibility in *Il.* 5.845, shows that this disputed etymology of Hades was operant for the poet; see Burkert (1985) 462 n. 13.

defined in certain moments of the performance, even if not quite defined in a literary way. Proems situated these performances in a particular place and time and also defined the singer and audience. The invocations then moved from that occasion to a timeless and universal realm in which the stories subsist with ideal integrity. In this transcendent realm presided over by the Muses, the stories of men are made permanent and are fixed as sequels to the stories of gods. The Muses are tightly bound up with this kind of poetry; indeed, they are central and make the difference between poets and nonpoets, so that the "art" of poetry is finally to be favored by the Muses. In the notion of genre which Homer constructs out of the oppositions of past and present, presence and absence, his singing, like much of Hesiod's, was a special presentation of the past, manifested in the effect I call vividness. In the next chapter we will see how this defining difference of the poetry of the past was rooted in a kind of seeing attributed to the Muses. Their seeing lies at the very heart of the difference between poetry and other tales of the past; a survey of celestial forms, it made the past appear in a way no other speech could. It is not surprising that we are permitted to hear such poetry only after prayer upon prayer.

CHAPTER 2

THE POEM
Homer's Muses and the Unity
of Epic

Poetry and Its Others

I have given an idea of how epic defined its place among
other forms of Greek poetry and how it constructed an internal
organization for itself, setting its themes within a comprehensive
order and its singing within the larger field of unsung poetry. The
difference that the presence of the Muses makes I have found not
in artistic shaping or in factual truth but in that especially convincing and absorbing quality I have called vividness. But insofar as I
have specified the "outside" limits of poetry, its differences from
nonpoetry, I have repeated Homer's own definition, which is a
vicious circle with a god in the middle: the Muses are what make
the difference between a singer and a teller, but a singer is simply
someone favored by the Muses. The central Muses, then, merit a
closer examination since they define singing as a whole in relation
to other uses of language, for the nature of poetry also depends on
how it is different from other discourses.

My approach to this limit of epic will be through the phrase *klea
andrôn*, the "fames of men." Clearly a traditional term for what the
poet sings, it has been taken by some as Homer's word for poetry,
or as epic's word for itself. But we will see that *klea* can designate
the entire range of oral tradition, and *klea andrôn* is any traditional

story from the past, not just those purveyed by poets. The phrase is indeed significant for defining epic, but for defining it from the outside, for Homer takes pains to distinguish his singing from "mere *kleos*." The distinction of "singing" from other forms of oral tradition (of *aoidê* from *klea*) serves instead of categories like poetry and prose to explore how epic claimed a unique and valuable place among the many discourses of the past.

The key ingredient that separates poetry from the fames of men or from any other discourse is expressed as a vision the Muses have of the past which serves to elevate the account they sponsor above other reports. We will find in Homer not a formal distinction between verse and prose but a claim for the superiority of sight over hearing which is converted into the triumph of singing over mere report. But this victory—achieved, after all, through language, not sight, and made by a singer traditionally portrayed as blind—is not easily won. In fact the great vision and scope of the Muses shadow the poet, and the comprehensiveness of their knowledge may threaten the integrity of his single song.

Here arises in Homeric form the problem of unity, the mainstay of all classically influenced criticism and the bugbear of Homeric studies since the Enlightenment. To demand strict unity of an oral work has long been regarded as problematic. We may again take our provocation from Albert Lord:

> We have exercised our imaginations and ingenuity in finding a kind of unity, individuality, and originality in the Homeric poems that are irrelevant. Had Homer been interested in Aristotelian ideas of unity, he would not have been Homer, nor would he have composed the *Iliad* or *Odyssey*. An oral poet spins out a tale; he likes to ornament, if he has the ability to so do, as Homer, of course, did. It is on the story itself, and even more on the grand scale of ornamentation, that we must concentrate, not on any alien concept of close-knit unity.[1]

If it was not Homer's endeavor to weave a seamless garment or to fashion a well-wrought urn, the problem of epic unity may nevertheless be found in his work, expressed as a tension between the

---

[1]Lord (1960) 148. Similar claims had been made by Perry (1937); Van Groningen (1958); and Notopoulos (1949).

coherence of the single song he performs and the totality of songs the Muses "see." For the poet, the tradition is the Muses, and so the relationship he establishes with them in his invocations is the place to find out how he managed to settle this problem. If we eavesdrop on Homer's prayers, we cannot fail to learn something about the poet's project as he conceived it and in particular about a crisis he faced which needed gods to overcome. The solution to this question, which is also the anchor of the special nature of his singing, I will call *the Muses' sublime*.

Klea Andrôn and Oral Tradition

To define the singer's art, *aoidê*, from the outside, let us contrast it with a traditional expression for the themes poets treat, *klea andrôn*. Etymologically, *kleos*, means "what is heard" and hence "fame"; and this phrase seems to attest to an ancient association of epic with Indo-European praise poetry, characterized as conferring "fame" on its subjects.[2] In Greek the connection is strong: Demodocus sings to a lyre the "fames of men" in the *Odyssey* (8.73), as does Achilles when he has withdrawn from battle (*Il.* 9.189); the phrase is also associated with singing in Hesiod and the Homeric hymns (*Theog.* 100–101; *Hymn* 32.18), and the verb *kle(i)ô* means "to celebrate," especially through poetry, as when Penelope speaks of "the deeds of men and gods, on which bards confer fame [*kleiousi*]" (*Od.* 1.338; cf. *Theog.* 32). But it has been further argued, in particular by Gregory Nagy, that "*kleos* was the formal word which the singer himself (*aoidos*) used to designate the songs which he sang in praise of gods and men, or, by extension, the songs which people learned to sing from him."[3]

Yet it must be realized that the etymological sense of *kleos* is still quite active in epic: simply as "what is heard," *kleos* may be report, reputation, or rumor.[4] And neither is the formula "fames of men"

---

[2]Schmitt (1967) 61–102. For *kleos* in Homer, see Murnaghan (1987) 149. n. 6, with references.

[3]Nagy (1974) 248, and cf. 244–255 and (1979) 16; cf. Segal (1983).

[4]Greindl (1938) 16–18, citing, e.g., *Od.* 16.461 ("talk about town"), 3.83, 4.317; cf. Redfield (1975) 32–34.

confined to traditions handed down in poetry: when Phoenix tells Achilles the Meleager story from the "fames of men" (*Il.* 9.524–525), he is no bard, any more than Achilles was when he sang the *klea andrôn* in his tent. Perhaps Phoenix heard this tale from a poet, but he doesn't say so, and it is given not as epic poetry but as exhortation.

Literally, *klea* only implies that the stories of heroes have descended through time in an oral tradition: what bards sing is indeed *kleos*, but fame or tradition may also be handed down in other ways. Indeed, we should not properly speak of oral tradition in the singular, for there are always many ways of passing down information in an oral culture, with various officers and styles. (Eric Havelock, in speaking of Homer's epic, uses the unfortunate metaphor "oral encyclopaedia," as if it were the single, comprehensive embodiment of all one needed to know.) Even in Homer it is clear that there are many people apart from poets who know about the past, and some figures specialize in it: Nestor has lived through three generations and is not reluctant to share his experience with younger men; in the *Odyssey* we can compare Echenous ("keeping intelligence"), who functions as a kind of "prose" epic historian: oldest among the Phaeacians, he surpassed them in speaking (*muthois*) and he knew "many ancient things" (*Od.* 7.156–157). Homer's task is not to define poetry against prose but to set his own art apart from the oral histories of these others, the "mythologues" that Plato refers to, or "men of tales" (*logioi*) as they are called by Pindar and Herodotus.[5]

Homer singles out the singers' presentation of *klea andrôn* not on formal grounds (as poetry versus prose) but by defining his Muses as lifting that song above the realm of mere rumor or hearsay:

> Tell me now, Muses, who have your homes on Olympus—
> For you are goddesses, and are present, and know [*iste*] all,
> but we hear only *kleos* and do not know [*idmen*] anything—
> [*Iliad* 2.484–486]

In a line of nearly incantatory assonance (2.485: *este, pareste te, iste te*) Homer attributes three things to the Muses: first of all, they

[5]Pindar *Pythian* 1.94, *Nemean* 6.52, and cf. 33; Herodotus 1.1.1.

exist, and they are goddesses and immortal; second, they are present, to the poet as he calls them and also presumably present as spectators at the events of which he wishes to speak; finally, they "know" these things, in the special sense compressed in the Greek verb, by having seen them.[6] With this repeated word (*iste/idmen*) the poet emphasizes the direct, unbroken contact that the Muses maintain with heroic history, as opposed to Homer and his generation (= "we"), mere mortals, who do not know, have not seen, but only hear the report (486).

The Muses, then, have an eyewitness knowledge of the past, and for Homer, in the Greek tradition, the surest and clearest knowledge is of that which you see yourself: it is not only a philosopher who says, "The eyes are more accurate witnesses than the ears," but a popular historian too: "The ears are less trustworthy than the eyes."[7] The opposition between sight and hearing of course became a part of sophisticated Greek epistemology, but I am not attributing advanced skeptical thought to the early Greeks if I say they knew the difference between what they saw with their own eyes and what they only heard, and were cunning enough and wary enough of being deceived to guard the distinction.[8] This commonsense skepticism need be no more or less significant than the aphorism of a literate culture "Don't believe everything you read"; but we should listen closely when an oral poet says, "Don't believe everything you hear."

"Poets are always chattering that we neither see nor hear anything accurately," Plato complains,[9] but Homer seems to have used this opposition to situate his own poetry as uniquely privileged in

---

[6]Snell (1924) 24–27 and (1964).

[7]Heraclitus 22 B 101a D-K; Herodotus 1.8.2; cf. Thucydides 3.38.4, 1.20.2 and Clay (1983) 13, in a valuable chapter: "This kind of cognition (sc. eye-witness knowledge), as opposed to knowledge through hearing, was considered by the Greeks the highest possible form of knowledge." Further references at her note 8.

[8]For the later philosophical development of this opposition, especially in reference to Xenophanes, see Fränkel (1974) 118–131. The idea is reversed for paradoxical effect by Empedocles (31 B 3.9 D-K) and by a literate poet who cherished texts before recitations, Callimachus fr. 282 Pfeiffer.

[9]*Phaedo* 65B; cf. *Phaedrus* 250D, 274. Plato may have in mind many reflexes of the idea in tragedy, e.g., Aeschylus *Persians* 266; Sophocles *Oedipus the King* 6, 1238, *Trachiniae* 747; Euripides *Suppliants* 684, *Trojan Women* 481–482, *Iphigeneia in Tauris* 901, *Hippolytus* 86, *Medea* 652.

the world of report. The fiction of the Muses serves to distinguish heroic poetry from other oral traditions: it elevates such poetry above mere "report" into a contact, mediated to be sure, with an actual witness to the events.[10] By contrast, the selection from the fames of men that Phoenix "remembers" and communicates to Achilles is only what "we learn of" or "find out" (*epeuthometha*) from mere report (*Il.* 9.524, 527).[11] Most of oral tradition consists of such secondary reportage, as when Agamemnon speaks to young Diomedes:

> Alas, son of shrewd Tydeus, breaker of horses,
> why do you cower, avoiding the turbulence of war?
> Not indeed was it Tydeus's way to cower so
> but far in the forefront of his friends to fight the enemy.
> So they say, the ones who saw him about the work of war; for my
> part,
> I never met him or saw him; but they say he excelled over all
> others.
>
> [*Iliad* 4.370–75]

The point of such a qualification is surely not to cast doubt on the speaker's veracity; it is rather to categorize this story within the structures that the society recognizes for old tales and their uses.[12]

In this context Homer uses his all-seeing Muses not only to exalt epic but even to disparage other accounts of the past as "mere"

---

[10]Cf. Dodds (1957) 100 n. 16: "I take it that what the poet prays for here is not just an accurate memory—for this, though highly necessary, would only be the memory of an inaccurate *kleos*—but an actual vision of the past to supplement the *kleos*. Such visions, welling up from the unknown depths of the mind, must once have been felt as something immediately 'given,' and because of its immediacy, more trustworthy than oral tradition." To this extent I would agree with Nagy (1979) 95: "The conceit of Homeric poetry is that the sacred mnemonic power of the Muses is the key to the *kleos* of epic."

[11]For the association of "finding out" and "hearing" (*p(e)uth-* and *akouô*), see *Od.* 2.118, 3.193, 4.94, 688, 15.403 and Clay (1983) 13 n. 8.

[12]A close parallel to this passage has been noted in an archaic poem by Mimnermus (14.1–4 *IEG*), stirring up his audience with the recollection of a great warrior two or three generations earlier:"His was not such might and warring spirit, / so I learn (*peuthomai*) from my elders, who saw him / scattering the crowded ranks of Lydian horsemen / On Hermus' plain, a spearman." For the historical context see West (1974) 73–74, though it is just possible that, as Bowie (1986) 29 suggests, the lines come from a fictional battle narrative.

kleos. This theme may be seen particularly clearly in relation to the oral tales that are heroic genealogies. Genealogy was one of the most important uses of the past for both Homer's characters and his audiences, and yet it is not to be thought that the basis of genealogy as words, discourse, escaped the Greeks. When Athena asks Telemachus whether he is really Odysseus's son, he expresses a skepticism of genealogies that sounds proverbial: "My mother *says* I am Odysseus's son, but for my part / I don't know. No one knows firsthand [*autos*] his own begetting" (1.215–216).[13] In fact, the more important and impressive a genealogy is, the more it will have to reach back into the past and ground itself in what has not been seen but can only be claimed, whether this be a great founder many generations back or a scene of divinity descending to mate with a mortal, often in secret or in disguise.

Naturally enough, then, heroic poetry interests itself greatly in genealogies, but it claims a superior knowledge of them. From his Olympian Muses, Homer knows which foundational stories are true, and he lets his audience know (e.g., *Il.* 5.541–549; *Od.* 15.225–226); but he puts his characters on a plane of limited knowledge about the past, so that for them, as for Homer's audience, genealogies are only a matter of what people say. As a consequence we often see heroes preface a recitation of their ancestors with a dismissal of the use of what people say (e.g., *Il.* 6.145–151, 21.153–160), and heroes often dispute the genealogies of their foes as part of the flyting preceding an engagement. A simple case is when Heracles' son Tlepolemus challenges Zeus's son Sarpedon: "They lie when they say that you are the son of aegis-bearing Zeus / since you fall far short of those men / of former times who were begotten of Zeus." (*Il.* 5.635–637). Dramatically, of course, this is a piece of bravura and not an epistemological essay, but it is also an ironic statement in that the abuse of genealogy is put into the mouth of a son of Heracles himself. If heroes can challenge a tale of ancestry only a single generation long, the problem in Homer's day may be only that much greater. Such moments allow Homer to make points for his own audience about the special place of song in

---

[13]A similar phrase is Menander fr. 227. Martin (1990) chap. 2 examines the rehearsing of genealogies as a kind of speech act.

preserving the past and, indeed, to assert a very noble "genealogy" of epic.

The most extensive genealogy offered us in Homer is also the
one most hedged by reservations about the trustworthiness of traditions. Indeed, the flyting here is so intense and extended that it
reaches beyond condemning a particular boast and casts asper-
sions on the entire realm of oral tradition. In book 20 of the *Iliad* we
are shown an encounter between Achilles and Aeneas which
proves also to be a confrontation of two divine genealogies, an
inconclusive match between the son of Thetis and the son of Aphrodite.[14] The genealogical theme emerges at the start, when Apollo, having taken human form, urges Aeneas to take Achilles on:

> They say you are born from Aphrodite, daughter of Zeus
> and Achilles only has Thetis, the daughter of the old man of the
>   sea,
> don't therefore turn back.

> [*Iliad* 20.104–106]

This is to be a test of divine parentage, and the issue of genealogy
dominates the subsequent flyting. Very much in the style of
Tlepolemus, Achilles taunts Aeneas by asking how he dares to
come to the forefront of battle, reminding him that he had only
barely escaped the last time they met; Achilles suggests that
Aeneas has possibly been mislead by that piece of luck into thinking he enjoys divine favor (20.178–198). The poet knows, and has
earlier (*Il.* 5.311ff.) let the audience know, that Aphrodite, Aeneas's
"mother who had borne him," is indeed willing to snatch her child
from a threatening foe. But Achilles remains to be convinced of the
hero's relationship to the gods. Aeneas counters with an interesting speech on the uses of genealogy:

> Son of Peleus, don't expect to frighten me with words as if I were
>   a child,
> since I too know quite well how to wrangle and insult.

---

[14]Nagy has a rich chapter discussing this scene (1979) 265–276, though I think
there is no warrant for saying (271–272) that "Aeneas and Achilles . . . have complete *poetic* access to each other's lineage" (emphasis mine).

We know [*idmen*] each other's lineage, we know [*idmen*] each
    other's parents.
by hearing the sayings [*epea*] that have been heard before [*prokluta*]
    among mortal men;
but as for actually seeing them, you have never seen [*ides*] my
    parents, nor I yours.
They say that you are the offspring of blameless Peleus
and that your mother was fair-tressed Thetis of the sea;
for my part, I claim to be son of great-hearted Anchises
and my mother is Aphrodite;
one of these pairs will mourn their child
today, since I don't think that with mere childish words
we will separate from this encounter and go back from battle.
But if you wish, listen to this, so that you may well know
my lineage, many are the men that know it.
Zeus the cloud-gatherer first begot Dardanus. . . .

                      [*Iliad* 20.200–217]

Aeneas dwells on the frailty of our knowledge of the past in the
same terms that engage the poet: we "know" about heroic genealogies only through "hearing" the tales passed down in oral
tradition (*prokluta epea*); it is not something that one has seen (*ides*).
Aeneas's anaphoric pair, "we know" (*idmen*, 202), resounds hol-
lowly against the "you know" / "we know" (*iste*/*idmen*) that the
poet had addressed to the Muses, and it puts such recitations in
the category of "mere *kleos*." Hence he specifies that "they say"
Thetis was Achilles' mother. As far as his own heritage is concerned, he is willing to lay claim to his title and to go on for fifteen
hexameters tracing his royal line back to Zeus-born Dardanus; but
he adduces this genealogy only as a "claim" or a boast, something
generally acknowledged, what "all men know."[15] Even for these
god-sprung heroes genealogies are a matter of *kleos*. They get them
the same way Phoenix got the Meleager tale, by hearing the words
that have been spoken before.

---

[15]On the importance of Aeneas's "I claim" (*eukhomai*), see Muellner (1976) 76–78.
Cf. *Il.* 14.113–127 (Diomedes in council): "Hear me, though I am young. I claim to
be of a good father"; he justifies this claim by reciting three generations but adds
"you are likely to have heard whether these things are true" (14.125).

Aeneas concludes his catalog of ancestors by again downgrading oral report and calling for the test of arms:

> Such is my lineage and the blood I claim to come from.
> But Zeus is the one who gives men might or takes it away,
> as he wishes, for he is most mighty.
> Come then let us no longer talk back and forth like children
> standing in the midst of hostile battle.
> There are many things we might say to insult each other,
> so very many, a hundred-benched ship couldn't carry the load.
> For the tongue of mortals is slippery, and there are many tales in
>   it,
> all kinds of tales, and the great rangeland of words reaches far and
>   wide.
> The kind of thing you say is what you are likely to hear.
> But what need have we for quarreling and abuse,
> standing her insulting each other, like women
> who fall into a rage over some soul-destroying quarrel
> and heap abuse on each other when they meet on the street,
> some of it true, some false, and some provoked by anger.
> I am bent on valorous action and you won't put me off with words
> before fighting face to face with bronze. Come then
> and let us try each other's strength with the bronze of our
>   spearheads.

[*Iliad* 20.241–258]

Aeneas's speech might raise questions about how we get our heroic stories. Do our heroic lines come from the slippery tongues of mortals, men who can say anything, who can say everything? There are no Muses guaranteeing this genealogy here; it is mere oral report, shifty, uncontrollably large, its truth subject to the mood of the speaker.[16]

Reliance on oral traditions alone, speech without the test of strength, is consigned by Aeneas to unheroic categories: it is womanish, childish, weaker than action. When, in the event, Achilles discovers that Aeneas's genealogy is true, it is by action and not words. After Achilles shatters Aeneas's shield with his spear and moves in to dispatch him, Poseidon intervenes to save the Trojan, actively and verbally confirming his lineage, "so that the race of

---

[16]The notion that what you say determines what you hear in return is proverbial; cf. Hesiod *Works and Days* 721; Alcaeus 341 Voigt.

Dardanus shall not die, without seed, obliterated, / Dardanus whom Cronus's son loved most of all his sons" (*Il.* 20.303–304). Poseidon spirits Aeneas away in a mist, and when the clouds clear, Achilles is astonished to see his spear on the ground but Aeneas gone. He then concludes: "Aeneas after all was dear to the immortal gods. / I thought what he said was empty boasting" (20.347–348). A generation of Dardanians has been saved, and along with it a genealogy has been proved to go back to the gods; this *kleos* proved to be true, but it needed proof.[17] But the poet's song is also indirectly validated, for he knew the true story that even a goddess's son could doubt. Deriding all but his own divine lineages is the privilege of one behind whom the Muses stand, somewhat as Poseidon stood by Aeneas.

The Unity of a Traditional Song

Perhaps the most striking metaphor in Aeneas's description of oral genealogical tradition is his characterization of it as a "great rangeland of words" (*epeôn . . . polus nomós* [*Il.* 20.249]). The figure of the "range" of things said as a spatially extended field or pastureland (*nomós*), like Homeric metaphors for poetry, depicts language as an extended field, and it seems not to be idiosyncratic.[18] This idea of words as spread out like a grazing land for flocks is also found in the *Hymn to Apollo* (19–21) but applied to song:

How shall I hymn you, who are so completely well-hymned?
For in every direction, Phoebus, the range of your song has been
    extended [*nomós beblêat' aoidês*],[19]
on the mainland and through the islands.

[17]Bacchylides 17 Maehler (1982) is a notable instance of a similar test of divine descent. Midas asks his father Zeus to prove his paternity with a "sign that can be clearly seen" (*sêma arignôton* [57]); and the god consents to make his status something all can see (*timan . . . panderkea* [69–70]). Theseus in turn gets a miracle from his father, Poseidon.

[18] Hesiod's *Works and Days* says that the lazy man (who is unwilling to farm, n.b.!) may go off begging; but soon "you say much, but in vain / and the range of your words will bring no profit" (402–403). Cf. Pratinas for the metaphor of "ploughing the furrows of poetry" (*neôn arouron* [712 Page]).

[19]I have modified Allen's (1946) text of line 20: *nomós beblêatai ôidês*. The manuscript's *nómos . . .ôidês* is not to be read; see Càssola (1975) 485–486 for a discussion.

To say that the "range" of Apolline song extends everywhere means that hymns in his honor have been dispersed throughout Greece. This seems to have been a regular *topos* for glorifying Apollo (it is repeated at 207–208), but here the poet's pose of aporia before a rich tradition invokes the same image as Aeneas used of the field of genealogies.[20] In this proem, then, the poet, like Aeneas, charges oral traditions with being too immense. The verb *beblêato* here may be taken as "strewn," in which case the field of song is seen as littered with hymns, covered over or filled up with tradition.[21] Both resemble the *Iliad*'s Glaucus, who prefaces the recitation of his lineage with an unforgettable simile on genealogy as a forest of symbols.[22]

> Great-hearted Tydeus, why ask after my genealogy?
> Like the generations of leaves are those of men.
> The wind sweeps the leaves to the ground, but the wood
> in bloom grows them again, when spring returns.
> But if you wish to know these things. . . .
>
> [*Iliad* 6.145–151]

The significance of imagining the poetic tradition as a crowded or littered field can be better appreciated if we contrast a later, literate poet's use of the same motif. When the tradition had become increasingly available in definitive, authored texts, mentioning the already great "expanse" of existing song in a proem was also a way for a new writer to define his own hoped-for achievement against a written canon. As these poets looked jealously at the abundant and quite tangible texts of their predecessors, we may sense in their conscious nostalgia for an earlier, simpler, and more fertile time what Harold Bloom has named an "anxiety of influence."[23] In the proem of Choerilus's fifth-century epic on the

---

[20]For more on the "aporetic mode" here and at lines 207–208, see Bundy (1972) and Miller (1983).

[21]Diehl (1940) 94 compares the description of a distracted Laertes sleeping outdoors (*Od.* 11.193–194): "In every direction along the knoll of his vineyard / leaves were strewn [*beblêatai*] as beds on the ground for him."

[22]Aeneas and Glaucus introduce and conclude their genealogies with identical formulas: *Il.* 6.150–151 = 20.213–214, 6.211 = 20.241. The metaphor of fallen leaves for limitlessness is anticipated in 2.468.

[23]I may cite Bloom (1973), though I am anxious enough to say that I have found all his work stimulating and, mutatis mutandis, relevant to Greek poetry, as will appear especially in Chapter 3.

Persian War, the field of song appears too crowded, and the poet longs for clearer ground:

> Ah happy was he, who knew singing in that time,
> a servant of the Muses when the meadow was still uncut;
> but now when everything has been divided up,[24] and arts have
>   reached their furthest limits,
> we have been left behind like the last runners on the track, and
>   there is not any way,
> though searching in every direction, to drive the chariot, newly
>   yoked.
>
> [317 Ll-J-P (= 1 D, K)]

The difference between this text and Homer is instructive. In an age when texts are being more widely produced and collected, a new song can be measured against preexisting ones, and the singer may feel impelled to become an author, a maker of a unique and different song. Lost in a dense overgrowth of tradition, Choerilus has to peer anxiously in every direction to claim some place as his own (*paptainonta, pêi . . . pantêi* [4–5]).[25] For an oral poet, by contrast, tradition was common property, and there was no point in putting one's name on any part of it; so we do not hear any anxiety about making an original contribution in Homer or Hesiod.

But Homer already viewed his tradition as a very large field, even if it was not carved up by authors: Phemius "knows many / deeds of gods and men" (*Od.* 1.337–338), and other bards know "all kinds of things" (*pantoia*).[26] The words have more force if we consider that the triumph of the Panhellenic poetry that Homer represents was to weave into one another a variety of local, di-

---

[24]I interpret the formula "everything is divided up" on the basis of *Il.* 15.189, where it refers to the division of the sky, the earth, and the sea/underworld among the three greatest Olympians, and *Od.* 15.412, which refers to the division of lands between two cities.

[25]Often in epic *paptainô* describes the worried search for some way out of a desperate situation, e.g., *Il.* 14.507; *Od.* 12.232–233, 22.43. A comparable text is Theocritus *Idyll* 17, esp. 9–12. On the influence of "books" on Hellenistic literature, see Bing (1988).

[26]Hesiod says the Muses make a man "capable of saying or conceiving many things" (*poluphradeonta* [fr. 320.1 M-W]) and says that Linus the Kitharist "had learned wisdom of every kind" (fr. 306 M-W). In *H. Herm.* 484 the lyre, if approached with skill, "speaks, and teaches all kinds of things [*pantoia*] pleasing to the mind."

vergent tales, synthesizing thereby a massive mythic history embracing the whole Greek people.[27] This interweaving was thorough and extensive: local accounts of local heroes were entwined with those of other heroes from other places and other times until they meshed and eventually covered the expanse of unknown history. Reading Homer, one soon realizes that the mention of any proper name almost invariably brings with it a patronymic; the father's name in turn may evoke recollection of his place of origin or of some characteristic exploit, and these tales may involve yet other characters (and their patronymics) in various times and locales, until the history of a single hero begins to entwine with that of all the other heroes in the dense undergrowth of tradition.

At such a moment in a tradition, the problem of making a song was not how to say something new or in a new way but what to say in the face of so many endless tales. The highly literate but deeply Greek Aristotle seems to know this too, for the final motive he ascribes to Homer in shaping the *Iliad* is not a search for novelty or artistic expression but the necessity to reduce a too-vast tradition to an intelligible part:

> Homer, as we have said of him before, on this point too might seem divine in comparison with the others, in that, though the war had indeed a beginning and an end, even so he did not attempt to make the whole of it the subject of his poem, since he realized that, if he did so, the narrative was going to be too vast to be easily embraced in one view, or if he limited its extent, the variety of incidents would make it too complicated. As it is, he selected one part of the war as his theme and used many of the other parts as episodes, the Catalog of Ships, for example, and the other episodes with which he spaces out his poem. [*Poetics* 23.1459a30–37, after Hutton]

Surely we may agree that the *Iliad* was shaped in this conscious way: its beginning and end trace but a small arc on the larger cycle of legends; its middle is copiously filled out, yet filled only so much. But from Aristotle's discussion we can see that selection is also reduction. For him, though the legends of Troy's fall compose a unified action, the poet must forgo this unity because it would be

[27]See Nagy (1979) 6–10.

impossible to represent: it would be either too long or too compressed to be comprehended.[28]

It is finally because the tradition is so unwieldy that the poet
must be selective. Selection is both necessary to the traditional
poet's art and crucial in giving coherence to his performance, but it
is also a less simple matter than it may appear after the fact. What
belongs essentially to the Wrath of Achilles and what lies outside
the story may seem clear to us, but would it have seemed so to the
traditional performer? On the one hand, the traditional poet absolutely depended on the mass of stories that his society had accepted, approved, and enjoyed; a "true" traditional poem presupposes
the tradition and situates itself within it. On the other hand, if any
single poem is to be a self-standing whole, it must dispense with
most of tradition as peripheral, even though the tradition may not
easily yield to such omissions. The unique lineaments of these
poems had to be painstakingly detached from tradition, removed,
ideally without severing any vital connecting thread, from the total
concatenation of events of which they were a part.

What the poet gains in intelligibility he pays for with a loss of
totality. Such a sacrifice may seem trivial and is surely inevitable,
human powers being what they are. But there is more going on in
Homer than that. In fact, his invocations show that the greater
whole that cannot be contained in the individual wholes may
threaten to encroach on them. It is, after all, in the nature of tradition to be repeated, not to be forgotten. To make one story whole,
to remember a tale, one must forget much, and be sure that what
one forgets does not belong.

Selection then is a crisis: it is a judgment, a reasonable measure
taken to ensure intelligibility; but it is also a troubling point at
which the whole truth must be reduced to the essential. How does
an oral poet come to terms with his tradition? How did Homer—
that is, the maker of our *Iliad*—come to terms with the problem of
what to include and what to leave out of his epic? Was he troubled
by the double-edged process of selection, which gains unity and at
the same time sacrifices totality? I believe that Homer had an
awareness of the perils and power of selection in his poet's way. In

[28]On the necessity of an intelligible size in art, see especially *Poetics* 7.1450b32ff.

fact the crisis of what to leave out, recurrent for Greek poets, finds its first and most influential statement in Homer, most strikingly in his address to the Muses in the second book of the *Iliad*.

The Muses' Sublime

The longest and most revealing of Homer's invocations is the ten lines introducing the catalog of ships in the *Iliad*. The passage is well known: after the intense close-ups of Greek leaders in the first book, we are presented with the entire Greek army marshaled together for the first time in the poem; Homer stresses the enormity of the host in a series of splendid similes (to which I will return), and then proposes to list the names of the chiefs. At this point he stops and invokes the Muses to help him with this daunting task:

> Tell me now, Muses, who have your homes on Olympus—
> For you are goddesses, and are present, and know all,
> but we hear only *kleos* and do not know anything—
> who were the leaders and the lords of the Danaans;
> the multitude [*plêthun*] I could not tell nor could I name
> not if I had ten tongues and ten mouths,
> and a voice unbreakable, and a breast of bronze within,
> unless the Olympian Muses, daughters of Zeus of the aegis,
> should bring to my mind how many came under Ilion;
> but the chiefs of the ships I will tell and all their ships.
> [*Iliad* 2.484–493]

The poet says the Muses can "bring to mind" (*mnêsaiath'* in 492) the names of those at Troy; but the invocation is not simply a demand for information. Apart from anachronistically imposing a clear distinction between form and content on this oral art, such an interpretation misses a key point: Homer also mentions his need to be selective in what he will represent. Crucial to understanding this passage is the translation of *plêthun* in line 488. Many commentators (e.g., G. S. Kirk) rightly take the word here in its common sense, referring to the plebeian multitude, the *dêmos* as opposed to the leaders. Accordingly, Homer says that he cannot name "all those who came under Ilion," but he can name the leaders. Often, however, *plêthun* is rendered as referring to the multitude of leaders, as in Richmond Lattimore's translation: "Tell me Muses . . . who were the lords and chiefs, I could not tell the multitude of them nor name them, not if I had ten tongues." But this reading gives too little weight to the passages in which, as here, *plêthus* is explicitly opposed to the leaders, the *hêgêmones*.[29] Furthermore, taking *plêthun* as the multitude of leaders is senseless in context, for there is no physical impossibility in naming all the leaders of men—Homer proceeds to do just that with his one mouth and his mortal heart—but it is quite conceivable that naming every last soldier that came under Ilion, naming what he elsewhere calls the "boundless demos" (*dêmos apeirôn* [*Il.* 24.776]), would wear him out.

The logic of this passage seems to be something like this: Homer proposes to name the Greek leaders and tell who they were, and he asks the all-knowing Muses to inform him. But as for naming the entire host, that would be beyond his physical powers. He then adds, somewhat parenthetically, that even if he had superhuman physical stamina to go on naming forever, even if he were some kind of sounding bronze, he would still require the Muses to bring the names to mind. Then by ring composition he returns to his main theme: the leaders, nevertheless (*arkhous d' au*), he will tell.[30] Homer's invocation, then, contains not only an appeal for knowledge but also what turns out to be his special form of *recusatio*, a refusal to give a full presentation of complex things.[31]

This interpretation is supported by a number of passages in which one or another of Homer's characters recounts some exploit, for the need to be selective attends all human storytellers. In comparing a few of these we will come to appreciate the poet's complex

[29]E.g., *Il.* 15.295–296; cf. Cunliffe (1910) s.v. *hêgemôn* 2.

[30]Cf. *Od.* 4.494–497 for the opposition of leaders (*arkhoi*) to the multitude. With my general reading of this passage compare Virgil's renditions of Homer's invocation in *Aeneid* 6.625–627 and 7.641–646.

[31]I use *recusatio* beyond its limited application to Roman Augustan poets because I believe, along with Nannini (1982), that the Latin practice ultimately derives from archaic Greek literature (though Nannini does not notice the Homeric *recusatio*).

view of the problems a narrator faces. Consider Helen in the *Odyssey* when she tells Telemachus a story about his father; she begins with a prologue like a poet's:

> I could not tell nor could I name them all,
> as many trials as stout-hearted Odysseus had;
> but such a great deed was this the mighty man did and dared
> in the land of the Trojans where you Achaeans suffered woes.
>
> [*Odyssey* 4.240–243]

In the same words with which Homer refused to name the multitude, Helen declines to tell all Odysseus endured. (The wording is the same, with the innumerable *plêthun* replaced by the ineffable *panta*, "all.") Helen then solves her problem by selecting (*all' tode*) one episode from the Trojan campaign—Odysseus in the Trojan horse.[32]

Nestor is put in the position of narrating poet when Telemachus asks him for news of Odysseus. His *recusatio* is, not unexpectedly, more ample:

> O friend, since you have put me in mind of the woe
> we suffered in that land, we sons of the Achaeans, unconstrained
>   in rage,
> how much in ships upon the misty sea,
> wandering after booty wherever Achilles led,
> and how much about the great city of lord Priam
> we struggled; when as many as were best of us were slain there.
> There lies Ajax, man of Ares, there Achilles,
> and there Patroclus, equal to god in council,
> and there my own son, both strong and fair,
> Antilochus, excellent runner and fighter;
> and many other evils we suffered in addition to these;
> what man among mortal men might tell them all?
> Not if you were to stay here five years—not six—
> could you ask about each thing as many evils as the Achaeans
>   suffered there;
> before that you would go back home wearied out.
>
> [*Odyssey* 3.103–117]

---

[32]Nearly identical is *Od.* 11.516–519, in which Odysseus recounts to Achilles one among the many exploits of Neoptolemus.

"You have put me in mind of the woe we suffered": like the Muses' promptings, Telemachus's questions have brought to the old man's mind many tales of woe, whose multitude is emphasized by the polar "on sea . . . on land." Like a poet, Nestor then indulges himself in a short catalog of fallen Greeks. But mercifully he pulls himself up short and does not quite name "as many of the best"— *hossoi aristoi*—as died. He says that no mortal could ever tell all the woes, the many in addition to the ones he has named. How long this might take is left unclear: more than five years, more than six, and still the listener would fail before he got the full account.

These speakers seem unable to tell all they know; they have seen too much and there is too little time to tell it in. Even after Odysseus kept Eumaeus up for three nights and three days, he still didn't come to the end of his stories (*Od.* 17.513–517). And when asked by Queen Arete to give an account of himself and where he came from, he confesses he is unable to recite his personal *Odyssey* to date: "Hard it is, O queen, to relate my cares full through, / for the gods have given me very many; / but this which you ask me I will tell" (*Od.* 7.241–243). None of these speakers can recount their experiences fully, and each, including the poet, takes time to mention this.

In all these passages there is a gap between the multifariousness of experience and an account of it in speech; and this gap is repeatedly portrayed by Homer as a gap between the powers of sight and speech. The truest account of experience would replicate all one has taken in. But the problem arises because sight includes its objects in a comprehensive sweep, whereas speech is basically a catalog, *kata-legein*, a naming that articulates each element of what is seen.[33] Sight can represent a complex reality to the mind at once, whereas to tell things requires a sequence, which takes time. Such is the nature of speech, and it is no problem until people contemplate a full speech, a full account: this is always "refused," for it would take a full time, and mortals have only so much of that. Human representation may have to stop before we have quite come to the end of our tale. This is exactly Odysseus's difficulty when he tries to tell the Phaeacians about his journey to the under-

[33]For this sense of *kata* in *kata-legein*, see Krischer (1971) 102, 104.

world. He starts a full catalog of the noblewomen he saw there, but he cannot finish his catalog of women, and breaks off:

> All the women I could not tell nor could I name
> as many wives and daughters of heroes as I saw;
> before that ambrosial night would wane.
> It is time now for sleep.
>
> [*Odyssey* 11.328–331]

To name every woman he saw would outlast even the longest nights; it is time to close the eyes in sleep.[34]

The gap between seeing and saying what you saw reaches its extreme for the epic poet, who wants knowledge of an immense action in a vanished past, and the invocation in *Iliad*, book 2, confronts this gap. Homer invokes Muses whose unlimited gaze takes in all epic tradition in a magnificent panorama, but he must add that he could not set it all down. To tell everything that happened at Troy would take a more than human poet. The poet's problem is not simply the finitude of human existence; it is also an aesthetic problem, a difficulty with representation itself, with the project of recounting experience. The issues of representation at stake here are illuminated if we note that the invocation enacts a drama that Kant analyzed as the mathematical sublime.[35] For Kant, this sublime is prepared for when the mind is confronted by an immeasurable multitude in nature, in his example the innumerable sands on the shore. Before such an infinite object the mind cannot represent to itself each thing in its individuality, and there is a momentary blockage, a checking of powers, as the world outruns the

---

[34]Odysseus twice seems to tell a tale full through, though not directly to us, and in each case the time it took is mentioned. On Aeolia, amid constant banquets (8–9) the wind god delays Odysseus a month asking him "each thing" about "Ilion and the Argive ships and the return of the Achaeans"; Odysseus claims to have "recounted all [*katelexa*] according to its proper portion [*kata moiran*]," perhaps meaning that he tailored his story to his host (*Od.* 10.14–16; see Fränkel [1973] 13). In book 23 Odysseus and Penelope trade their stories in a more magical setting as Athena holds back the dawn (241–246); she tells him "as many things as she endured" (302) and he tells "all, as many pains as he made / for others and as many woes as he suffered" (306–307). The poet notes that "she listened with pleasure and did not close her eyes in sleep until he had recounted all" (308–309).

[35]In Meredith's translation, see esp. 90ff.

representative powers of mind. At this point a sublime elevation may occur. Reason steps in and comprehends the whole, and the mind is uplifted by having represented an infinite reality to itself. So in the *Iliad* the poet is faced with an ineffable number of men; in his similes leading up to them he says that they are like mingling flocks of birds, like swarms of insects. He observes that Agamemnon and his chiefs marshal this mass into order "like goatherds who segregate their flocks, which have been grazing together" (2.475–476); he would like to order his characters as well. But at this moment he stops, thinking like other human narrators of the limits of his frame. Here not reason but the Muses enter. It is in them that all history is comprehended into a whole. Note that the Muses do not appear in order to organize the material for the poet, for he has his organizing question ready beforehand ("who were the leaders?"). What the Muses do for the poet is to take on the burden of knowing all and representing all, first, presumably to themselves, for whom seeing and knowing are one, and then somehow to the poet. They sustain the totality to which his poem may belong; if he speaks with them, his poetry, though only a part of theirs, will have the great Homeric aesthetic virtue of being *kata kosmon*, in accordance with the order of things.[36] They enable him to give a true account of an uncountable reality.

The Muses play a similar role in their other appearances in Homer. When they are invoked at the beginning of each poem, this is the moment at which the poet must intervene in the immense cycle of tales which extends from the beginning of the world to beyond the end of Troy. Hence at the opening of each epic the poet first mentions the many traditions—the myriad woes that were heaped on the Achaeans, the many, many sufferings of Odysseus—and asks the Muses to help him start: the Wrath of Peleus's son Achilles might ultimately be traced to the twin egg of Leda, but Homer will start "from the time when the son of Atreus and Achilles first stood apart in contention" (*Il.* 1.6–7); Odysseus suffered much on land and sea, but of this rich store, the poet asks the Muse, "of these things, starting from some point at least, tell us now" (*Od.* 1.1–10). Again, the poet knows he wants to sing the Wrath of Achilles and

[36]This phrase is discussed in Chapter 4.

not, say, the Fashioning of the Horse, but he needs the Muses at
this point to give him entrée into this unutterably long story at the
right point.

Three other times the poet of the *Iliad* stops his narrative to
summon the Muses, and readers have wondered what gives rise to
them in these places.[37] It seems to me less necessary to formulate a
rule that infallibly predicts when a poet will reinvoke the Muses
than to note that on each occasion we find a certain similarity of
scene: the poet is confronted with a tumultuous battle, with
swarms of soldiers running pell-mell; among this confused and
confusing action the poet raises his voice above the din and asks,
"Who first came to face Agamemnon?" or "Which Greek first won
his spoils?" or "How did fire first come to the ships of the
Achaeans?"[38] We might add to these passages *Iliad* 12.176, where
the poet aims to describe a massive attack on the Greek defensive
wall:

> Some men were fighting at one gate, some at another.
> Hard it is for me to say all this, as if I were a god;
> for everywhere around the stone wall the god-kindled
> fire arose.
>
> [*Iliad* 12.175–178][39]

The warriors rushing about indiscriminately are like the many traditions that crowd a poet's mind, seeking expression.[40] A god
might tell them all, but hard indeed is it for the mortal poet to say

[37]Minton (1960) is most often cited now. He rightly notes the close connection of
invocations and catalogs (293, n. 3, citing Gilbert Murray); but his claim that they
mark turning points in a pattern of "crisis-struggle-defeat" is finally no less subjec-
tive than earlier views of invocations as "heightening attention" which he seeks to
replace.

[38]*Il.* 11.218ff., 14.508ff., 16.112ff. Sometimes the organizing question occurs without mentioning the Muse, e.g., *Il.* 5.703–704, and sometimes the poet simply proceeds to make his way through a welter of slaughter by saying who was killed first,
and next, 16.306–307. Pindar (*Pythian* 4.70ff.) and Bacchylides (15.47ff.) direct similar questions to their Muses in similar contexts.

[39]On the athetesis of this section, see van der Valk (1963–64) 1:579–580.

[40]Very similar is *Il.* 17.257–261, where the poet breaks off a catalog of Greeks
fighting in defense of Patroclus's corpse: three heroes are named, but "of the others,
who might, relying on his own wits, say their names?" This passage too has suffered athetesis; see van der Valk (1963–64) 2:39.

what was there to be seen, as the old man in the *Hymn to Hermes* notes:

> Hard it is to say as many things as one sees with one's eyes
> for many travelers pass back and forth on the road,
> some good, some bad,
> and it is difficult to know each one.
>
> [*Hymn to Hermes* 202–205]

The appearance of the Muses in the *Iliad*, book 2, then, is not simply a scene of instruction but also one of selection: it is the point at which both the immense Greek host and the ineffable oral tradition must be cut down to manageable, significant figures. For poets embarking on great tales or in the midst of them, to grapple with an enormous tradition and call in the Muses as saviors was a grand gesture that managed to augment their song without increasing it. Without exactly imposing order themselves, the Muses assure the poet that his account, incomplete though it be, is yet part of the total account they intend. As a man must make a partial poem, but it may also be a part of the sum of all poems, which is the past as reality.

Excursus: Later Appearances

Kant's mathematical sublime illuminates these passages with its emphasis on the incomprehensible multitude that provokes an appeal to the transcendent, and his illustrations of sublime phenomena are strikingly similar to Homer's: when the Greeks are marshaled, Iris takes human form and reports the spectacle to the Trojans, "never have I seen so great an army as this; / for very much like leaves or grains of sand they cross the plain" (*Il.* 2.799–801). Kant is also useful in drawing attention to the uneasiness that accompanies Homeric invocations in their metaphors of vision and blindness, timelessness and decay. It is not the way that Hesiod, for example, handles similar situations. In the *Theogony* (367–370) he manages to cut short a catalog of river gods simply by referring us to local traditions:

> So many other rivers are there, noisily flowing,
> sons of Oceanus whom Lady Tethys bore,
> their names it is hard for a mortal man to tell,
> but the people who dwell beside each of them know them.

Here the appeal is not to the Muses but to epichoric traditions, which cannot be included in a Panhellenic river catalog. But in its context the function of this muffled *recusatio* is the same as that of Homeric invocations: with these words Hesiod is able to leave water divinities and turn to the topic of sky gods.

In calling invocations instances of the Homeric sublime I wish to draw attention to the way that the triumph of knowledge is purchased by an initial anxiety in which the greatness of the tale and the powers of the Muses are so magnified as to reduce human narrative to the blind and ephemeral. But it is not a question of imposing Kant on the text or of postulating a universal feature of the human mind. It seems to be rather that Kant's idealist formulation is only a later version, in its own context, of an old, especially epic way of understanding representation. For the peculiarly Homeric note of the sublime, the somewhat daunting evocation of an infinity, a cosmic order within which the poet blindly seeks his way, is often struck in the invocations of later poetry and in similar contexts.

The clearest reflex (and perhaps imitation) is in the sixth-century lyric poet Ibycus. One of his fragments opens with a long list of themes and characters from the Trojan War that the poet will *not* sing about. He simply lists them, in language redolent of epic, saying he has no desire to hymn them (10ff.). But when he comes to the heroes whom Agamemnon led in their hollow ships (16–22), lack of desire becomes impossibility of execution:

> As for these things, the Muses of Helicon,
> skilled in song, might embark on such a tale,
> But a mortal man, a man of flesh and blood,
> could not say how each thing happened,
> how great the number of ships, having set forth at Aulis
> and crossing the Aegean, made their way
> from Argos to Troy, nourisher of horses.
>
> [282 Page = *SLG* 151.23–30]

Like Homer, Ibycus is stopped at the point of counting the ships and saying how each thing happened; and it is here that the poet mentions the Muses and their superiority to mortal men.

The crucial opposition between sight and blindness comes into play when Pindar opens a song with a prayer for "resource-fulness," that is, abundance of material:[41]

> I pray to] the fair-robed daughter of Uranus,
> Mnêmosunê, and her daughters, to grant me resourcefulness.
> For blind are the wits of those men,
> anyone who, without the Heliconian ones,
> walking in wisdom [?], searches along the steep road;
> but to me they have handed over this immortal task.
>
> [*Paean* 7b.1–7]

The Muses can lift him out of the condition of blind-witted men by granting him resourcefulness (*eumachania*).[42] But so great is their wisdom that for the mortal to whom they transmit it (*diadidomi*) poetry becomes an "immortal task" (*ponon athanaton*). In another poem Pindar asks for a starting point for a tale (Apollo's defense of Troy against Hera and Athena); here limited human "resource-fulness" must be aided by the Muses and Mnêmosunê who "know" far more:

> And whence the immortal [struggle?] began,
> about these things the gods can persuade wise men's minds
> but mortals have no resources [*amachanon*] to discover it;
> But since you maidens, Muses, know [*iste*]
> all, together with your father of black clouds
> and Mnêmosunê,
> you have this power ordained [*tethmos*] for you.
> Hear my prayer now.
>
> [*Paean* 6.50–58]

[41]Cf. Bundy (1986) 13–17 and (1972) 57–77 for many examples from Pindar and epideictic oratory in which we find the more general *topos* of praise in which "the merits of the *laudandus* provide material in such abundance as to make it impossible for the laudator to recount, or the audience to hear, the whole story" (Bundy [1986] 12).

[42]On this passage, see Bundy (1986) 29 n. 71 and Richardson (1985) 388ff. for this sense of *eumachania* and Pindar's process of selection generally.

Here that same verb that in Homer combined the Muses' knowledge and vision is used of the Muses with their mother and inscrutable father. Their great scope of vision has been "ordained" for them as a law of nature (*tethmos*), and contrasts with Pindar's limited powers; it is human mortality that presses on this poet, as in *Nemean* 4.33–34, when "the pressing hours and my *tethmos* prevent me from telling the story [of Heracles at Troy] at length."[43]

Whether we wish to think of these later poets as indebted to Homer or to a traditional posture that he among others adopted, we should not miss the note of anxiety at confronting the realm of songs when one opens a long tale. Plato did not miss it; he has his Socrates break into a long account of a philosophic conversation in epic style (*Euthydemus* 275c): "As for what happened after that, Crito, how could I give you a good account of it? For it is no small task to take up and go through a wisdom so unmanageably great [*amêchanon*] as theirs. So I, at any rate, must begin my tale like the poets, calling on the Muses and Memory. At that point then Euthydemus began, as I think, from. . . ." The sublime epic Muses, then, proved to be a recurrent way of depicting the selective process, an appropriate response of Greek oral poets during the Panhellenic synthesis of large poetic traditions in the early archaic age. Though he refused such knowledge for himself, to envision it and attribute it to the gods was a major gain for the epic poet, and the Muses in the second book of the *Iliad* are what enables Homer to get on with his story, to keep speaking truly in the face of an overwhelming tradition. But we return to Homer and ask how such a singing can be ended, how a can shape be imposed on this song?

The Whole Poem

If the Muses connect the poem to a larger order, they do not make it whole. They may help the poet begin, putting his feet

[43]On *tethmos* in this passage, see Norwood (1945) 167–170 and Miller (1982); cf. the *brachu metron* that restrains Pindar from telling "all the contests that Herodotus and his horses won" (*Isthmian* 1.60–63). On the many passages where Pindar cuts down the long account he might give, see Hubbard (1985) 27–32.

firmly on the path, but how will he know where to stop, when it is enough and he can be finished? The point of closure in an oral performance is not a given, and the very form of epic poetry lends itself to infinite continuation: it is composed in short, generally self-contained phrases, paratactically strung along; these often fall into end-stopped hexameters, placidly laid one after another. Epic has no strophes to draw the poet's circle just.[44] In addition, as I noted apropos of Hesiod in Chapter 1, traditional epic poems never actually conclude: they leave off; open-endedness is the law of the genre. In Homer, we find that the last book and a half of the *Odyssey* have been taken to be a later addition, and even the end of the *Iliad*, so much praised for its exquisite resolutions, was in one ancient version immediately followed up by a lead-in to the *Aethiopis*. Even after Homer has said his all, there is more that might be said. How then can this little piece draw itself up into a unity without falling back into the unutterable totality of events to which it belongs? If there is an answer to this question, it is not an easy answer. I think that Homer adds to an awareness of the immensity of tradition an anxiety about his hopes for completeness, a fear that it is not so easy to disentangle oneself from this great tradition once it is called forth. The meetings with the Muses do not have the atmosphere of an easy feat, a perfect transmission from divine to human intelligence. The sublime Muses in Homer intervene on a moment of stoppage: they are summoned in turmoil and greeted in weakness; there is always a sense of the passing ambrosial night as the tales go on.

This overwhelming aspect of the Muses emerges in their figuration as the *Odyssey*'s sweet but fatal singers, the Sirens.[45] Like the Muses, the Sirens offer Odysseus the "pleasure" of "knowing more" (*Od.* 12.188); like poets, they enchant with their singing (*Od.* 12.40, 44). In language reminiscent of that of the *Iliad*'s Muses, they claim to know and to have seen very much:

> For we know [*idmen*] all the things, as many as in wide Troy
> the Greeks and the Trojans suffered under the will of the gods,

[44]Epic style is what Aristotle calls the "strung-along" style, of which he observes: "Apart from the matter treated, it has no end or goal in itself" (*Rhet.* 3.9.1409a 25ff.).

[45]On Sirens as demonic Muses, see Buschor (1944), with J. T. Pollard's review, *CR* 66 (1952): 60–62, and Pucci (1979).

and we know [*idmen*] everything that happens on the nourishing
earth.

[*Odyssey* 12.189–191]

These far-seeing goddesses can offer the entire *Iliad* and more, not
only the past but all events on earth. The chthonic Muses may not
necessarily offer a total poem—for example, they do not sing the
generations of the Olympian gods—but the poem they present is
open-ended, and because such a poem never comes to an end, it
threatens any listener. The problem is, of course, that this thrilling
song destroys its mortal listeners, who lose their ability to return to
wife and children, finally withering away (12.39–43).[46] In the Sirens, "infernal counterparts to the Muses," the enchantment of
poetry reveals its sinister side: their song is a binding spell for
Odysseus, for the price of listening to it is to be fixed fast.

Here this eerie art shows the dangers of an unmediated contact
with the heroic tradition. And these dangers become particularly
clear if we compare another occasion on which the interminable
adventurer directly encountered the heroes of old and again was
threatened with a kind of paralysis. Odysseus's journey to the
underworld was a seeing into the past, a direct vision of a parade
of heroes and heroines reaching back to the very children of the
gods; this vision, as he tells his Phaeacian audience, could never be
recounted in full. Yet though he was desirous to stay and see even
more, curious Odysseus had to leave this marvelous place and its
sights. After his mother's shade had departed, he says, he was
determined to stay and see even earlier heroes: "And now I would
have seen yet earlier men, whomever I wanted, / Theseus and
Perithous, illustrious children of the gods."[47] But then "countless
crowds [*muria ethnea*] of the dead gathered around him / with an

---

[46]Compare *Od.* 4.594–598, where Telemachus says Menelaus's tales please him so
terribly (*ainôs*) that he could endure to stay in Sparta for a year without longing for
home or parents. Though these stories are not, for him, from the absolute past,
Helen's Egyptian nepenthe, "inducing forgetfulness of all evils" (4.220ff.), makes
him like Hesiod's poetic auditor.

[47]*Od.* 11.630–631. It is interesting that the heroes Odysseus names had themselves made a descent into Hades. One early remnant of this tradition (Hesiod fr.
280 M-W; cf. *Minyas* 1 D = 1 K) depicts Theseus in colloquy with the early Meleager,
thus hearing face-to-face the story Achilles gets in a more mediated way.

awesome din [*êkhêi thespesiêi*], and green fear seized him / lest Persephone might send up a Gorgon's head from Hades" (*Od.* 11.632–635). The desire to look yet more and see still earlier reaches a vision stunned by multitudes raising an unearthly noise. Odysseus is flooded with a too great vision of the heroic world, an inarticulate sound and a fear of paralysis.

Homer too, I think, shies away from the perfect song with something like a superstitious terror of paralysis. His image of the more than human poet, impervious to decay, is finally chilling. Like Odysseus, the invoking poet experiences an influx of total vision which threatens to fix him fast: he imagines himself half paralyzed, as bronze and iron.[48] The immense tradition is not easily mastered by mortals; it takes a magical spell to control such numbers, a knowledge like that which Apollo boasts of through his priestess at Delphi: "I know the number of the sands and the measures of the sea" (Herodotus 1.47.3). Pindar says that only gluttonous men "chatter" praises of the great, not knowing that saying too much is vain; a wise poet tempers his praise: "As the sand escapes numbering, who could ever tell as many benefactions as [my patron] has done for others?"[49] The "tether" or the "short measure" with which Pindar says he reins in his songs, like Homer's *recusatio*, defends him from excess. The great invocation, then, is partly an apotropaic prayer against the spellbinding spirits that control the fatal powers of complete enumeration.[50] Only the proverbially

---

[48]The poet's "breast of bronze in me" (*khalkeon de moi ētor* [*Il.* 2.490]) is only one letter away from a phrase Hesiod uses to describe death: "his heart is of iron *and his breast of bronze*" (*khalkeon de hoi ētor* [*Theog.* 764]).

[49]*Olympian* 2.95ff. See Bundy (1986) 29 n. 71. Cf. *Olympian* 13.43–46: Pindar would compete with many to tell all his patron's victories but could not tell the number of the pebbles in the sea.

[50]The poet who plays most with this sublime enchantment is Catullus. In poem 7 the interrogator is a lover, the question erotic, but the answer sublime: "Quaeris, quot mihi basiationes / tuae, Lesbia, sint satis superque? / quam magnus numerus Libyssae harenae / . . . aut quam sidera multa." ("You ask how many of your kisses, / Lesbia, are enough and more than enough for me? / The number is as great as that of Libya's sands . . . or as many as the stars"). The answer, finally, is to invoke a flood of kisses to ward off any evil magic: "quae nec pernumerare curiosi / possint nec mala fascinare lingua." ("which busybodies may never count up / nor an evil tongue bind with spells"). One can compare, too, the end of poem 5: after "many thousands" of kisses, he and Lesbia will heap them together (*conturbabimus*) to avoid the evil eye (*invidere*).

foolish poet Margites (the "glutton"), "who knew many things, but all badly," would be so stupid as to try to count the waves of the sea.[51]

The poet then selects and reduces not with the confidence of an artisan who fashions the well-wrought urn, tossing off the dross, but in a spirit of resignation. Whatever the Muses give the poet, they withhold the all; there is an inevitable reduction from divine knowledge to *kleos,* which may be poetry or rumor or hearsay but never vision. The true account is still the total account, and who would happily forgo the sweet, complete, and fatal song of the Sirens?

How did Homer hope to recoup the grave losses of selection? Let us return to the *Iliad,* book 2, and look at the selection he makes to see what it entails. Homer's principle of selection is evident and may be termed aristocratic: out of the innumerable masses who came to Troy he chooses to name the chiefs and to ignore the *plêthus.* In this, Homeric aesthetics mirrors heroic politics: epic heroes and nobles are those who step out of the ranks into the forefront of battle; thus foregrounded they fight single combat to win fame and a name. To hang back is to remain obscure and to be swallowed up in the confused din of the mob. The great "marshaler of heroes," *kosmêtôr herôôn,* as Homer was styled in epitaph, is in league with the marshaler of men.[52] But if Homer is aware of the power of this organization, he knows too that it is not achieved without some suppression. Before it is possible to muster and name the troops a voice from the *dêmos,* that of Thersites, must be silenced. Not only does Thersites threaten the political order by challenging Agamemnon, but the rabble-rouser is an aesthetic offense as well: ugly and misshapen, his speech is abundant but without order (*akosma epea, ou kata kosmon*). The order he violates is at once political and aesthetic. His lack of measure in speech (*ametroepês*) and lack of distinctions (*akritomuthês*) threaten the hierarchies that make heroic action possible and the ordering that makes an account of that action possible. So he is drubbed by

[51]See 2, 3, 4, [4a]b *IEG.*

[52]For Homer's epitaph, *Certamen* 238.337 Allen (1946) vol. 5 and cf. 237.310; on *kosmos,* which may mean "marshaling," "arrangement" or "decoration," see Chapter 4.

Odysseus, who wields the staff of genealogy and authority, and slinks back into the mob, not to be heard from again. The poet and the great rhetorician make him a scapegoat so that order may be imposed, and everyone rejoices.[53] But the speech that must be silenced is quoted, and when we recall that many readers have found that the language of Thersites echoes that of Achilles, we may wonder if he can be driven out completely.

The scapegoat is necessary to the community, for the whole is defined and made orderly by excluding the disorderly, by silencing the extra voice that has no measure. In a sense this is how Homer uses his tradition: the crucial but shadowy part that Thersites plays here seems to me much like the function of the total knowledge of Homer's Muses: like the unspeakable, the ineffable is no sooner evoked than it is cut off. But with the brief appearance of the sublime Muses, Homer is able to incorporate the all that he cannot tell, to name the all as the sustaining ground and support for his stories and at the same time to banish its threatening power from his poem. The text constantly makes us aware of other stories that cannot be told, other parts of the stories that are told, so that we feel there is a great exterior in which all is supported and fits together. This outside of the poems, the whole of legendary history of which they are a part, guarantees the value of these partial accounts and makes them suffice though incomplete. But this whole must always be put outside the text, for the text cannot at once contain it and rely on it as basis and ground.

These intricate problems and their evasive solutions in attaining a complete poem appear as theme in the last passage to be compared. It is a story Hesiod tells in his epic on the adventures of seers, the *Melampodia*. I give the account we have from Strabo (14.462 = Hesiod fr. 278 M-W):

> It is said that Calchas the seer came here from Troy on foot with Amphilochus, son of Amphiaraus, and died of vexation when he chanced to meet at Clarus a seer who was greater than himself, Mopsus, the son of Manto, Teiresias's daughter. Hesiod works up the story in some such form as this: Calchas sets Mopsus the following problem:

---

[53]On Thersites as comic scapegoat, see Thalmann (1988).

"Amazement strikes my heart at how many figs this fig tree has, though it is quite small; can you tell me the number?"

And Mopsus answered:

"Ten thousand they are in number, but a bushel in measure; one is left over which you can't put into the measure."

So he spoke, and the number of the measure was discovered to be true. Then did the sleep of death close over Calchas.

We may not be surprised at this point that to give a complete enumeration of a manifold thing, even something as clearly defined and visibly present as a fig tree, is a problem worthy of seers. Nor that when the Eastern vizier gives the exact number (one of the myriads Homer cannot tell?)[54] the result is fatal for the Trojan seer. But note too that though Mopsus might take in the number of figs at a single glance, and name it in a word, they can not be encompassed in a single measure. There is one left out, a residuum that cannot be inserted into the whole. Without this one fig the figs would not have been namable, at least not in a single word that encompasses each one individually. The Greek for 9,999 would take some time to say and might not fit the meter. So the measure leaves something out of the total account, but this extra thing gives an exact name to the whole. The single fig fills the bushel, even from the outside.

This magically inflected view of wholes and parts may have more in common with the Homeric conception of unity than our text-oriented searches for organic and mechanical perfection. A literary notion of unity as a complete, unalterable composition was perhaps not inconceivable for the oral poet but conceivable only as a divine ideal or a paralyzing total vision. The unity that interests him as poet is not that of a plant or of a text removed from a context, but the unity of the whole as an object of divine contemplation. These epic stories must be parts of this but can only be parts. Of course that does not mean that they are all merely chaotic

---

[54]Note *Poetics* 1457b11: "Odysseus wrought myriad noble deeds." See Gudeman's commentary (1934) on 1451a3 for Aristotle's use of "myriad" in connection with epic traditions.

fragments and incoherent tatters. First in history and now in the mind of Zeus and his daughters, the heroic deeds stood ordered together in a line; and in their telling too there is an ordering in the paratactic line, in ringing speeches, in juxtaposed scenes and episodes. But for the singer to value a closed unity, even a moderately regulated unity of the sort envisaged in Cedric Whitman's attractive theory of a geometric structure in the *Iliad*, according to which the events of the first book are mirrored in the last, and the intervening books are woven together in the same way,[55] would be against basic demands of his traditional art. Homer sought to sing a story true, and that meant fully and completely, and that in turn meant that his singing was part of a whole whose final unity was not happily forgone. His songs are begun late and finished early; he weaves into them other stories as his audience directs or as his heart moves. Closure arrives with a change of mood, an interruption, waning hours, the urging of sleep. And until it arrives, until the all is added up, the singing can go on; to stave off that closure and closing is to keep the singing going; resisting the summary, the resolution, keeps the verses going down the line, as varied and inconsequential as the deeply connected sequence of life.

The extra part, the unassimilable piece, is necessary to unity. The part left out, the voice suppressed, still speaks and reassures the measure of its wholeness and integrity. Despite its evasiveness, we depend on this residue, which makes poems whole even as it leaves them a little incomplete: it is to that incompleteness that we add our interpretations. In that little space between what has been said and what might be said we read and, if we will, supply the connections that make a greater whole out of the part. Negligible as it seems, that little space between the lines contains room enough so that for us reading Homer is not merely repeating what he says but interpreting it, as he read without merely reciting the poets before him.

[55]Whitman (1958), esp. chap. 11.

CHAPTER 3

THE POET
Tradition, Transmission, and Time

The Poet and Other Poets

In the previous chapter I reconstructed the poet's conception of the Muses and what they do for him as poet. In Homer's invocations these goddesses are a complex personification of the poet's indebtedness to his tradition, but at the same time they cover over another important relationship that defines the poet, that to other poets. It may be a relief, or at least dialectically fruitful, to turn from these mythical and magical conceptions to the hard realities of poetic performance and transmission. For if we situate the invocation in the context of eighth-century performance, we find that there is a conflict between the hypostasis of Muses as bestowers of song and the ways poets actually worked and got their words. Poems, after all, come not from the gods but from other poems, and if Homer was at all like the poets we know from other traditional oral societies, his true teachers were the poets he heard and the poets they had heard.[1] But these very poets, who developed over centuries Homer's richly varied themes and language, are overridden by the direct appeal to a single,

[1]Bowra (1952) chap. 11; Lord (1960) chap. 2; Finnegan (1977) chap. 5.

transcendent source of epic song. The theology, if we may call it that, of inspired poetry claims that poetry is not transmitted historically but manifests itself, when the gods will, in ever-renewed epiphanies. Satisfying and useful as the fiction of the Muses may be, nothing could be less true to the real experience of poets as they made and performed their songs in a traditional culture; in fact the Muses substitute for, and even deny, the actual processes that brought them into being and gave them voice.

We may accept the Muses as a fiction, but we should not credit too much Homer's proud dependence on them and ignorance of any rivals. For if we do, we may begin to see him as a solitary artist, locked in struggle only with his imagination, and may mistake his project for a romantically conceived idea of creativity. If we allow the Muses to make us forget Homer's predecessors and peers, we may distort the crucial actualities of bardic performance in a traditional oral society and miss the way it was received by its hearers. The tension between the theology of poetry as a divine donation and the actual processes of poetic transmission and performance is the concern of this chapter.[2] I point out immediately that there is no reason that Homer should not represent transmission as he, or as the tradition, prefers to envision it. If we charge him with neglecting the existence of other poets, both the predecessors on whom he depended and the rivals whom he vanquished to gain his preeminence, he is surely entitled as artist to enter an august plea of *nolo contendere*. But I will show that Homer's choice, free as it may have been, was after all a choice, and was deliberately and consistently at variance with the reality he and his audience knew.

The account of its own transmission given in the poem is worth examining not only for tentative reconstructions of literary history; it also sends a message to the audience about how to receive the poetry, how to imagine that it has come down to them through time. For the poem's theory of transmission is also its theory of the relation of this performance to reality—in epic poetry, of this performance to the distant but real heroic age. If Homer is singing to an eighth- or seventh-century audience about events far outside

[2]Pucci (1977) 29–34 has explored the same tension in the proem to the *Theogony*.

the range of certain knowledge, he was obliged, at least for his audience's sake, to connect his late telling in some way with the early events. He had to have a version of how he got this story, for he claimed to have got it and not made it. Like the storyteller's "once upon a time," the epic poet's invocation immediately settles the question of transmission: it posits for the entire performance a descent of song from deed to Muse to poet and then to audience. The ideal epic then is presented to us as the Muses' knowledge mediated only by a single singer, and this singer is removed from his historical context and influences: once the tale begins, he is not an individual standing at the end of a long line of singers or in a crowd of competitors. The most persuasive, compelling, and vivid poetry of the past has no history itself.

The schemes of transmission offered in the poems, then, are fictions, but fictions designed to secure for the poetry its special status and aesthetic power. When the poet claims that the Muses enable us to overcome our separateness from the past and release us from dependence on the slippery tongues of men, he encourages the listeners to be transported out of their particular situation and brought to a direct, unmediated experience of the heroic age. But for the poet to deny his dependence upon and rivalry with other poets is also a way to avoid the issue of being late in time, of having only the most tenuous link to the great past. In Homer this denial is sustained not only in invocations but also in his portraits of poets, who, like him, are related only to the Muses above and the audience around them. By neglecting the possibility that two mortal poets might differ in their versions of a given story, the poet encourages us to regard the story as the enunciation of earlier deeds in their timeless structure. As a way of confirming the special place of the poets I think Homer went to some lengths to deny that they had other poets around them with whom they might ever compete. And in fact, a key moment in the *Odyssey,* when an epic poet confronts an epic hero, raises these submerged concerns all the more strongly. As we will see, the discrepancy between Homer's idealized self-presentation of poets of the past and the competitive realities of his own day could be exploited for significant aesthetic ironies in epic performance.

Thamyris and Poetic Competition

Homer invokes his Muse with confidence that she will grant him the ability to bypass all other traditions and will bestow her own song on him. But the tensions this strategy covers up are well evoked by Father Ong in what he calls "the old poetic tradition associated with rhetoric":

> It had kept the poet engaged, struggling, not only with an audience but with other poets as well. Rhetorically colored poetic was a poetic of virtuosity, setting poet against poet. The earlier poetic was not always explicitly conscious of its agonistic underpinnings, but the underpinnings were there nevertheless, to be seen if you looked. . . . This is a pristine rhetorical world speaking, thinking of composition, including poetry, as proceeding by "invention" (*inventio*), retrieval of matter from the accumulated stores of mankind, stores organized by means of the places or commonplaces or topics (*loci* or *topoi*). This topical poetic clearly calls for an agonistic stance, for if the poet deals with the common store of awareness available to all, his warrant for saying or singing again what everybody is already familiar with can only be that he can say it better than others. The invocation of the Muse can be paraphrased, "Let me win, outdo all other singers." In pre-romantic, rhetorical culture, the poet is essentially a contestant.[3]

Ong's vision of the agonistic poet engaged in staking his claim on a tradition available to others, so contrary to the image presented in Homer, was expressed by the Greek poet who said, "The keenly contested gifts of the Muses are not prizes lying out in the open for the first comer to win."[4] And it is likely that Ong is right to see in Homer's invocations a disguised claim for his own excellence. Such an interpretation is consonant not only with the heroic ethic pervading the poetry—always to be best, always to be first—but also would seem to be demanded by what we can reconstruct of the

[3]Ong (1977) 224–225.
[4]Bacchylides (?) fr. 55 Maehler (1982) (= adespota 959 Page). Cf. Bacchylides fr. 5 on the transmission of poetic wisdom (*sophia*): "One man becomes wise from another / both long ago and now; for it is not easy / to discover the gates of words that have never been spoken [*arrêtôn epeôn*]."

poet's professional and social milieu. Though Homer consistently
maintains the fiction of a divine, ahistorical poetic transmission,
Hesiod and the Homeric hymns testify that in their proems archaic
poets were quite willing to lay claim to the title of "sweetest of
wandering singers" and to validate such a claim in the great Greek
way, through contests in poetry.[5] Contests were not, of course, the
only forum for making and "publishing" epic poetry in archaic
Greece; Homer shows his poets at court providing after-dinner
entertainment, and such a venue is readily conceivable for this
kind of song in the eighth century, provided only relatively short
pieces of epic (a book or two?) are given each night. In addition,
comparative evidence suggests that less formal settings would
have been available and performances in wayside inns or mar-
ketplaces can readily be imagined. But contests interest me particularly because they were the crucible in which traditions could be
melded, refined, and worked into shape. A bard singing night
after night in the same palace or tavern may give pleasure for a
long time, but let another bard who treats the same themes wander
in and our poet will quickly find what parts of his own repertoire
his Muses had best forget the next time he invokes them, and also
what of the other poet's they might remember. Eris, "competition"
or "strife," is a god, Hesiod says, and she can be fruitful: wealth is
increased when "potter strives against potter, beggar against beggar, and singer against singer" (*Works and Days* 21–26).

Even more important, some kind of poetic competition or comparison of poems seems to me an essential prelude to the very
choice of two Homeric poems to be written down at all. For we are
told that oral poets do not make any fine distinctions between one
version of a theme and another and tend to regard two different
performances of a theme as the same song, even when they differ
in length and detail. But to write down such a poem is to convert it
from a form in which it was comfortably available to a wide range
of people and to reduce it to a form that only a few could use. Such
an astonishing step requires that people say first that one version is
different from another and then that it is better. Finally, these per-

[5]*H. Ap.* 165–172; Hesiod *Works and Days* 654–659. For other references to epic
contests in archaic literature, see Svenbro (1976) 78–80 and Edwards (1985) 11–13,
with bibliography.

ceptions must be so clear and important to people that they are moved to do a rather absurd thing for an oral culture, to point a finger and say stop there, catch and preserve that poem, it is the best and we want to hear it and no other on this theme. It seems to me that in archaic Greece a contest between poets would have best afforded the opportunity and incentive for comparing and preferring one version of an oral poem to another (there weren't, after all, Milman Parrys running around with tape recorders). In fact, contests are the first context in which we hear of Homeric *texts,* and I think, with others, that they must have provided the impetus for fixing a song in amber.[6] In any case, the serene, celestial Muses would have taken on quite a different aspect when they were invoked by two bards in succession eying a single prize tripod between them.

The poems, however, show very little trace of competition. The invocations that open these assured, autonomous texts do not seem to be troubled by antagonism, and when Homer depicts bards in his poems the divine model of strifeless transmission sustains them. To be sure, there is a "*race* of poets that the Muses love," but each one works alone and depends only on the goddesses as far as we can see. We have seen that the boast of one such poet explicitly equates inspiration with independence from other singers: "I am self-taught, and the Muse has made stories / of every kind grow in my heart" (*Od.* 22.347–348). For these poets, as for their author, the Muses lift the process of poetic transmission out of history. Accordingly, Homer's singers never perform with another poet near; indeed, as far as we can tell, none of them has ever met another poet.

The image of poetic tradition we get here may be characterized as vertical transmission: great deeds acquire a fame that reaches broad heaven, and from high Olympus the Muses breathe that song down on the race of poets. There is no exchange, no strife, interference, or even acknowledged influence on the horizontal plane where the poet might meet other poets. If we wish to ask Homer what has become of this fruitful exchange, we need not expect a direct answer; certainly he was not obliged to fill his

6Cf. Ford (1988) 305–306.

poetry with explicit commentary on his peers and antecedents (far less to be honest if doing so). But occasionally the poems allow their "agonistic underpinnings" to show through.

The best example is the story of Thamyris, told in an excursus on the city Dorion in the catalog of ships:

> there the Muses
> encountered Thamyris the Thracian and stopped his singing,
> as he was coming from Oichalia and the house of Oichalian
>   Eurytus;
> for he made a boastful vow that he would emerge victorious
> even if the Muses, daughters of Zeus, should come to sing in
>   person;
> and they became angry and maimed him, and at once
> took away his divine gift of singing [*aoidê*] and made him forget
>   how to play the lyre.
>
> [*Iliad* 2.594–600]

The story pattern is familiar: a mortal's self-assertion of excellence; ensuing anger on the part of the patron god in that realm; a contest between god and mortal followed by the inevitable punishment of mortal presumption. A number of such stories involve the arts— for example, Marsyas's ill-fated challenge to Apollo in flute playing—and clearly Thamyris embodies that myth as it applies to poets like Homer himself.[7] A lyre player and singer, Thamyris is something of a minstrel, on his way from the palace of Eurytus in Oichalia down into Nestor's realm. Poets like Homer must indeed have moved from place to place, though he generally represents bards as firmly established at court.[8] More important, Thamyris is boastful and competitive, and this passage shows what might happen when such a poet met potential rivals on his travels.

This is the only overt Homeric allusion to poetic competition,[9]

---

[7]For a survey of contest myths in the arts, see Weiler (1974) 37–128.

[8]There is a reference to traveling bards at *Od.* 17.382–385; cf. *Margites* 1 Allen (1946) vol 5. On the puzzling Mycenean geography in the Thamyris tale, see Kirk (1985) 181, 214–216.

[9]It is so taken by Schadewaldt (1965) 64 and Maehler (1963) 16; so too [Plut.] *On Music* 1132a, which assigns to Thamyris an appropriately early and hubristic theme, the Titanomachy.

and it is muted to near inaudibility. In the first place, it is not a
proper contest, because Thamyris's antagonists are not other poets
but the Muses. Second, readers have not even been able to decide
from this brief passage whether the contest actually took place or
whether the goddesses simply struck at him for his boast. The
latter point is trivial, since the main point of the myth is to assert
that there must be limits to self-assertiveness for poets as for anyone else. But the fact that Thamyris's antagonists are the Muses
may have a special significance in this version of the story.[10] In this
dark and peculiar tale, Homer represents the only kind of poetic
contest possible under the reign of the Muses: where all horizontal
relationships between poets are ignored, interpoetic strife can be
played out only along the vertical axis of Muse-poet. Thamyris
represents for Homer essentially an *early* singer: he serves a king of
the pre–Trojan War generation of Heracles and comes from Thrace,
land of the most ancient mythical singers, including Orpheus.
Thamyris, the only named and identified singer in the *Iliad*, stands
in that poem for preceding poets, and his contest shows that mere
temporal earliness is not enough to guarantee a strong transmission of song if the Muses are not honored.

The Thamyris tale, then, may be an admission by the *Iliad* poet
that rivalry attended epic from a very early time, though in the
heroic form of mortal against immortal. Indeed, it seems to offer a
kind of negative *aition* for the "normal" epic competitions of the
eighth century. In addition, it encapsulates a repeated Homeric
strategy for transposing his own art into the heroic age.[11] The story
transmogrifies two competing rhapsodes as they might have appeared in the eighth century into one very ancient singer competing with the Muses; if the Thamyris story is a replacement for any
account of poets competing with other poets, it is a way to escape

[10]Devereux (1987) argues that the tale is an "unrecognized Oedipal myth" based
on (later attested) variants in which, e.g., Thamyris is the son of a Muse/the Muses
or the prize is the right to cohabit with them. Inasmuch as I will follow in this
chapter Harold Bloom's idea that the denial of poetic influence can be disguised as
inter-generational anxiety, I find the suggestion that rival poets vie for exclusive
access to these goddesses useful.

[11]For Homer's "archaizing" in his representation of poets, see Schadewaldt (1965)
54–86, esp. 59.

the pressure of one's rivals by projecting an ideal image of one's art as it was earlier, before them and closer to the origins of song. When we hear the Thamyris tale we look at the poet differently, as one whose art is not being shaped now but is very old, one whose true competitors can only be gods.

The *Odyssey* presents a slightly different version of the mortal-immortal contest story, which may suggest that Thamyris's fault (and perhaps the fault of the *Iliad* poet as well) was not simply to deny the gods but to deny his own lateness in time. When Odysseus is challenged to compete in athletics on Phaeacia, he asserts himself and his superiority in a speech of intricate tact. He says he is willing to take on the best of the Phaeacians, his host excepted, "for a man would be a fool to offer strife [*eris*] to his host in that man's country" (8.210–211). He then boasts that he is a better archer than any hero of his time (excepting, again, the paragon of Greek archers, Philoctetes), but this boast is immediately qualified: "I would not strive [*erizemen*] against the men of former times / not with Heracles, nor with Eurytus of Oichalia" (*Od.* 8.223–224). He goes on to recount the story of Eurytus, who challenged Apollo to a contest in archery (*erisdeskon* [8.225]) and was destroyed. We note that Odysseus declares himself to be later than Eurytus (indeed he has inherited his bow through Eurytus's son [*Od.* 21.11–33]); hence he has put competing with an earlier hero on a par with such an early hero's taking on the gods themselves. The mythological logic of the story as Odysseus tells it is that hubris against the gods is parallel to hubris against the precursors in one's art. The refusal to acknowledge the natural distinction that separates god and mortal is the same as the refusal to acknowledge the differences in time, the qualitative differences between early stronger and later weaker generations.[12]

Perhaps we may apply the lesson of athletic Eurytus to the musical exemplar of Thamyris, for his contest with the Muses is said to have taken place near that same Oichalia, as he left the palace of

---

[12]The undeveloped reference in 8.224 to Heracles, the quintessential crosser of all these borders, is relevant too. Some myths have him attacking Hera and Hades with a bow, and even killing Eurytus (n.b.) after being cheated of a prize. See Heubeck, West, Hainsworth (1981) on 8.224 and 225 and Clay (1983) 92 n. 70.

that same Eurytus.[13] Like Eurytus, Thamyris would not respect the limits of artistic ambition and disastrously set himself against his patrons, the sources of his power. But if presumption against the gods is analogous to the presumption of a later figure who encroaches on an earlier, stronger one, Thamyris's attempt to take on the Muses is also a battle to claim priority and authority for the single singer against the tradition. Thamyris's hubris in denying his dependence on the Muses is an extreme instance of the *Iliad* poet's own stance toward the poets before him. Each denies what must be prior, religiously and temporally. Accordingly, the Thamyris story for Homer meditates on just how far a poet can go in denying his predecessors as the poet's battle against the consequences of being later in time, against his debts to tradition, risks becoming a battle with his Muses. What is at stake for the poet of the *Iliad* may be a competition for vividness conceived as the gift of earliness, an unmediated closeness to the events that are the source of song. Though he strives for an absolute earliness and proximity to the heroic age—to be best is to be first—there must be a limit to poetic self-assertion if the traditional poet is to be able to continue singing. A poet who follows the example of the *Iliad* will not admit to being at the end of a tradition but will claim to be next to the source of song; but the *Odyssey* warns that one should not trespass further, should not strive with one's host in the host's country.

Thamyris's fate is exceptional, a onetime event and a transgression of the normal piety that other Homeric singers seem to exhibit. But it shows that the epic fiction has not quite excluded the antagonism at the root of a growing poetic tradition. In what follows I study more closely Homer's picture of how tradition is handed down through time, bearing in mind that the poet's happy direct relationship to his Muses is shadowed by the tale of Thamyris. The text that offers most on this theme is the *Odyssey*, for

---

[13]The three contest passages share a vocabulary of rage (*khôomenos*): Odysseus is "enraged" by Euryalus, Apollo by Eurytus, the Muses by Thamyris (*Od.* 8.238, 8.227; *Il.* 2.599). The bow of contention is appropriate to the context of *Od.* 8 as a weapon unfavored by the Phaeacians (*Od.* 6.270), but symbolically the bow was early the counterpart of the lyre.

not only is it the more self-conscious of the two epics, but it also seems to have a stronger sense than the *Iliad* of coming late in the tradition and of the need to establish its worth as a tale by setting itself against others.[14] As we shall see, the *Odyssey* manages to say in its first book that it is the "newest songs" that men praise, and recent readings have seen in this assertion a response to the discomfiting greatness of the *Iliad*.[15] In view of the oral nature of epic performance and exchange, however, it is perhaps unnecessary to determine to what extent the *Odyssey* poet's "anxieties of influence" are focused on that particular poem conceived of as a text or are more generally directed at such well-known sagas as the Argonautica (whose wandering heroes cross many of the same waters as Odysseus) or even early legends about Heracles and Eurytus such as later nourished the *Sack of Oichalia*. For the "other" to epic poetry in the *Odyssey* is not any one of these poems seen as a text; the *Odyssey*, rather, sets itself against saga, against what men "say" about what they have seen and heard. The uninspired, toilsome, decidedly historical process of saga making is a sustained interest of this epic, which goes to some lengths to show us how mortals with their limited knowledge collect from human testimony the accounts of noble deeds in the recent past. When these tales are juxtaposed to representations of epic songs, in particular to those of the Ithacan bard Phemius and Demodocus on Phaeacia, saga takes on the role of a kind of "naturalized" epic, a wholly mortal counterpart to divinely bestowed heroic poetry. Placing the god-given songs of epic singers against a background of evolving human saga allows the *Odyssey* poet to reflect on the origins and growth of heroic traditions and the place of poetry within them. This reflection reaches its climax in book 8, when the timeless communion of poet and Muse is shattered as the last of Troy's heroes meets one of the first of her singers. When Odysseus follows Demodocus's epic songs with his first-person accounts of his heroic adventures, it would not be straining to say that we are

[14]On the *Odyssey*'s concern with poetry generally, see Schadewaldt (1965) chap. 6 and, among more recent studies, Clay (1983) chap. 1; Thalmann (1984) chap. 6; Murnaghan (1987) chap. 5.

[15]Redfield (1973); Edwards (1985); Pucci (1979); and more dialectically, Pucci (1987).

presented with the birth of the first *Odyssey*. It seems that if Thamyris could meet his match only in the Muses themselves, the Odyssey poet has structured a subtler meeting between a very early poet and an *Ur*-poet, the hero himself. No more than the *Iliad* does the *Odyssey* dethrone its Muses, but it explores and in a new way settles poetry's origins in time. It reaches an accommodation between its own theory that song is a god's gift and not a construction of poets and the knowledge that there were always earlier tellers of these tales, going back even to the autobiographical hero.[16] Finally, I ask of each poem what is won for the poet in this steadfast denial of historical transmission if it is not a romantic voice expressing individuality and originality.

Song and Saga in Ithaca

If we consider the *Odyssey* strictly as a poem about how Odysseus made his way back to Ithaca from Troy, it must be said that the path of song begins with a detour.[17] At the opening of the poem Athena formulates a plan to free our hero from the island of Calypso, but he will not be set into motion until book 5. In the interim we are concerned with Telemachus on Ithaca and particularly with the quest he undertakes for news of his father. Because these first four books of the *Odyssey* do not plunge us directly into its central theme, and because they seem to possess a certain coherence in themselves, they have been set apart by analytical critics as a separate poem. Yet it has been pointed out in turn that the so-called Telemachy in many ways fits in with the main story and prepares us for it. We are offered a view of the hero's son, coming of age and winning his own *kleos*, as Orestes did. We get to know important figures on Ithaca, and we have, for contrast, vivid sketches of Nestor, Helen, and Menelaus at home and, indirectly,

[16]Fränkel (1973) 20 n. 26 sketches out the logic behind this "theory" (though I think it is unnecessary for his reading of *Od*. 22.347ff.).

[17]Scholium to *Od*. 1.284: "Since the *Odyssey* does not have in itself sufficient variety, the poet depicts Telemachus's journey to Sparta and Mycenae so that a good deal of Iliadic material may be mentioned in passing [*en parekbasesi*]."

of other notable Greeks and their fortunes in trying to return from
Troy. Finally, there are some very telling anecdotes about the great
hero himself, which keep Odysseus in our minds. But the part of
the Telemachy that interests me here is the story that acts as scaf-
folding for all this exposition, Telemachus's extensive but fruitless
search for his father's whereabouts. For this framing story serves to
introduce the poem in the largest way. Throughout these books the
questions on everyone's lips are Where is Odysseus? and Will he
come home? In this prolonged opening gambit, a game of hide-
and-seek for our hero, the *Odyssey* opens and announces itself as
the greatly desired answer to the most urgent and unsolved question. There is an agreeable irony in the poem's self-glorification in
creating an appetite for itself through its own characters. But beyond this self-centering, in depicting its theme as news of the past,
the *Odyssey* also explores the relationship between song and saga
and between new songs and old.

Athena no sooner plans her favorite's release than her thoughts
turn to Ithaca, which is in social upheaval: arrogant suitors harass
Penelope with demands of marriage and threaten the position of
young Telemachus in his house. This desperate situation prevails
not simply because the rightful king is absent but because no one
knows exactly where he may be. The social crisis on Ithaca is fundamentally a crisis of knowledge, as Telemachus explains when the
goddess visits him:

> Once upon a time this house was wealthy and excellent
> while yet that man was here among his people;
> but as it is the gods have planned otherwise, devising evil,
> and made that man unseen [*a-iston*] beyond all others,
> since, even if he were dead, I would not be in such trouble,
> if he had fallen among his companions in the land of Troy
> or among friends when he had woven the war to its end.
> In that case the Achaeans would have joined together to make him
>   a tomb
> and he would have won for his child a great *kleos* thereafter.
> But now the gusts of wind have snatched him away, without
>   leaving *kleos* behind [*a-kleiôs*],
> he has perished unseen [*a-istos*], without leaving any report
>   [*a-pustos*], and left me only groans.

[1.232–243]

Had Odysseus died among men that knew him, society could accommodate the change and effect an orderly transition of power: a tomb would mark for all to see the spot where he lay, and his *kleos*, his glorious and enduring reputation, would preserve his status in an account of who he was and how he ended. In that case Telemachus too would have his rightful place as the son and heir of a great king. Hence, though Telemachus might wish that his father would come home and rout the suitors, he would prefer to the present uncertainty to be the son of a man who had died among his possessions, a well-witnessed death that would secure his own position and patrimony (1.217–220). But as it is, everything is in doubt because Odysseus has vanished without a trace. For his part, Telemachus has stopped believing in the reports that are carried to Ithaca, and puts no stock in the seers his mother consults (1.413–416).[18] He supposes his father is dead, though even in this his uncertainty is global: he doesn't know whether Odysseus's bones are rotting somewhere on land or washed in the waves of the sea (1.161–162).

What is needed, then, are answers to certain questions: Is Odysseus alive or dead? If alive, will he return? If not, what was his end and has he been properly buried? These concerns for Telemachus are naturally emotional and religious; moreover, definite answers, whether the news be happy or not, would at least make clear the social, political, and religious obligations of son and mother. Accordingly, Athena's plan for Telemachus is a mission "to inquire about [*peusomenon*] the return of his father, if he should hear any news / so that he might win *kleos* among men" (1.94–95). The remedy to a crisis of knowledge must be a heroic quest after certainty, and the first four books of the *Odyssey* follow Telemachus as he searches after the character our poet has concealed.

In the event, the quest will not be quite successful; when Telemachus returns to Ithaca, his key questions will remain unanswered and the problems at home will only be exacerbated. The poet has been stringing us along, and the game of hide-and-seek has turned into something of a shell game: we saw the hero concealed right before our eyes, but turning to one witness after another has failed

---

[18]Misleading reports from wanderers in search of gain are referred to in 14.122ff. and 378ff.

to disclose him. This game has a significance as it is played out because it highlights another issue, one relevant to the poet and his audience. On our way with Telemachus we see how heroic figures find out and fail to find out about events that are of great import but obscured by time or distance. These models of how stories from the past survive are quite relevant to the status of the *Odyssey* itself.

Indeed, a quite specific emphasis on the means by which an oral society establishes "facts" important to it runs through Telemachus's complaint. He says that no one has seen Odysseus, no one has brought back a credible report, there is no agreed-upon version of his fate which circulates as part of his *kleos*. Here, as in the *Iliad*'s description of the Muses, there is a careful and consistent use of the vocabulary of seeing and hearing. The best knowledge would come if someone had seen Odysseus (expressed in the root (*w*)*id*/(*w*)*oid*-); failing that (expressed in the privative prefix *a*-), one can find out by inquiring (root *p*(*e*)*uth*-), which is listening (*akouô*) to what others have to say, without seeing the proof for oneself.

Athena is equally explicit in her instructions to Telemachus:

Go to inquire about [*peusomenos*] your father so long gone,
if by chance some mortal might tell you, or you hear
a rumor [*ossan*] from Zeus, which chiefly carries *kleos* among men.

[1.281–283]

Telemachus's position is like that of Homer's audience: he cannot expect to see Odysseus and thus to know surely where he is; he will have to rely on hearsay (cf., *akoê* [5.19]). What a mortal chances to say cannot be traced to its source; it is as unreliable as a rumor— literally the "speech of Zeus," which is, like *kleos*, a tale that has currency without a definite origin among men.[19] When Telemachus subsequently undertakes his journey, the focus on just how people find things out remains constant, carried through by this recurrent vocabulary to mark firsthand knowledge as opposed to the report of such knowledge. This journey extensively illustrates a

[19]See Heubeck, West, Hainsworth (1981) on 1.282–283.

process of collating oral reports in an attempt to substitute for a clear knowledge or view of heroic reality.[20]

Once the chase is afoot, the first stop is Pylos and garrulous old Nestor. Telemachus asks him for any news of his father, "whether by chance you have seen him / with your own eyes, or have heard the tale from another, / a wanderer" (3.93–95). Again, the report of an eyewitness is best; next is the account gleaned secondhand from an eyewitness, which would be perforce a slightly wandering account in the case of Odysseus. Nestor begins with his divagating *recusatio* but manages to bring Telemachus abreast of things as far as the time he parted with, and thus last saw, Odysseus, at Tenedos at the beginning of the way back to Greece. After that he himself made good time home,

> So that, dear boy, I have found out nothing [*apeuthês*]
> and don't know [*oida*] at all about them, which Achaeans survived
>   and which died.
> But as much as I have found out [*peuthomai*] while sitting here in
>   my palace
> this, as is only right, you shall learn, I won't hide it from you.
> They say that the Myrmidons. . . .
>
>   [3.184–188]

Nestor doesn't "know" about the returns he goes on to recount because he has been sitting at home far from the actual events, but he is willing to give the hearsay, what "they say" about the returning army.[21] He has heard about how Achilles' troops fared, and about other Greek contingents, but as for Odysseus's present fate, he can only offer a pious hope that Athena still stands by him (3.230ff.). Telemachus is not comforted by Nestor's report and continues to suppose his father dead (3.240–242).

We get further along with the story with Menelaus, who was the last to make his way back from Troy. Telemachus tells him that he has come after news (*klêêdona* [4.317]) of his father, and repeats the request he had made to Nestor for anything Menelaus might have

---

[20]The importance of this theme is well noted by Murnaghan (1987) 156–160. Cf. Peradotto (1990) 116–119.

[21]It is also from what "they say" that housebound Nestor knows of the current troubles on Ithaca (3.212).

seen with his eyes or heard from some traveler (4.323–325 = 3.93–95). Menelaus turns out to have some hearsay about Odysseus, and it comes from an unusually good source, Proteus. The prophetic sea god told Menelaus a good deal about the returns of various Achaeans and said that he "saw" (4.556) Odysseus alive but trapped on Calypso's island, with neither vessel nor crew (4.555–560). What the god has seen and deigned to say must be true, and so it will prove to be (4.557–560 = 5.14–17); but what may have happened to Odysseus since then is not known, and it hardly seems likely that he will be able to make his way home. Menelaus knows only that things look very bad for his old companion and fellow warrior: "It is likely after all / that trouble came on him, and on me an unforgettable sorrow / for him, so long gone, I don't even know / whether he is alive or dead" (4.107–110); some angry god, he hazards, has taken away his return (4.181–182).

Telemachus then returns to Ithaca without the crucial information he was seeking but having learned much about other heroes. Most of it is reliable report, for it comes from eyewitnesses of established credentials and good will, Odysseus's comrades in arms or someone such as Helen, who contributes her own encounters with Odysseus in Troy. He also has the report of one divine sighting of Odysseus, but it offers little insight into his present situation. If his firm knowledge of Odysseus's prospects for returning has not essentially been advanced from the time when we first saw him, "imagining in his mind's eye" (*ossomenos . . . eni phresi* [1.115]) how his father might come home and scatter the suitors, nevertheless his quest has provided an extensive illustration of how a great and complex action is converted into an accepted story.

What we are shown here is in effect the formation of an oral tradition recounting how the Greeks fared on their perilous return from Troy. The tales are passed from witness to reporter to reporter, and Telemachus in his travels can collate them to make a larger whole. The particular stages by which such a tradition grows can be resumed in a consideration of Agamemnon's exemplary fate, which is rehearsed four times in these books. First of all, the events have occurred and, even if done by guile, have been open to the sight of the gods, to all-seeing Zeus in particular. In the scene that opens the poem, we get the Olympian view, as Zeus calls to mind

(*mnêsato* [1.29]) Aegisthus, how he killed Agamemnon on his return and how he was in turn slain by Orestes (1.29–35). On earth,
the tale is carried to Ithaca by Athena, disguised as a traveling
merchant: "Haven't you heard," she asks Telemachus, "what *kleos*
Orestes got / among all men when he killed his father's mur-
derer?" (1.298–299). The story is evidently already widely circulating, and Nestor assumes it has reached Ithaca: "You yourself,
though you live far away, have heard about Agamemnon / how he
came back and how Aegisthus contrived his wretched destruction"
(3.193–194). Menelaus was even more removed from Mycenae at
the time of his brother's death, being detained in Egypt, but he can
give the fullest version of all, because he got it from Proteus (4.519–
537). The next step for a story like this, which has moral and
dynastic implications that give it universal and enduring interest,
is to become *kleos*, the hardened and lasting form of report which
passes through the wide world and through time. So Athena says
Orestes has won *kleos* with his vengeance, and Telemachus predicts the future career of the story: "Indeed that one took a great
revenge, and the Achaeans / will carry his fame afar, even to be a
song for men to come" (3.204–205). Action, report, *kleos*, and finally song; Athena and Nestor compress the whole sequence when
they counsel Telemachus to be brave at this time so that men born
later may speak well of him (1.302 = 3.200).

As the poem opens, then, Agamemnon's great fall is already
achieving fame, and stories about the other heroes are circulating.
From his various sources Telemachus can piece together an account
of the *nostoi*, the perilous returns of the Greek heroes from Troy.
The human tale is incomplete, but there is of course another way to
find out what the Greek heroes did and suffered, one that comes
not from the tongues of men but from the gods, inspired song. In
fact there was a large range of epic which took these very returns
for its themes. The *Odyssey* is the greatest and earliest extant example of such *nostoi*, or "return poems," but its author by no means
invented the form. Indeed, such a poem is being sung by the very
first bard we see, Phemius, who sings in the palace of Ithaca "the
Wretched Return of the Achaeans / from Troy which Athena
brought about" (1.326–327). This return song plays in the background while Athena and Telemachus discreetly talk about Odys-

seus's possible return.[22] The human account of the Greek returns is thus matched with an account given in "divinely inspired song."[23] If Proteus will sometimes tell men what he has seen, the Muses also tell men the *klea andrôn* that they and their father have witnessed. On Ithaca both epic and human inquiry as forms of recollection aim to give an account of the same events, and both have strong psychological effects on their hearers. Athena tells Telemachus about her last meeting with Odysseus, and her conversation "put him in mind of his father more strongly than before" (*hupemnêsen* [1.321–322]). The song sung by the bard moves Penelope to an "unforgettable sorrow" because she is "always thinking of" (*memnêmenê*) her husband (1.342–343). Both Athena, who bears the name Mentes, "inspirer of thought," and the "mindful" bard play the role of *mnêmones*, reminding guardians of the past.[24]

We would like to know more about this song of Phemius, which seems to parallel human inquiry as a source of heroic history and incentive to action, and a good deal is supplied in the ensuing scene. Penelope appears and asks the bard to sing one of the many other enchanting songs that he knows but to stop this sad one (1.337–341). What exactly is the subject of "this" song? We are told only that it is the "Wretched Return of the Achaeans." Because Phemius's song makes Penelope long for her husband, it has been suggested that Phemius is singing a lying song about Odysseus's death to please the suitors.[25] Yet no bard in either epic sings an evidently false song, and Penelope elsewhere seems uncertain of his fate. His "fame spread wide throughout Greece" to which Penelope refers (1.344) must be of his heroism in the Trojan War, well known by now. But what is missing is any *kleos* of his return (1.242), and for Penelope this must remain in doubt, despite her

---

[22]Homer creates a foreground and a background here by having Telemachus draw Athena (and us) out of earshot of the entertainment for their talk at 1.156–157. It is normally his practice to depict simultaneous events as happening consecutively, but Phemius seems to begin singing at 1.155 and to have been singing all the while (cf. 1.159) until Telemachus returns to the suitors, 1.324–325.

[23]Such I take to be the implication of *thespin aoidên* in 1.328, on which, see Chapter 5.

[24]Svenbro (1976) 31 n. 88.

[25]E.g., by Svenbro (1976) 20–21; Pucci (1987) 198–199, following the scholium on 1.340.

interest in divination. It is rather because she thinks of him always that the tales of other returns remind her of him who has not come home.

A striking point is made in Telemachus's reply, which offers a significant commentary on song in the heroic age. He tells his mother that the bard is not responsible for the fates men get, but Zeus is; the bard must be free to pursue the course of song "wherever his mind moves" (1.346–349). "He is not to be blamed for singing the evil fate of the Danaans / for men praise most of all that song / which rings newest in their ears" (1.350–352). The palpable irony of this statement is not always noted,[26] but it could not have failed to strike an audience whose greatest delight was for songs of a dim and distant past that the heroes within the *Odyssey* take for their entertainment the newest themes. The fundamental character of epic as poetry of the past is reversed when it appears in the looking glass of epic. What were the "fames of men" for Homer's audience were fresh rumor and recent news for the heroes; the literate's trope would be to say that the faded parchments we keep in museums were the daily newspapers of old. And this makes sense, for it is an appropriate glorification of these men greater than we to say that, just as their own deeds and lives are destined to become the stuff of immortal poetry, so the poetry they prefer comes closest to these deeds.

Book 1 of the *Odyssey*, then conscientiously juxtaposes the two forms of heroic narrative by setting up an urgent inquiry after Odysseus and then characterizing poetry as a source of the latest news about glorious action. With this irony, poetry is put alongside oral report as a parallel source of knowledge about the *klea andrôn*. When the story begins, however, each source of knowledge has reached the same impasse. Phemius sings the latest poetry, the sequel to the Trojan song, but the *nostoi* do not yet embrace Odysseus's return. The path of god-given song has advanced only so far in the process of transmuting deed into account. And this is exactly as far as human tradition has progressed. Telemachus manages to piece together a fairly complete saga of the returns, but the great

[26]An exception is Jensen (1980) 118.

missing piece remains the return of Odysseus, as he says to Nestor:

> For all the other heroes who fought at Troy
> we have found out where each one met his painful end,
> but this man's death the son of Cronus has made unknown
> [*apeuthea*],
> and no one is able to tell us clearly where he died,
> whether he fell on land, at the hands of foemen,
> or on the high seas in the waves of Amphitrite.
>
> [3.86–91]

No one can say where Odysseus is, and no one can sing his return. Phemius, "man of fame," has the latest poetry, but this is no more than one might learn by going abroad.

In the Telemachy, then, we see oral traditions about the heroes' return and the poetry of that return stopped at the same point. How will the tale go on? The answer is of course the *Odyssey* itself, and the poem very explicitly situates itself in its prologue as that latest song, sought by all but not yet accomplished:

> At that time all the others, as many who escaped utter destruction,
> were home, having escaped the war and the sea;
> but him alone, eager for his homecoming and his wife,
> the awesome nymph Calypso kept back, shining among
> goddesses.
>
> [1.11–14]

Others have come home, or not; some have won *kleos;* others are in the process of winning it; reports abound. But Odysseus's return is covered over; he is held by Calypso, the "concealer," on her "far-off island" (5.55). The *Odyssey* dedicates its opening books to depicting a world in which it is itself on the verge of being realized, at the precise moment when gods and heroes are most eager to retrieve the story of far-off Odysseus.

Song and Saga in Phaeacia

The *nostoi* is completed by the *Odyssey:* the newest of new songs tells how the last of the heroes came home. Yet the poet has not finished sketching out the relationship of saga and poetry, for what has happened to Odysseus since Troy is told to us by Odysseus himself in a long first-person narration filling books 9 through 12. Moreover, this hero's report of his own heroic doings is also juxtaposed to the poetry of an epic bard, Demodocus, the court poet in Phaeacia. The Phaeacian episode, like the Telemachy, puts heroic reminiscence alongside epic poetry, but with a significant difference: here at last a reporter is found who can add to the tales of return. Our source for the missing account will prove to be an excellent witness, in fact he is the only Greek on earth who could tell the story as an eyewitness.

On Phaeacia, Odysseus's oral report supplements heroic song, but the situation is in fact more complicated. Odysseus's performance is not simply juxtaposed to that of Demodocus but so intertwined with it that the two nearly meld together as if they were the offerings of two poets. It has been noted that Homer repeatedly compares Odysseus to a poet in his tale-telling and that in these books the hero in many ways acts as his own bard.[27] Alcinous explicitly compares Odysseus to a bard (11.363–369), and the poet twice says that his long heroic narrative cast a spell over his audience, which is precisely the effect Phemius's songs have on his hearers (11.333–334 = 13.1–2; cf. 1.337–340). But the comparisons are more extensive than is usually noted; in the aggregate they suggest that Odysseus is not merely the "prose" counterpart to Demodocus but in a certain sense his poetic antagonist.

As far as the plot of the Phaeacis is concerned, Odysseus's tale is an interruption of the song of Demodocus, indeed, only the last in a series of impulsive interruptions by Alcinous that seem to send the action in book 8 reeling from palace to public square and back again. But threading together all of Demodocus's performances and tying them to the tale of Odysseus is a consistent and explicit focus on the forms of poetic performance. In describing the performances of Demodocus and Odysseus, Homer highlights their formal aspects, noting how they begin and end and so suggesting how they might be connected. Specifically, he uses a number of

[27]The main allusions are collected in Moulton (1977) 145–151. Further discussion and references can be found in Segal (1983) 24–26; Thalmann (1984) 173; Murnaghan (1987) chap. 5, references at 149 n. 4.

expressions that are rare or unique in his corpus but usual in Hesiodic proems and the Homeric hymns as technical terms relating to the rhapsodic presentation of piece after piece of heroic poetry. The constellation of these quasi-technical terms here (and only here in the two epics) draws our attention to the place of Odysseus's story in Homer's "topical poetic," a poetic conceiving of poetry as themes selected from a common store and connected one to another.

Demodocus is moved to sing by the Muses and selects as his theme, *oimê*, the "Quarrel of Odysseus and Achilles, son of Peleus" (8.75). This particular theme is not known to us elsewhere, but comes from sometime in the beginning of the expedition.[28] Later Odysseus refers to this performance and then asks the poet to skip forward on the path of song: "But come, move along [on the path of song] and sing the Fashioning of the Horse" (*Od.* 8.492). Demodocus complies: he "took his beginning from the god [*theou arkheto*]" (8.499). The phrase *theou arkheto*, like the verb *metabainô*, is unique in Homer, but like *oimê*, both seem to belong to the quasi-technical language of early *epos*, and their effect here is to draw attention to the formal breaks in the performance and to the performatory procedure by which subsequent tellers pick up and carry on the previous theme.[29] Similarly, when Demodocus takes up Odysseus's

[28]The quarrel is "the beginning of woes" for the Greeks. Whether one locates this event at the marshaling of the fleet at Aulis, with Pagliaro (1951) 17–20, or later at Tenedos, with Nagy (1979) chaps. 1 and 3, the sequence is not affected.

[29]Another possible proemic locution in this context is the Homeric *hapax humnon* in 8.429, referring prospectively to Demodocus's second palace performance. As mentioned in Chapter 1, *humnos* does not at this time mean "hymn to the gods," but if it is a general term for "song," it is remarkable that Homer does not avail himself of it more often as a variant for *aoidê*, which occurs more than thirty times. This anomaly would make sense if *humnos* named singing particularly in its aspect of an individual performer's contribution in a series of performances. Hence it would have been established in the Homeric hymns, for example, in the transitional formula in which the poet "moves" from his proem "to another *humnos*" (*H. Aph.* 295 etc.); Hesiod uses *humnos* twice in the proem to the sailing section of the *Works and Days*, where he speaks of "winning a tripod by my hymn [*humnôi nikêsanta*]" (657). Whatever may be its precise sense as opposed to *aoidê*, *humnos* seems an appropriate expression for song in its aspect as a competition piece—not "singing" as an activity but the woven, defined presentation of an individual, possibly for a prize. Such also seems to be the force of the word in the psuedo-Hesiodic hexameters describing a mythical contest between Homer and Hesiod at Delos (note the proemic first person) 357 M-W: "Then first in Delos did I and Homer / make festive music for Apollo, weaving song in new hymns, / for the one with the golden sword, whom Leto bore."

request, Homer tells us the starting point (*enthen helôn*) from which
he began the episode of the wooden horse and the ensuing sack of
Troy (8.492–503; cf. 514–515). These two songs, then, roughly span
the Trojan War, and their sequel can only be the returns. The great
capstone to the returns, the part that Phemius was unable to sing
on Ithaca, is the return of Odysseus. But here Demodocus is inter-
rupted by Alcinous, who turns to his vagabond guest and asks him
only what one might ask any long-suffering suppliant:

> But come now tell me this, and recount it straight
> where were you buffeted and what lands did you visit
> where men dwell, and what well-inhabited cities
> both the ones that were cruel and savage, unjust,
> and the ones that welcomed strangers and had a mind of
>   reverence?
>
> [8.572–576]

But this is the same topic, in some of the same words, as the
Odyssey's own: the man much buffeted, who knew cities of many
men, and their mind (1.1–4). Odysseus is being invited to follow
Demodocus's songs with a personal version of the *Odyssey*.

Odysseus begins his tale with a prologue (9.2–38), in which he
manages to execute the primary functions of a proem: honoring
the host and the present occasion (2–14), identifying and praising
the speaker (19ff.), posing the aporia about beginnings (14–16), and
settling on a starting point (37–38). His topic is his "Return of many
Cares / which Zeus imposed upon me from Troy," which rings like
an invocation in its title, relative clause, the mention of woes and
the will of Zeus. Setting apart its unique ethos, Odysseus's tale is
very much a heroic story, and he begins just where Demodocus
had left off: the first word of his narrative proper is *Iliothen*, "from
Ilion" (9.39).

The sequence of paths, of *loci* or *topoi*, remains strikingly evident
throughout. Odysseus's narrative runs on until 11.327, when he
tries to conclude it with a *recusatio* closing his catalog of women in
Hades. There is a pause; Alcinous bestows gifts and compliments
and then moves the song along:

> But come, tell me this, and recount it unswervingly
> whether you saw any of your godlike companions, who with you

went to Troy and met their fate there.
This night is quite amazingly long, and not yet is it time to sleep.

[11.370–74]

When Odysseus complies, he converts Alcinous's request into a conversational version of the invocation. "I would not begrudge you," he says,

the Cares of my Companions, who died then,
the ones who escaped a groanful death from the Trojans
but on their return died, through the will of an evil woman.

[11.382–384]

Odysseus announces that he is taking up the epic theme again in the titling syntax, the paratactic relative clauses alluding to suffering, and even the parodical mention that all this happened through the will of—not a god—that evil woman Helen.[30] He takes up his story from where he left off: after Persephone scattered the shades of the women "there came the shade of Agamemnon" (11.387).

From the perspective of a topical poetic, Demodocus and Odysseus manage through starts and pauses to give a long continuous tale tracing a large part of the heroic traditions. The poet has not only enjoyed the irony of bringing the living hero into the heroic poet's audience, he has so structured and described their performances as to make them join together into one grand epic. At first Demodocus had sung "in whatever direction his heart moves" (8.45), as Phemius did in Ithaca (1.347); but with Odysseus's intervention, he enters the song on cue. In fact, the sequence of themes here suggests nothing so much as a competition in epic poetry; at least this is exactly the procedure that we hear was practiced later in Athens with the poetry of Homer. Ancient testimony traces to some time in the sixth century the "Panathenaic rule" that rhapsodes take up their themes from one another in a prescribed succession. Diogenes Laertius attributes to Solon a measure stipulating that at the great Athenian festival for Athena "the Homeric

---

[30]"Through the will of," *iotêti*, is usually used of divine will in Homer, and always in this metrical position; cf. its use in 12.190, where the Sirens sing what the Greeks and Trojans suffered "through the will of the gods."

poems should be recited by a process of giving cues (*ex hupobolês*), that is, at whatever point the first poet stopped, the one who came after him should start from there" (*Solon* 1.57).[31] And a work attributed to Plato assigns a nearly identical law to Hipparchus: "He compelled the rhapsodes at the Panatheneia to go through them [the Homeric poems] taking up the pieces in order [*ex hupolêpsios ephexês*], just as they do now" ([Plato] *Hipparchus* 228B).[32] The performances of Demodocus and Odysseus happen to replicate very closely the art of rhapsodes as it is later attested. Their individual contributions might be stitched together into one long continuous song.[33]

These testimonia are late and attribute the procedure to different innovators, but they agree on the procedure for competitive epic performance at festivals, and we simply cannot say when Homeric poetry first began to be performed in this way.[34] Other details seem to add to the picture. When Demodocus takes to the *agora* we

[31]When Demodocus left off his Trojan narrative, the verb used was *lêxeien* (*Od.* 8.87), which is the technical expression used by a rhapsode to end a performance or a part of one: *H. Dion.* 17–18; Hesiod fr. 305.4 M-W and *Theog.* 48; Diogenes Laertius 1.57; see West (1981) 122. Dunkel adds *Il.* 9.191 and suggests that this language may go back to the vocabulary of Indo-European song contests (1979) 268–269.

[32]Pagliaro (1951) 30–38 argues that these non-Homeric terms belonged to the archaic terminology of the singer's art and especially described aspects of competitive performances. He has further claimed that the *Odyssey* preserves a technical expression for the first performer in a series of rhapsodies in describing Demodocus's beginning, *aneballeto kalon aeidein* (*Od.* 8.266, etc.); but *Od.* 17.261–262 clearly indicates that the traditional explanation of the phrase as referring to an instrumental prelude, without special reference to a series of performers, cannot be excluded from Homer (contra Pagliaro, esp. 32).

[33]It has occasionally been suggested that festival contests, lasting several days, were the occasion for monumentally long compositions such as the *Iliad* and *Odyssey*; e.g., Murray (1934) 187–192 and Webster (1964) 267–272. The scholium to Pindar *Nemean* 2.1 (concerned to offer an etymology for the much disputed term *rhapsode*, "stitch-singer") says that "originally each contestant gave at a competition whatever piece he wished. . . . Later, when the two [Homeric] poems were introduced, the contestants, so to speak, sewed together the parts of the poems to each other and went through the entire poem."

[34]Davison (1955) 9–12 and (1962) questions the accuracy of the testimonia, but there is no reason to think that this manner of performance cannot be archaic. For a recent strong defense of the old hypothesis that Homeric texts were first formed at Athenian festivals, see Jensen (1980) chap. 9 (relevant texts reprinted on 207–226); she argues that the Homeric epics were dictated in Athens at the end of the sixth century by the poet who won the Panathenaic rhapsodic contest.

find several peculiar details that may evoke a singing contest as much as an entertainment. For the poet's performance *aisumnêtai kritoi dêmioi* appear. It is hard to judge from the obscure archaic word *aisumnêtai*[35] what these "selected public umpires" did. Ostensibly they have no contest to judge; their job is to smooth out the dancing place and broaden it (*eurunan* [8.260]), probably by sitting the people away from the arena, which is just what Achilles does as he prepares the athletic competition in *Iliad* 23.257–258. Further, the place they broaden, which is where Demodocus will perform, is called here not simply a "dancing place," (*khoron* [as in *Od.* 8.264; cf. 6.157]), but an *agôn* (8.259, 260); this word, used generally for "assembly" in epic, bears elsewhere in this book (8.200, 238) and in the Iliadic description of Patroclus's funeral games the specific sense "place of contest."[36]

Taken as a whole, the series of songs offered here contains many elements typical of a succession of rhapsodic performances. Demodocus offers several themes in succession and comes tantalizingly close to entering the lists; and it is suggestive that his "Affair of Ares and Aphrodite" resembles in many respects a displaced Homeric hymn,[37] since Homeric hymns would have been an especially appropriate way to lead off a festival rhapsodic contest. The reference to poetic contests in Hesiod makes it certain that Homer must have known of poetic competition, however idyllic the world in which his bards operate. Hesiod speaks of a contest held at a king's funeral, but more relevant to our context may be the testimony of the Homeric *Hymn to Apollo,* usually dated to the seventh century, which describes rhapsodic competitions at festivals.[38] For the larger context of the Phaeacis provides a number of other suggestions of a festival setting for poetic contests.

[35]Eustathius (1594.62) and the scholium on 8.258 gloss *aisumnêtês* with *brabeutai,* which can denote the judges at a musical agon (cf. schol. on Aristophanes *Peace* 733); but *aisumnêtês* is rare in archaic Greek, and its meanings remain obscure. See *LfgrE* s.v. and, for its later political use, Romer (1982).

[36]*Il.* 23 passim, 24.1; cf. *H. Ap.* 150, *Hymn* 6.20, and H. J. Mette in *LfgrE,* s.v. 2.*f, g.* Cowgill (1978) has proposed to connect this word (via *ageirô*) with *agorê,* "public square."

[37]See Allen, Halliday, and Sikés (1936) lxxxvii–lxxxviii, who note that the only elements missing are the invocation, epilogue, and the address to a deity—i.e., the rhapsodic elements have been shorn off.

[38]*H. Ap.* 146–150. It is hypercritical to doubt that the passage refers to contests; for

In its outline, book 8 interposes athletic contests between two epic recitations by Demodocus. The mere depiction of a festivity that combined athletic competition with musical performance would have been suggestive in the archaic age of the matching poetic and athletic contests which were the core of great festivals such as the one on Delos for Apollo. But in this book things are managed in such a way as to make the resemblance the result of spontaneous impulses: Alcinous is searching for ways to entertain his guest. The action of the book is complex but fairly well articulated by the movements of characters in and out of Alcinous's palace. At its opening Alcinous and Odysseus leave the palace to join a public assembly of the Phaeacians in the *agora* (8.5); there, the king proposes to entertain this unknown wanderer and convey him home (28). Then a select royal party repairs to the palace to entertain the guest. Demodocus is specially invited, and he performs the Quarrel of Odysseus and Achilles after the feast (73–74). When this presentation distresses Odysseus, Alcinous tactfully suspends the entertainment and proposes that the company turn their attention to athletic contests; accordingly, they return to the *agora,* where they are joined by a multitude of spectators (107–109). After the games and gift giving, the royal party returns to the palace (421–422). Here there are further civilities and a feast, after which Demodocus performs another Trojan theme (499–500). The spatial movements serve to emphasize their different contexts: one is a public spectacle, the other a royal entertainment; one is competitive and the other not. Even when Alcinous collapses these distinctions by inviting Demodocus to perform at the games, it is as though singing were incorporated with the games as an afterthought. Homer marks the incursion of the singer into the public space as exceptional: Alcinous must dispatch a herald to fetch Demodocus's lyre, which had been left hanging in the palace hall (8.254–255; cf. 67).[39]

---

a discussion, see Förstel (1979) 138–140, 383–384. Another suggestion of festival contests in epic may lie in the very name Thamyris, which Hesychius glosses as *panugêris,* a word meaning "crowd," and particularly one gathered for a festival.

[39]This kind of detail is not beneath Homer's notice; cf. *Il.* 9.188, where it is explained how Achilles happened to have a lyre at Troy. Similar is *Il.* 5.192ff.

It is as though Alcinous is improvising here, and his improvised entertainment of Odysseus happens to include the activities that the Greeks were wont to enjoy at festivals. Contests between poets, formal or informal, were especially suitable for such a setting. Eustathius, the learned twelfth-century bishop of Thessalonica, was troubled when he read this scene by a naïve question— Why would a blind poet go out to watch games?—but he shrewdly sensed that Homer has brought Demodocus out here as to a competition:

> Demodocus is led out where the best of the Phaeacians go . . . to admire or watch the athletics, not only so that he may enjoy the contest by listening to it, but also, as it were, to compete himself and to display that musical art in which the Phaeacians take so much pride because of him. And if the poet had been able to fashion some rival artist [*antitekhnon*] for Demodocus, on the pattern of those who later competed at musical contests, he would not have hesitated to do so. (1587.49ff.)

Eustathius is wrong about the chronology of poetic contests and fails to note that Demodocus meets his match in Odysseus, but he senses from the logic of book 8 both that Demodocus is somewhat out of place at the games and that he is a rhapsode manqué.

The Competition for Truth

The unachieved contest at Phaeacia is only one of several analogous displacements of eighth-century festival life to be found on this exotic island. The first thing Odysseus sees when he is washed up on shore is Nausicaa and her maids at play. The girls are playing a ball game (*paisdon*) while Nausicaa leads (*êrkheto*) them in a "song and dance" (*molpê* [6.99–102]). These terms were also typically used in archaic Greece to describe any virginal choragus who led a festive maidens' chorus, and the poet strengthens the allusion when he compares the scene to that of Artemis dancing (*paisdousi*) with her nymphs (6.106), making her mother rejoice.[40] This image of Artemis leading a maiden's dance to the delight of her parents, well known to the Homeric hymns (*Hymn* 27.16–20; *H. Ap.* 197–199, 204–205), was a paradigm for maidens' choruses in which proud parents would show off their marriageable daughters at Delphi or the Panatheneia. Artemis is invoked for a second time by Odysseus himself, who adds that Nausicaa's parents must be gratified when they see her enter the chorus (*Od.* 6.151–157). But on Phaeacia the formal maidens' choral ceremony is no more than a seaside game of a princess and her maids.

One detail from the Phaeacian episode supports these hints and epitomizes their subtle disguising. At 6.162–167 Odysseus compares Nausicaa to a palm he once saw beside the altar of Apollo at Delos. H. T. Wade-Gery has suggested that the poet's audience would recognize such a reference from having attended the Delian festival.[41] This sole Homeric mention of the palm certainly suggests the sacred tree at Delos, which was frequently mentioned in Apolline poetry as supporting Leto when she gave birth to the god. But again the context denies that the palm in Homer could be Leto's ancient palm, for the altar of Apollo is already there and the tree is only a shoot (*ernos*) and still growing, surely too frail to support a goddess in travail. A Delian palm it is though, unique, awe-inspiring, and in the sacred precinct. It is, in fact, the very same tree, but like the other aspects of a god's festival, including the competition among poets, returned in time to its heroic infancy.[42]

The archaizing or heroizing of poetic competition in the *Odyssey*, book 8, is thus part of a larger reduction from the present to the past and from the ritual to the spontaneous. On this fantastic isle Homer imagines a very early kind of festival, complete with a very early kind of contest. With its spontaneous choruses and games and musical performances, the Phaeacian episode preserves hints

[40]For *exarkhein* (cf. *Od.* 4.19), see Pagliaro (1951) 19–34. On *paisdein* and *molpê* in this context, see Calame (1977) 164–166, 90–91.

[41]Wade-Gery (1952) 1–6; so too thought the scholiast on the passage and perhaps whoever wrote the hexameters about Homer and Hesiod competing on Delos ([Hes.] fr. 357 M-W).

[42]In a comparable piece of archaizing, Pindar imagines the early Olympic festival before olive trees were planted there (*Ol.* 3.21–24).

of the major entertainments of a festival honoring a deity, such as
the Ionians established for Delian Apollo.[43] If we add the sacrifices,
the feasting, and the procession arranged by Alcinous, in which
delegates from the Phaeacian tribes bring gifts to Odysseus, Homer
seems to have staged a day of singing and contests as the scene for
a competition, or at least confrontation, between heroic poet and
narrating hero.

All these details suggest the most magnificent forum for epic
success in Homer's day, and yet it is not quite a contest: although
Alcinous may say that Odysseus is like a poet, he is of course
finally not a poet. Hence this peculiar meeting is rather like
Thamyris's encounter with the Muses: in this imaginary land, at
the very end of the Trojan tale, Homer imagines an epic poet so
early in time that he can meet one of the subjects of his song. In
each case the poet translates the familiar antagonism of two poets
beneath one Muse into a very early kind of contest between the
poet and his tradition personified. For a poet who declares his
independence of rivals and predecessors, this can be the only interesting contest. In leaping out of the competitive context of his
own day to find his only adversary in a figure so early as to be of
another order, the poet tries to make singing timeless. The contest
at Phaeacia, adumbrated but not realized, effectively solves the
question raised in book 1 of how a tradition manages to grow:
Telemachus sought an eyewitness account of Odysseus from the
ones who had seen him most recently or seen him best; in later
times, when all the heroes are gone and Proteus may be silent,
Homer's own poetry is the sole satisfying account of the past. The
prize at stake is the hope of giving a true account of the past, which
turns out to mean the account closest to the deeds themselves.

Odysseus's meeting with Demodocus is usually read for what it
says about the hero. In book 8 he reveals his excellence according

[43]For the chorus of maidens at Delos, see Calame (1977) 194–204. There are many
other parallels between the Phaeacians and the Ionians, who are also noted for their
ships and wealth (H. Ap. 153–155). These might be explained by assuming that the
composer of the Delian hymn was influenced by the fictions of the Odyssey in
describing a real island, but again these traditional texts contain patterns that are
more widely dispersed, see Richardson on Od. 8 and H. Dem. (1974) 179–180, 339–
343, who suggests that H. Dem. may have been modeled on Od. 8–13 but allows
that many of these similarities may be part of a tradition, 180.

to the classic heroic standard of being a doer of deeds and a speaker of words: he shows his athletic prowess in the contests and
shows that he knows how to speak prudently in his contretemps
with Euryalus (esp. 8.166ff.). But by bringing Odysseus together
with Demodocus, Homer adds a further quality to the hero "with
whom no mortal could contend" in speaking (*Il.* 3.223): his mere
reminiscences are as spellbinding as a poet's and so he shows the
special self-conscious, artful, and affecting qualities that are so exploited in the rest of the poem.[44]

All this seems fair enough. But the scene also says something
about the nature of poetry and its relation to other oral traditions,
a theme we have seen in the Telemachy. It contrives to pit the
inspired bard against the eyewitness hero. The meeting between
Demodocus and Odysseus is thus a meeting of song and saga, as
the poet makes clear when Odysseus addresses Demodocus:

> Demodocus, to you beyond all other mortals I offer praise:
> either the Muse taught you, the child of Zeus, or Apollo.[45]
> For quite rightly [*kata kosmon*] do you sing the destruction of the
>   Achaeans,
> all that they did and suffered and wrought at Troy,
> as if somehow either you yourself were present or had heard of it
>   from someone else who was.
> But come, move along and sing the Fashioning of the Horse,
> the wooden one that Epeius made together with Athena,
> which godlike Odysseus once brought to the acropolis as a trick,
> filling it with the men who sacked Ilion.
> And if you narrate these things to me correctly [*kata moiran*],
> then I shall proclaim to all men

---

[44]So Murnaghan (1987) 153: the depictions of Odysseus as his own poet "are
expressions of just how rare and how complete his success in the *Odyssey* is."
Similarly Thalmann (1984) 174 speaks of Odysseus's verbal facility and his extraordinary mastery of deed and word. Redfield sees Odysseus as making poetry out of his
experience, as mediating and settling "somehow" the relation between poetry and
fact ([1973] esp. 153). Segal (1983) 27 speaks of the irony that "calls attention to the
fact that the glory of heroic deeds exists only in song."

[45]Apollo's association with "singers and kitharists" is archaic (*Theog.* 94–95; cf.
Allen, Halliday, and Sikes (1936) on Hymn 25). But it is suggestive that Homer
names him as patron of poets only here, along with other apparent references to a
Delian setting already noted.

that on you the god in her favor has bestowed divinely spoken
song.

[8.487–498]

Again the opposition of seeing and hearing is pregnant: the poet
speaks "as if he were there," as if he saw the events for himself,
though we know he wasn't and we see he is blind. Yet he has
"heard it from someone else who was," since the all-seeing Muses
supply his eyes into the past. In addition, Odysseus has implicitly
pointed out that his own forthcoming account will not come from
the Muses but will be a tale told by one who was there.

Odysseus's praise of Demodocus must be read as indirect praise
for the epic poet singing the song, but it is necessary to specify in
what his song excels. This passage is often read as an indirect claim
for the "truth" of the poetic tale from an actual eyewitness, but we
have seen that any basis for such judgments would have been
inaccessible to Homer's audience. In fact, we should note here that
as a vagabond from unknown parts, Odysseus has no credentials
in Phaeacia to authenticate the "factuality" of these events. He is
speaking only as another member of the audience; he remains
aware of his own concealed identity enough to speak disin-
genuously of "Odysseus" in the third person.

In context, the only kind of "truth" that the vagabond can assert
is that limited kind denoted by *alêtheia*. Such a judgment is also
implied in Odysseus's key commendatory phrase, *kata kosmon*
(8.489). Literally, "according to order," this phrase has yielded the
antithetical interpretations "true" or "well ordered" as well as com-
binations of both.[46] Yet the phrase should not be pressed too quickly into meaning "true." As "order," *kosmos* is an arrangement that
is good, efficient, approved: in military terms it is well-deployed
forces; in social terms it is the high seated above the low.[47] It is how

---

[46]E.g., Lanata (1963) 12–13, who presses the phrase to mean both "true" and
"well-structured." Cf. Thalmann (1984) 129: "not just in sequence but 'accurately,'
'truly'" and Walsh (1984) 7–9.

[47]The best attack is "well according to order" (*Il.* 11.48 = 12.85). A routed army is
not "orderly" (*Il.* 12.225). The Phaeacian nobles sit "in order" (*kosmôi* [*Od.* 13.77]),
that is, according to precedence. Actions *not* "according to order" are those done
without regard to decency or social propriety, such as the assembly called at night,
to which everyone comes sodden with drink (*Od.* 3.138; cf. *Il.* 5.759, 8.12, 17.205;
Od. 20.181).

one goes about preparing a sacrificial animal (*Il.* 24.622). The order may have an aesthetic aspect ("cosmetic" order) when the most efficient order is the neatest; so weapons stored in three neat rows are "well according to order," and more clearly, when a horse's cheek piece is beautifully made, it is an "adornment" to be stored away in a chamber and not borne by horsemen.[48] In relation to language, *kosmos* is usually used of speeches when they are "*not according to order*" (*ou kata kosmon*), and in these cases social proprieties are violated more often than factuality. So I take it of Thersites' disorderly speech (*Il.* 2.214), and when Odysseus says Euryalus's abuse of him was "not according to order" (*Od.* 8.179), he means that it was inappropriate to their relative status rather than that it was false. The swineherd Eumaeus calls the tales of disguised Odysseus both "reckless lying" and *ou kata kosmon* (*Od.* 14.361–365); the first phrase indicates that he doesn't believe them and the second that it was not fitting for a suppliant beggar to try to abuse his host's credulity.[49] In the passage I have quoted, I translate the phrase "rightly," so that it might express accordance with social propriety as well as that sense of truth as "scrupulously told" which Thomas Cole describes.[50] This idea of the well-ordered speech, which is at once well put together and suitable to the situation, is also apparent in the phrase *kata moiran* in 496, literally, "in due portion," which seems to be synonymous.[51] I note the force of the *kata* in both these phrases as suggesting going through something, proceeding thoroughly, without evident omissions and contradictions. What one can judge is the way a tale is told, cir-

---

[48]*Il.* 10.472; 4.145; in *Od.* 8.492, the "ordering of the wooden horse" can be both its "fashioning" and its "deployment."

[49]Following Adkins (1972) 13.

[50]Cole (1983) 14. Webster (1939) 175 glosses the phrase: "Everything that happened must be in it, and there must be no gaps in the narrative." He goes on to compare geometric painting, citing as its principle the notion that "intelligibility is more important than a convincing visual impression." Putting geometric art aside, I would say that in Homer's verbal art "intelligibility" and recreating the visual impression are one.

[51]Svenbro (1976) 24–26 stresses the social aspects of speaking "in due portion," but social and rhetorical criticism are indissoluble when Nestor uses the phrase to compliment youthful Diomedes. Nestor says Diomedes is the best speaker of the younger warriors, for he speaks "prudently and *kata moiran*" (*Il.* 9.59). "But," he adds, "you did not get to the end of your speech"; he, who is older, "will take up your speech and go fully through the matter" (*Il.* 9.55, 61). Similar is *Il.* 19.186.

cumspectly, with a regard for details.[52] For Odysseus, who does
not as yet acknowledge that he has seen what happened at Troy,
this is the quality he must be commending to Alcinous and the
court: the fullness and appropriateness of Demodocus's song have
earned him Odysseus's praise.

The same criteria and the same limited basis for judgment come
into play again when Alcinous judges Odysseus's tales:

> Odysseus, as we look on you, we do not liken you
> to a cozzener and cheat, the kind of man
> that the dark earth supports far and wide,
> framing lies, whose source one cannot see.[53]
> There is shapeliness on your words, and your heart is noble
>   within.
> And you recounted your story like a skillful poet,
> the wretched Cares of the Achaeans, and your own.
>
>   [11.363–369]

This passage too has been overread as asserting the truth of the
tale, but again Alcinous is in no position to utter such a verdict.[54]
He says as much when he characterizes the tales of wanderers as
those whose sources one cannot see, and he cannot claim to have
any certainty about these fabulous goings on. All he has before his
eyes is the hero himself ("as we look on you") and he judges from
Odysseus's words and actions that he is not the lying wanderer he
might well have been. The "shape" of his words is like the "form"
of a poet's song: a convincingly articulated and conscientiously
reported account that has the appearance of truth and so must be
one with that truth, since form is finally content. This aesthetically

---

[52]The *Hymn to Hermes* seems to offer an illustration: in his theogony (427–429)
Hermes honors Mnêmosunê first and then the rest of the gods "according to who
was born first" (*kata presbin*, [431]). The song merits Apollo's compliment *kata kosmon*
(433) both because it has a structure—i.e., it corresponds to (*kata-*) the temporal
order—and because it is "appropriate" for the very young god to acknowledge
precedence.

[53]Following Stanford (1974) on *hothen ou tis idoito* in 8.366: "from sources
which . . . no one could see [i.e., test] for himself." The rendering of Heubeck,
West, and Hainsworth (1981), "such lies that no one is able to see through them,"
seems to me a modern idiom.

[54]See the excellent analysis of this speech by Heath (1985) 261–262.

convincing truth is the common property of the song of Demodocus and the memoirs of the hero. For Homer and his audience,
who can expect no direct confirmation of these old stories, such
truth was the special and defining quality of the poetry of the past.

Vividness and Closeness to the Past

Oichalia is the scene of two fatal contests, but Phaeacia is
where threatening conflicts are tactfully defused. Such a conjunc-
tion of god and man, hero and poet, could not take place anywhere
else, for the true and permanent location of Phaeacia is at the
convergence of the paths between gods and men, past and present, and hero and his poet. In predicting their role in the poem,
Zeus introduces the Phaeacians with a riddle, saying that Odysseus will be conducted home (*pompêi* [5.32]) by neither gods nor
men. The Phaeacians solve this riddle because they are marginal
people who live far from bread-eating men and "near the gods"
(*ankhitheoi* [*Od*. 5.35, 19.279]). They live at the limits of the world,
like the Ethiopians, and like the Ethiopians, they have a special
closeness to the gods. At the limits of space and humanity, the
Phaeacians are also at the limits of time. Alcinous and his people
live like prelapsarian heroes in perpetual abundance (7.114–128),
without hostility from others (6.201–203); theirs is a pristine society
where the gods come undisguised to the feasts (7.201–203).[55] They
live in that golden age Hesiod characterizes as "that time when the
gods and men had banquets together and were seated together"
(fr. 1.6 M-W).[56] Nor will these rare encounters ever take place
again. Odysseus comes to this island just as the Phaeacians are
about to fall from their blessed state on account of the anger of
Poseidon. After the island is ringed with stone, the concourse between the Phaeacians and gods will be sealed off from men; elsewhere festivals will be like the Delian panegyris, and poets will
have to compete with other poets in telling tales of far earlier he-

---

[55]Cf. Vidal-Naquet (1981) 92.
[56]Cf. *Theog*. 535. The gods also feast with the Ethiopians in *Il*. 1.423; cf. *Od*. 1.25.

roes. But in this place for a last moment the poet can meet the hero face-to-face and win from him confirmation of his right to succession, on the verge of the fall into competition.

The meeting of Demodocus and Odysseus, then, is a way for the poet to lay claim indirectly to a particular kind of value for his song. The implication of their encounter for Homer must be that his song, if not exactly a historical tale, it is a tale so well and fully told that it could be rivaled only by a hero who was there. The Muses give the epic poet truth as an effect of speech, a convincing fullness of detail that could come only from one who has seen what he describes, who holds each detail vividly in his mind. Beyond any claims of factuality, such a quality is constitutive of the aesthetic experience of epic as it is performed.[57] In blending his own telling with that of the hero, the poet transports his audience away from whatever festival they may be attending, from whatever princely hall or tavern where they may be sitting, to become the heroic audience itself. Indeed, in books 9 through 12 Odysseus's firsthand account becomes indistinguishable from the account we the audience hear, so that for a time the voice of a very late poet melds into that of the early hero. In performance, the effect of this double ethos would have been astounding if a poet followed another epic poet by presenting a song in which Demodocus yielded to the first-person epic of Odysseus. The extended irony of having Odysseus encounter Demodocus proves to be another way of giving the poetry the striking immediacy for its hearers that I have called vividness.

Mnêmosunê, mindfulness, is so closely related to *lêsmosunê* (forgetfulness) by Hesiod because the poetry of the past must make its audience forget its own present; for this to happen the here and now of the performance must give way to create a space for the earlier age to appear. The epic poet dismisses the living present in which he sings and his audience hears him. What is essential for vividness is to obliterate the narrative distance between action and its telling: the "they say" frame of the tale must be reduced as close to zero as possible. Hence, as Aristotle noted, the invocations in

---

[57]Compare Redfield's fine remarks on what he terms the "epic distance" (1975) 35–39.

Homer are very brief, and he "straightaway brings on some character speaking."[58] But in each poem what is cast out returns, each
poet mentions heroic poetry within the heroic world at least once.
And with the mention of poetry, the question is raised about the
relation of the deeds unfolding in the heroic present to the song
they will become: tradition implies transmission, and transmission
raises the problem of time. How the poet manages the relation
between early event and present singing will determine how vivid
his narration is. The *Iliad* and *Odyssey* take different stances toward
this singing, however, and their stances are expressed in the models of transmission they convey. Here I am not interested, like the
rhetorical critics, in the specific tropes by which vividness is produced; I am concerned with the largest trope, the way the poem
presents itself not as a story told but as a drama unfolding.

The *Iliad* for the most part dismisses any thought of itself as
performance in order to present the deeds as unfolding "now." It
drives us firmly back into the time of the actions themselves, which
will only later become song. This is not a time before song—
Thamyris has already been there—but it is decidedly a time before
the *Iliad*. Achilles sings in his tent about the deeds of former men,
but his own glory has yet to be achieved. "For a long time, I think
the Achaeans will remember our strife," he says in reconciling with
Agamemnon (*Il.* 19.64), but this remembrance will arise in the
future, and it is not clear what form it will take. Perhaps he means
no more than that his deeds will become an exemplary tale, like
Meleager's old story, which was repeated to him. In any case, the
Trojan War is very much in progress and this song is unformed as
yet. Helen is more self-conscious and, when we first see her, has
begun to put "the many Struggles of the Achaeans and the Trojans" into a tapestry.[59] But again the main action of the war and the
poem remains to be done, and she breaks off her weaving to go
and look at the army from the city wall (*Il.* 3.139–145). In a much-
noted speech she says more than Achilles about fame, that this war

[58]*Poetics* 24.1460a5–11. It seems to be because the narrative element in epic can
never be eliminated that Aristotle awards a greater degree of vividness to drama in
24.1462a 16–17.
[59]*Il.* 3.125–128. For Helen as quasi poet, see Murnaghan (1987) 152 and n. 1.

for her sake will be *sung* about; but again, this will be in later generations, "among men to come" (6.357–358). The only professional singers (*aoidoi*) who actually perform for us in the *Iliad* are the leaders of threnodies for Hector at 24.720ff. Their song is a ritual, tied to that one event and performed for the close audience of his female kin and townsmen. Later, perhaps, their song of how Hector died will be remembered, and his vow to die not without *kleos* will be fulfilled (22.304). Perhaps we may even think that this threnody will evolve into that more general song for all Greeks, the *Iliad*; but this is very much to come as the poem closes on the scene.[60]

Though not without its ironic moments of self-reference then, the *Iliad* takes a very austere stance toward its audience. It almost completely effaces itself as performance and postpones its coming into shape to the end. By this resolute self-repression it achieves a vivid presence in which the focus is kept on the actors in their acting. The *Odyssey* has a different stance toward song and achieves a different kind of vividness. It sees a longer history of singing behind it and portrays itself consciously as the last in a long line of song. Even before Troy a song of the *Argo* was on the lips of all (12.70). Its own characters, both the living and the recently dead, are already enshrined in Trojan songs whose fame has reached heaven; the poetry of the returns is already arising. It is in this song-filled world that Odysseus must find a place for his own fame. The *Odyssey*, then, decides to offer not the deed before the song but the newest in a long line of songs. Its poetic is summed up by its hero, who concludes his performance by saying "It is hateful for me to tell once again what has already been clearly told" (12.452–453). In this conscientious lateness it may be that the *Odyssey* is responding in some way to the *Iliad*, but in any case it man-

---

[60]Cf. Lynn-George's perceptive remarks on the *Iliad*'s references to its future as a poem (1988) 272: "This repeated anticipation has tended to be recovered as a self-reflexive text's glorification of its own achievement. . . . This is undoubtedly part of the story. But the *Iliad* seems to project itself beyond the bounds upheld by the critical belief in the autonomy of the work of art sealed in its own absolute present and the self-sufficiency of its performance. In its tale of the past for the future— already belated, after the event, and always ahead of itself, telling of what still is to come—the epic compounds a sense of finitude with a sense of the indefinite."

ages to achieve with this self-consciousness another kind of earliness. It retrojects songs to the start of its performance and even
before. As the story moves forward we move to newer songs, even
to the point of the first performance of Odysseus's return in books
9 through 12. And even after this tour de force is over its effects
reverberate through the rest of the poem, for thereafter we are
provided with a yet closer view of the action, the actual return to
Ithaca in deeds and not in speech.

By retrojecting song, the *Odyssey* poet makes his song early,
makes it come straight from the horse's mouth, as he speaks it. If
the *Iliad* banishes itself to get a direct vision of the heroic world, the
Odyssey retrojects itself into that world, so that performance is no
longer a late thing, after the event, but one involved with it and in
part preceding it. The differences between the stances of the two
poems toward their own past may be summarized. The *Iliad* sees
itself as song to come; it values action over representation, deeds
over boasts, as Aeneas values fighting over rehearsing genealogies
in book 22. The *Odyssey* sees itself as the newest song in the making, song extending itself. It values one who can tell his deeds as
well as do them.

Homer and his audiences knew, no less than scholars today, that
epic poetry is "traditional." They knew too that tradition is never a
static abstraction but exists only through transmission, the constant struggle of poetry to survive in time. Distorting as a fixed and
monolithic idea of tradition may be, Homer would encourage us to
see all the work of poets as nothing compared to the perfect and
unchanging song of the Muses. He would pretend that his song
knows no other version than what they give and always will give.
This pretense is established in his invocations and is supported by
his representation of poets. They confront tradition not in the form
of other poets, but in the *Iliad*'s meeting of Thamyris and the
Muses, or in the *Odyssey*'s encounter of poet and hero. Hence the
historical, diachronic process of transmission, with all its hazards
and losses, is represented by the synchronic conflicts of poetic
competition, and both are denied or disguised by the poet.

Homer's meditations on tradition are quite different from ours
and so are his reasons for giving it this particular representation.
For literate critics, the opposite of tradition is originality, and these

categories break down poetry into the new and the repeated, the variable and the fixed. But such appropriations are of no concern to Homer, for whom the opposite of traditional or transmitted poetry was not originality but vividness, a matter of how close hearing a song might come to being present at the events themselves. Poets strive not to coin the memorable phrase but to make their performances more striking, to intensify the sense of heroic presence. Vividness is explored by Homer not as a rhetorical effect but as a matter of being early, of singing as the first poet on the scene would sing. Representing his tradition, then, was a way of re-orienting his audience's sense of time, for this poetry aimed primarily to affect its hearer's sense of the present. Hence if the issue of transmission appears as the issue of competition, denying the fact of poetic competition or disguising it as a unique, primeval encounter was a way for Homer to deny his lateness in time.

The schemes of transmission offered in the poems, then, are not incidental but confer on the poetry a great power. In the *Iliad* action is taking place under the eyes of the gods, who will make it song, but under our eyes too. In the *Odyssey* we witness not only heroic deeds but early singing about those deeds, as both poem and hero wander toward their final destination. Song is very much a part of this early world, and so even as we listen to our bard, we are playing the part of heroes.

CHAPTER 4

THE TEXT
Signs of Writing in Homer

Fixing the Text

To this point I have been describing a view of poetry inherited from a time when writing was unknown, or, if known, had nothing to do with the profession of epic singing. In a sense I have been looking past or behind the texts for the theory of poetry that was formed to preside over their evolution. Inasmuch as this idea of poetry, like its concomitant modes of oral composition, was hallowed by tradition and proved by success, it was carried over into the texts of the poems when they were written down. Yet they were indeed written down; at some point in the archaic period the oral art of epic issued in at least two monumental compositions, which have become the *Iliad* and *Odyssey*. In this chapter I shift my perspective to this moment, difficult though it may be to fix chronologically, and consider how writing may have affected the singer's idea of what he was doing. If the texts of the *Iliad* and *Odyssey* are manifestly products of an oral art interacting with writing, it may be that they bear some trace of the poet's attitude to this new art. If we imagine the first contributors to fixed texts, as I think we must, as still capable of the oral improvisational style, it is possible that the poems they composed for inscription bear some reference to or reflect upon this new device for preserving fame. It is at least clear

that Homer refers to writing, apparently alphabetic writing, once
in the epics. And the word he uses for it—*sêmata*, "signs"—can be
a signpost for us in thinking of how writing would be accommodated in his world. If we look at writing as one among the many
other fixing and fixed signs in Homer, we may read a lesson on its
powers and weaknesses. In particular, those "signs" that are monuments to heroic action may suggest one answer to how the poetry
met this technology and its peculiar powers. I turn, then, in this
chapter away from the traditional ideas of poetry embedded in the
texts and try to read, as it were, their topmost layer to discover the
poet's relationship to his text.

If we think of Homer as the "great master" at the end of the
tradition who fixed the poems, by definition he had come across
the fact of alphabetic writing.[1] Inscriptions show that the Greeks
had adapted a Semitic script to their language already by the second half of the eighth century B.C.E., and no one would put monumental composition much earlier.[2] In fact the writing referred to in
the poems seems to be a reflection of contemporary writing rather
than a traditional reference to some earlier Aegean script. In a
version of the Potiphar's wife story attached to the name of Bellerophon, Proteus sends him away to Lycia to be done away with by
one of his guest-friends. Toward this end he gives the unwitting
Bellerophon a closed diptych tablet on which are inscribed "baleful
signs . . . soul-destroying, many of them" (*sêmata lugra . . .
thumophthora polla* [*Il.* 6.168–170, 176–178]). The passage has been
explained away as a dim memory of Mycenean script or a reference
to some primitive system of signing, tokens, or pictograms; yet
recent finds from the Near East convincingly suggest that the writing here is oriental writing, as are the motifs and geography of the
story.[3]

By the time the *Iliad* was composed, then, alphabetic writing was
known in Greece. The still-open question is how widespread the
new technology was and whether it would have been used to
record an epic poem. Not a few Homerists have assumed or argued

[1]Webster (1964) 226–227.
[2]Heubeck (1979).
[3]Bellamy (1989) 289–307 provides Eastern parallels to the tablets and the tale; cf.,
too, Heubeck (1979) 126–146.

that Homer seized on the (relatively new?) invention near this early date and wrote himself.[4] But Albert Lord, on the basis of fieldwork in Yugoslavia, held that writing destroys the compositional powers of an oral poet: he was willing to allow only that the poet might have dictated his poems.[5] Lord's claim about the mutual hostility of orality and literacy is now seen as too sweeping.[6] Nevertheless, others have been troubled that, though the earliest inscriptions include many snatches of verse, there is no proof that the new technology was used so early for creating monumental public documents.[7] Even if we allow for the possibility that we may have lost a great deal of writing on perishable materials, it is not easy to imagine why such enormous texts would have been produced for a still largely illiterate age in which they would have been rarely read and nearly impossible to perform in toto. Hence, G. S. Kirk hypothesized that the poems were fixed in their oral stage and transmitted by memorizing rhapsodes until it was easier and more obviously useful to write them down.[8]

What remains constant in this variety of views is that, however late or early the scenario, an oral poet confronted writing, in the sense that he took the step of putting his fluent art into a single fixed and lasting form. The point was made in Adam Parry's perceptive review of the question. Allowing that Lord's suggestion of a dictating oral poet is not to be ruled out, he noted, "If the man who, on this hypothesis, put the poems into writing was more an amanuensis than a recording scholar in the manner of Parry and Lord, then the difference between this sort of dictation and actually writing by hand would not be enormous. . . . It follows that the name 'Homer,' if by this we mean the author of the our poem,

[4]E.g., Lesky, Whitman, Wade-Gery, Bowra, and Heubeck. A good survey of the many scenarios for the writing of the Homeric poems, with full bibliographical references, is Miller (1982) 99–102.

[5]Lord (1960) 124–129.

[6]Finnegan has argued (1977) 160–169 that writing and "oral" techniques of composition may at times interact.

[7]See Coldstream (1977) 307–311 on the earliest uses of writing in Greece and Heubeck (1979) 151–152 for the possibility that we have lost much that was written on perishable materials.

[8]Kirk (1962) 208–17, who observes, "The evidence is still too slight for anyone, however judicious, to settle once and for all these detailed problems of how the poems were composed and transmitted."

must be reserved for the poet who composed the *Iliad* at the time when it was put into writing."[9] In all scenarios we must posit as one step a confrontation between the traditional oral poet and this new technology. Even in Kirk's scenario, which Parry rightly characterizes as uneconomical and unlikely, a song that had been sung in many ways at many times is at some point reduced to a fixed version in the mind of the poet.[10]

The effects of the simple fact of writing on the idea and nature of poetry may no doubt be great. The works of Havelock and Ong aim to show that writing is not just a neutral technology but may effect a transformation of consciousness and create a new relationship between speaker and what is spoken; and no one living in the computer age will doubt that what may appear to be a mere refinement in information storage can have profound implications for art and thought. But it is also clear that revolutionary effects need not be instantaneous: this new way of transmitting poetry need not have immediately transformed the singer's conception of his art, and as I have said, his representations of his art are determinedly oral. Yet even in the earliest imaginable moment of the meeting between song and stylus, there was surely a radical transaction. It is easy to imagine that the prospect of a written poem could reconfigure the poet's relation to his art: because of writing, what had been a fluid performance may become a fixed and visible object; what had been the gift of the Muses can be owned, hidden away, referred to, and revised. At least potentially, writing makes it possible for the singer to become the maker of an artifact and for the song to become a finished text. The question for Homer is whether these new attitudes might have already begun to emerge in some form at the times the poems were written down.

The very old question of whether Homer could write is rarely raised in this form but usually asked in behalf of the text. If it was written, we might expect subtleties and a well-conceived general

---

[9]Parry (1966) 297.

[10]Kirk's position is nuanced in Miller (1982), citing also Notopoulos (1951) and Hainsworth (1970). Miller hypothesizes that, even if unwritten, an excellent performance may have been regarded as a "final version" in its macrostructure. But as he is forced to allow for "various local expansions, contractions, and other artistic and audience-specific modifications," it is hard to imagine any real function for the "final" text of such a necessarily adaptive structure.

scheme; if it was orally composed we need not resolve every incon-
sistency and apparent fault into a literary stratagem. But it can also
be asked in behalf of the poet: What was it for a poet descended
from an oral tradition to meet writing? Would he have immediately
perceived and embraced its potential to fix his songs in a stable and
enduring form? It is worth wondering whether the poet's attitudes
toward this new way of preserving his art were exactly what we
would suppose.

To literate readers and antiquarian scholars the advantages to a
poet in writing down his text are clear: one has captured the best
performance and is not likely to do as well ever again; one gets it
right because it can be gone over and revised; perhaps too, one can
make something more monumental and massive than had ever
been possible before. Moreover, with writing the singer has not
simply an ability but a precious object: it can be dedicated at a
God's shrine or passed down as a sort of heirloom. Finally, writing
offers a new way for the singer to aspire to poetic immortality: his
texts, his own words, will be repeated as *his* through time. Often
without thinking we assume that Homer would have ended his
dictation or writing with the same feeling as Horace, when he
penned the epilogue to three books of odes: "Exegi monumentum
aere perennius" ("I have brought to completion a monument more
lasting than bronze"). Yet I do not see much trace of such an attitude in Homer, and indeed, one Horatian scholar (and early con-
tributor to the Homeric question) seems to me rightly to repudiate
such comforting intuitions. When Richard Bentley read that Homer had "designed his poem for eternity, to please and instruct
mankind," he responded quite bluntly: "Take my word for it, poor
Homer, in those circumstances and early times, had never such
aspiring thoughts. He wrote a sequel of songs and rhapsodies, to
be sung by himself for small earnings and good cheer, at festivals
and other days of merriment. . . . Nor is there one word in Homer
that presages or promises immortality to his work; as we find there
is in the later poets, Virgil, Horace, Ovid, Lucan and Statius. He no
more thought, at that time, that his *poems* would be immortal, than
our *free-thinkers* now believe their souls will; and the proof of each
will be only *a parte post*; in the event, but not in the expectation."[11]

---

[11]In the Dyce edition (1938) 3.304 (originally published 1713.)

We are not as sure as Bentley was just when and how the poems were written down, but his point about the difference in artistic posture between Homer and these later, fully literate poets is well taken. Even if we allow that Homer might have chosen to be silent about his text's immortality, a portrait of him as literary artist presupposes a rather sudden rise of literary values and virtues in the eighth century. To assume that the availability of writing would have automatically brought with it expectations of Horatian perfection and enduringness may be a no less apocalyptic fantasy than the notion of a "literate revolution" in which the technology of the alphabet instantaneously transformed thought and speech. Certainly the historical evidence suggests that authorship and fixity were slow to come to the epic genre as a whole.

Apart from the problem of anachronistically making the monumental poet a wholly literary type, it must be borne in mind that, for all its powers and promises, writing would have been antithetical to the oral singer's art in real ways, if less extremely so than Lord suggested. "Verbal variability and originality in oral performance are extremely common, and almost certainly more typical than an unchanging transmission," says Finnegan, and this is not simply a primitive aspect of the art but one of its virtues.[12] One can imagine some practical disadvantages in adhering to a written text for a poet who had been doing very well relying on the Muses: once fixed, a song is inflexible, unadaptable to the moods of the audience, the proprieties of the place and time. Poets who had long been able to produce songs appropriate to given occasions hand this ability over to a device that makes the songs rather stiff and no longer subject to their personal control. Again, circulation becomes far more limited than it had been for an able-bodied poet: very few of the crowd in the agora would have wanted to read such a thing, and his noble patrons would no doubt have preferred seeing the bard come into their halls to hearing his poem from a scribe. Even if we suppose that the poems were first written only for poets, as a reference and reminder (this for devotees of the Muse!), still, under ordinary circumstances they were too long to be performed in toto, so that their monumental structure might become apparent. The

[12]Finnegan (1977) 153.

poets, then, who handed over their Iliads and Odysseys to alpha-
bets may have had more complex attitudes than may appear. This
new device for capturing fame need not have been wholly wel-
comed any more than photography, for example, is always thought
a benign marvel when seen for the first time. After all, the only
writing Homer does refer to is called "soul-destroying" and is the
secret, folded-up writing of a tyrant; it is the opposite of publica-
tion.

The idea of fixing the text is what interests me in this chapter:
whether the Homeric texts reflect any tension between the idea
that a text is in perfectly fixed shape and the sense that it has
become fixated and lost its motion and ability to change. To explore
this attitude, if it is accessible, is to look at the *sêmata,* "signs," the
texts speak of, for in calling writing "signs" Homer seems to have
made a deliberate choice: he does not use the regular word for
"writing" in later Greek, *grammata,* though he uses its parent verb
graphein, "to scratch," for the act of writing in this same passage.
Rephrasing writing as "signs" may be a means of disguising contemporary technology under terms and processes traditionally
found in the idealized, archaized world of heroes.[13] In any case, in
choosing the word *sêma* Homer has aligned writing with many
other "signs" in the poems, a large array of physical objects with
varying signifying functions. Indeed, Homer's heaven and earth
are full of signs, which the heroes, together with all the ranks of
priests, prophets, and soothsayers, try mightily to understand.
There are signs in the regularities of nature, as in the crane's cry or
the dog star's rising; there are signs in exceptional or fortuitous
events, such as flashes of lightning or the flight of birds; and prodigies of nature are inevitably portentous. The order that governs
the world, that is to say, the mind of Zeus, is proverbially inscrutable; but anything in the world that rises to strike the eye or mind
may be a sign of a meaning beyond it.

Homer's heroes live among man-made signs too. In particular
we are directed to understand the function of writing in relation to
the signs or tombs of warriors, which promise *kleos.* As these signs

[13]So Heubeck (1979) 140 and Jeffery (1962) 555, though the latter allows for the
possibility that the word may be an unconscious Greek repetition of a detail in the
Lycian tale.

are a visible, tangible, and artificial way of preserving *kleos*, their operations and qualities may parallel those of written epic poems. Writing itself may have been of little interest to Homer; he may have scarcely known it or hardly appreciated its consequences. But writing was to be given the same powers over his art as the sign had been given within the oral tradition, so that in thinking about signs Homer and the tradition were already thinking about those aspects of writing that concern us. In this chapter, then, as a way into the question of the oral poet and his relation to any art work, I consider not the art of writing, or even the arts in general, but signs, as concrete and efficient objects, how these actual signs behave and how they are related to the singer's project. In fact, the stories Homer tells about signs seem concerned with their power to preserve fame and seem to know that it is something like the power of epic. Indeed there are in each epic monumentally constructed signs to spread fame far in space and time which seem to intimate our idea of the text as a "monumental" composition. But at the same time, it can be seen that Homer's attitude toward his own posterity does not sound exactly like Horace's; there is a consistent awareness that signs cannot preserve all that they cover, and several climactic episodes show how physical signs are vulnerable to destruction.

Although the question of when and how the Homeric poems were written down remains open, it is at least clear that there came a time when a singer contemplated the idea of fixing his songs in a lasting form, and I think that this moment is actually reflected on in the poems through the archaic technique of grave making. But first we will need a typology of signs.

Strange Objects on the Ground

Although Homer knew the alphabetic writing of his own day, it is no part of the world of his heroes. The point is made, perhaps even insisted upon, in a little comedy of illiteracy played by the Greek soldiers as they draw lots to choose a champion among themselves (*Il.* 7.175–190). The procedure is a cumbersome affair: each hero inscribes a sign (*esêmênanto*) on a pebble; after they are collected and the champion's lot is drawn, a herald must carry it around until the one who marked it looks at his sign (*sêma*) and recognizes it again. Thereupon the winner tosses the pebble to the ground and proclaims to the army that he has been chosen. This is a primitive kind of marking one's name, unreadable except by the one who wrote it and needing the writer's voice to bring its message to others. Writing is hardly a significant part of the heroic world.

Once such a "text" has served its purpose, it is cast aside, and will remain only an odd, inscrutable scratched stone in the sand, a reminder, perhaps, that the other world, the one in which Homer sang, was also full of signs, and many of these must be assumed to have come in some way from a great past of heroic war. The landscape in which Homer sang bore traces of even earliest history, particularly in the form of signs that were hard, solid, and tangible, such as great stones or buildings. Some Greek myths evidently try to connect sights on the land with cosmic history: it is easy to see how such stories as the sacred legend about the stone at Pytho or the myth of Niobe functioned etiologically for the Greeks of Homer's day to explain strangely shaped or strangely placed stones. This would be all the more true for heroic history, for we know that in the eighth century the Greeks were often coming across bronze-age burial sites, some marked with dressed but uninscribed stones, some yielding deposits of ancient weaponry and artifacts. These remains of great human art, far beyond the competence of eighth-century technology, were in themselves awe-inspiring, and in Homer's time the Greeks began to make offerings at old tombs, usually without any idea of what lords lay within. Naturally such strange objects in the ground had to be accommodated to the legendary past, and the so-called Greek Renaissance was a time for coordinating these local sites and assimilating them to the oral legends of the national past. And Homer himself takes part by showing us his heroes trying to interpret marks on the landscape and indeed trying to mark it with their presence in turn.

This is natural enough, since he was singing on ground that many of these heroes had crossed and was putting before the eyes of his audiences things that had happened in the places they might

live in or visit or hear about from others. But the relationship between the stories Homer sang and these splendid warrior tombs
appears to have been the opposite of what we might expect.[14] His
purpose was not to provide the stories to go along with the various
local antiquities but rather to provide an account of the past that
transcended all the individual stories told at individual shrines. In
fact, the general picture that Homer presents of the death and
burial of heroes would have discouraged his contemporaries from
tying his poems to any physical remains of the Mycenean past:
Homer's heroes are cremated, their bones removed, and each individual's ashes covered over by a separate mound, his name preserved by oral tradition. This kind of burial was in contrast to the
Mycenean relics, which were as a rule collective inhumations, and
the cults first established there apparently did not name the hero
particularly.[15] Homer's eschatology, too, suggests that the dead
heroes are radically separated from the living and beyond the reach
of their local rites.[16] His Panhellenic world of heroes is deliberately
distinct from local figures of cult, and he works to bury and memo-
rialize his heroes in his own way.[17] This self-differentiation of his
lore from the cult at tombs opened up in his day involves Homer in
a meditation on how the great efforts of men from the past may
leave their mark on the landscape, or fail to, and, conversely, how

[14]The significance of the rise of hero cults in the eighth century is a complex
matter, involving social and economic factors (such as the growth of populations,
re-settlement of land, and rise of the city-state) and no doubt having particular
functions in particular places (Whitley [1988]). But as to the relationship of this
phenomenon to the poetry of Homer, I think we cannot follow Coldstream ([1976]
and [1977] 341–356), who sees the eighth-century rise of cults at Mycenean tombs as
the *result* of Homeric poetry (indeed of the poems we have). Rather, the first such
cults at tombs (embracing both the recently and long dead) are clearly not directed
at the heroes of epic. It is thus more probable that Homer is a parallel but quite
separate aspect of a general revival of interest in the past; see the next note.

[15]Archaeological evidence indicates that such ancient figures as were venerated
would have been anonymous for the audience of Homer. Hesiod would have placed
them in mythic history among the "Silver" race, unnamed but separate and earlier
than the epic heroes; see Snodgrass (1980) 38–40, (1982), and (1987) 159–165 and
Morris (1988).

[16]On Homeric eschatology, see Burkert (1985) 194–199.

[17]A main theme of Nagy's work on the *Iliad* (1979) is to show how Panhellenic
epic and local cult are complementary ways of preserving the past; see esp. 114–117,
159–161, 206–209.

the visible and tangible world around us may disclose or fail to disclose the past.

For the poet to reflect on the way actions might mark the landscape is the first level of the question of how one might fix one's own story fast. Etiology is not the sole concern of epic poetry, of course, but in accommodating the physical world to his poetry, Homer speaks of the signs of the past and tells us how they work and how they fail. These observations on signs may be read as observations on a prototypical kind of writing, for even the roughest objects left from the past suggest the possibility that a great action might leave its enduring, physical trace. And when human art contrives to leave such traces, it is possible to ask if fame can be inscribed in some way so that later generations might look at an object and learn the past. The stories surrounding these signs express a poet's view of how fleeting but momentous events might leave a memorial and are a preface for us to his idea of fixing heroic action in a text.

The signs in the Homeric world that come closest to writing as sign are the solid terrestrial signs, objects that some great event in the past has left on the ground to be "read" by later generations. As the regularities of nature were sometimes broken by portents and prodigies, the landscape was most mysteriously significant where it rose inexplicably in mounds or was marked with stones and boulders. Such objects may seem to invoke a kind of response that is simpler and more banal than "reading," but it must be remembered how impressive the solidity, durability, and strength of stone could be: its sheer massiveness and independence have evoked religious awe in many ancient societies, including Greece, as Pausanias says: "If one goes back in time, one sees the Greeks paying honor not to statues but to unwrought stones [*argoi lithoi*]." Stones could be signs of a meaning beyond themselves, and such rough objects as Pausanias refers to early served to mark a place as sacred.[18] In archaic Greek poetry something of this magic power in stones is still discernible, especially so when their permanence and unchangingness enables them to carry meaning through time. In the worlds of Homer and Hesiod, stones can be a machine to

---

[18]Pausanias 7.22.4; cf. Burkert (1985) 85.

preserve *kleos:* a physical rock is the solid counterpart to a speech handed down in time as a way of preserving meaning. And if a new machine is found, if it is possible for writing to fix fame and endure unchanged through time, it will be on the model of these strange objects on the ground.

The quintessential signifying stone was the *sêma* of Zeus at Pytho. This was an ancient rock in the heart of Delphi which the Greeks venerated from their earliest past, oiling it and offering it various ministrations. It is sacred because of its history, which is given by Hesiod: this was the stone that was wrapped in swaddling clothes and given to Cronus when he meant to swallow Zeus. Later, when Zeus came of age and released his Olympian siblings from his father's belly, the stone was the first to come out:

> First he vomited out the stone that he had eaten last;
> this then Zeus set fast on the wide-wayed earth
> in sacred Pytho under the glens of Parnassus
> to be a *sêma* thereafter, a marvel for mortal men.
>
> [*Theogony* 497–500]

What Zeus does to make this stone a sign is fix it, plant it in the earth; in itself the unwrought stone is no sure sign: it has already been disguised, misread, swallowed up, and moved. But once set fast, it becomes the most fixed sign of all, providing a point of orientation in the wide-wayed earth and signifying to wondering later men Zeus's continuing sovereignty. In Homer too, the gods make such immortal signs: Odysseus reminds the Greeks that when they were sacrificing under a plane tree at Aulis, "a great *sêma* appeared" (*Il.* 2.308): a snake crawled from the altar and devoured a mother sparrow and her brood; then "the very god who made it appear made it very conspicuous [*arizêlon*] / for Zeus the son of Cronus turned it to stone" (2.318–319). Odysseus calls the prodigious snake a "sign" when it first appears, for it is a portent; but it may also be termed a "sign" proleptically, for it will attain undying fame once it is petrified: Calchas announces that Zeus had sent this as a "portent late to be fulfilled, whose *kleos* will never die" (2.325). Here again, a sign is made by a magical fixation; once its motion is arrested, it can remain rooted to that spot by that fair plane tree, to be recalled and compared with what it signified.[19]

Mortals too took stones and tried to make them monuments of their own deeds to secure some remembrance of them in aftertime. A marked grave with a tumulus and perhaps a stone stele above it is also called a *sêma*, or sign of the place of burial. To call a tomb a *sêma* is to bring the making of objects as a means of preserving the past very close to the function of epic poetry. The warriors at Troy traverse a landscape that bears witness to older heroes who had been there before. The "*sêma* of ancient Ilus," for example, the tomb of one of Troy's ancestral heroes, lies next to a wild fig tree and has above it a stele "wrought by man" (*andrôkmêtos* [*Il.* 11.166–167, 371]). For the Trojans it marks a meeting place on the field of action, and for the poet it orients the movements of his characters (*Il.* 10.415, 24.349). Homer's heroes themselves expect such monuments in their turn, so that their own names and exploits might be remembered. So Hector, calling for single combat, prescribes the etiquette of ideal heroic burial: the winner may take the armor of the vanquished but must return his body to his people for rites of commemoration. "If I win," he says,

> the corpse I will send back to the well-benched ships
> so that the long-haired Achaeans may give it rites
> and heap a *sêma* for him beside the broad Hellespont;
> and sometime someone among later born men may say
> as he sails over the wine dark sea in a ship of many oars;
> "This is the *sêma* of a man who died long ago,
> a warrior, whom once upon a time glorious Hector killed."
> So sometime someone will say; and my *kleos* will never die.
>
> [*Iliad* 7.84–91]

This sign too will become a sign when it has been placed somewhere and set fast. It will preserve an undying glory not by being inscribed but by being conspicuous, being visible even from offshore in later times. Like Achilles' tomb on the headland of the

---

[19]*Il.* 2.307. in Pausanias's time (9.19.5) the remnants of this tree were preserved in the temple of Artemis at Aulis.

Hellespont, which the *Odyssey* describes as "shining afar to men on the high sea / to those now born and those who will be hereafter" (*Od.* 24.83–84), and like other signs called "conspicuous" (*arignôtos*) or "easily distinguished," the mere sight of the tomb mound will give rise to recollection of Hector's heroism.[20]

The purpose of these signs is like the purpose of epic, to fix a heroic exploit so that "those to come after may find out about it," and the parallel to the heroic tomb and the epic poem has been noted.[21] But the essential difference between them is also clear: the function of tomb is not to be read but to be conspicuous: it only gives the impetus to the speech that will interpret it. When Menelaus is wounded, Agamemnon imagines the expedition gone home in defeat and some Trojan dancing on his brother's tomb, boasting of the Greeks' failure, "So sometime someone will say, and may the broad earth then swallow me up" (*Il.* 4.182). The oral tradition is the necessary supplement to the durable, provocative, but unreadable sign.

In addition, Homer, perhaps with understandable self-interest, also points out that humanly wrought artifacts do not even succeed in their primary requirements of durability and fixity: they neither always last nor always stay in their original places. Consider the history of one such "clear sign" that old Nestor describes to his son as he points out to him the best turning point on a race course:

> I will give you a clear sign [*sêma*] that you cannot fail to notice.
> There is a dry stump standing up from the ground about six feet,
> of oak or pine; it has not been wholly rotted away by rainwater,
> and two white stones are leaned against it, one on either side,
> at the turning point of the course, and there is smooth driving
>   around it.
> Either it is the grave marker [*sêma*] of someone who died long ago,
> or was set as a racing goal by men who lived before our time,
> and now Achilles has made it the turning point of the race.
>
> [*Iliad* 23.326–334]

---

[20]Other "conspicuous signs" *Il.* 2.318, 13.244; cf. 23.326. Nagy (1983) studies the noticing, recognition, and "interpretation" of *sêmata*.

[21]On *kleos* and tomb, see Redfield (1975) 34; Murnaghan (1987) 157, references in n. 20; and Sinos (1980) 48.

The sign Nestor points out to his son is barely still a sign, or rather it is an old sign that has lost its original purpose and gained a new one: the rain has already started to work on the wood, so that one can no longer tell even what kind of a tree it was; the stones endure, and by their unnatural, propped-up position indicate that this is an object wrought by earlier men. Yet for these Greeks on a foreign shore the sign is nearly meaningless. Nestor cannot guess whose grave it was meant to mark, or even whether it was meant to mark anyone's fame at all. If there is some unnamed hero underneath, he is surely in danger of losing his fame.

Apart from the threat of erosion, monuments are vulnerable to the possibility that they might be moved. Fixity is the first important feature of Zeus's sign and especially important for funeral markers. A stone fixed over a grave had at first perhaps a magical property, holding the dead person's soul in place, to be rolled away only with resurrection; but in eighth-century Greece the gravestone could also serve to mark the place of cult tendance: only at that particular spot would libations and other offerings find their way to departed ancestors. Homer's heroes know nothing of this, but for them too the funeral stone ideally is fixed fast: in a simile a hero is bewitched by Poseidon and unable to move, like a stele (Il. 13.437), and Achilles' horses stand fast, "as a stele stays fixed in the ground [empedon], standing over the tomb / of some man or woman" (Il. 17.434–435). But the heroic age is also a time when stones are disturbed. Tydeus picks up and hurls a boulder described as "a great thing/work [mega ergon], such as no two men, / such as they are now, could lift" (Il. 5.302–304). And when Athena takes the field she undoes the work of men of old:

> Yielding, she picked up a stone with her large hand
> lying in the plain, black, rough, and huge
> which former men had put as a boundary of ploughlands.
> [Iliad 21.403–405]

This stone is unwrought, yet, like the stone in the race course, had once been significantly placed. But the goddess has erased the border; wherever it lands it will have lost its original significance.

In the Iliad, Hector, Ajax, and Aeneas also pick up and throw such stones.[22] If we live long after these disturbing heroes, we know that the landscape has been altered; we can't rely on the rocks and hills and trees to stand fast and let us read the past in them. Likewise, the stories in which they may have figured can be lost, as when Homer describes a hill standing out on the Trojan plain. It is steep, set off by a smooth track around it: "This men call by the name Bateia / but the immortals the *sêma* of far leaping Myrine" (*Il.* 2.813–814). The steep hill is a mark on the landscape; set off by the level ground like Nestor's blasted oak, it attracts our attention. Yet men can name it only from what is on it, "Briar Hill."[23] Only the gods know what is under it, know it is in fact a tomb. Who knows how many heroes of the past have had their name and fame buried under such nameless tumuli?

Of course the poet knows and can tell us in his god-sponsored speech. From this we see that Hector should not expect to find his undying glory in that *sêma* he bargained for; only in the poet's song will his burial be remembered. The oral traditions that center on various local antiquities, the stories one hears upon asking, "Whose tomb is that?" are not so durable or so reliable as this poetry, which turns not to the ground for the past but to the Olympian Muses. It is not surprising that the signs of the past need the oral tradition to explicate them or that, for Homer the poet, song alone can provide "immortal fame." But Homer seems to go beyond self-assertion here to undertake an aggressive war on the visible; he seems determined to show that no tangible, visible thing can be trusted to mark the fames of men accurately and enduringly. It is difficult to see the poet who takes such a stance toward the past as commending the making of artifacts out of his own tales. It is difficult to see a poet in this mood entrusting his song to marks that can be destroyed, removed, or misread. The true epic, the total knowledge of every hero who fell before Troy, is not inscribed on any stone, far less on leather or papyrus; it has no authoritative physical form. Such may be the meaning in the fate of the great Achaean wall.

---

[22]*Il.* 7.264–265, 12.380–383, 445–449, 20.285–287.
[23]On this passage, see Kirk (1985) 246–247 and Clay (1972).

The Achaean Wall and the *Iliad*

The strangest object on the ground at Troy is the great defensive wall the Greeks erect in book 7 of the *Iliad,* which is finally destroyed without a trace when the Greeks go home, as we hear in book 12. The episode is peculiar in many ways and has been written off as an interpolation into the poem, possibly added as late as the fifth century.[24] How early and how authentic the passage may be are less important to me than that it is clearly a part of the *Iliad* as we now have it. Whoever composed it and whenever he did, it seems that it was worked into a poem of approximately the scope of our text. In fact I maintain that this wall, which is also a tomb, in many ways corresponds to the text itself, insofar as both are immense constructs meant to preserve through time the memory of the action before Troy. Homer's persistent interest in the project of constructing this wall and its eventual fate may have been a way for him to think about making permanent heroic reminders like the *Iliad*. In such a case, the fate of the wall would seem to indicate that even such an artifact may not, for all its sheer massiveness and fixity, hope to escape destruction unless the gods will it.

During a temporary truce for burying bodies, Nestor proposes that the Greeks collect their dead scattered in the Scamander River and, after burning them and putting the bones in urns, that they heap up over the pyre a massive collective tomb, gathering the material "indiscriminately from the plain." This tomb he proposes to use as part of a great defensive wall to stave off Trojan advances (7.327–343). His plan is carried out and it is a "great work" (*mega ergon*), marveled at by the gods (7.444).

Hector derides the builders and the fortifications—"fools who have contrived these walls / meager, not worth a thought" (8.177–178)—but he is not wholly right. The gods take note of the great work, particularly Poseidon. When he looks down at it from heaven, he fears that it will eclipse the "intelligence and cunning of the

---

[24]For discussion and bibliography, see Webster (1964) 252 and Scodel (1982).

immortals"; he predicts that "its *kleos* will last, as far as dawn light is scattered, / and men will forget that wall which I and Apollo / built with great toil for Laomedon the hero" (7.450–451). Zeus assures his brother that his fame will not suffer diminishment and proposes that the wall be destroyed after the Achaeans go home (7.458–463). And the actual destruction is recounted, in prospect, as a digression later in the poem. After Troy was sacked in the tenth year, the poet tells us, and the Achaeans had gone home, Poseidon and Apollo contrived to create a flood of rivers, which, together with constant rain from Zeus, reduced the wall to flotsam; they uprooted the stone foundations that the Achaeans had laid with such toil and made the beach level again, smoothing it over with sand and returning the rivers to their courses (12.13–33).

The episode is peculiar in two ways. First, it is odd that we hear about the wall's destruction at all: Homer often alludes to events before and after the limits of his story, but he does not usually recount them. It is significant that here alone he reaches outside the range of his story to narrate the event. Second, the destruction of the wall is told from a different perspective from that of the rest of the epic: Homer not only leaves the plot outlines of the *Iliad* but also, with a single word, shifts his perspective to the here-and-now of his unheroic audience.[25] The key word occurs in a description of one of the flooding rivers, "Simoeis, where many cowhide shields and helmets / fell in the mud together with the race of the men who were half-gods" (12.22–23). "Half-gods" translates *hêmitheoi*, a word Homer uses only here for the "men" (*andres*) or "heroes" of former times. "Half-gods" suggests that the heroes are not just earlier men but a quite separate "race" between present men and the gods; this notion violates the normal epic representation of heroes as great though mortal warriors from the past. Moreover, the word expresses a different stance of the poet toward his past. The same word occurs significantly in *Works and Days* when Hesiod recounts to Perses a history of the races of men: in this history, which is told retrospectively from the late, corrupt iron age, the generations who fought at Thebes and Troy (as he puts it, those who fought for the flocks of Oedipus and for Helen), are called

[25]Nagy (1979) 159 has a valuable discussion of the passage.

"half-gods, an earlier generation on the boundless earth" (160).[26]
The word "half-gods" brings with it a unepic ethos: it is the word
one uses in speaking of heroes from a distance, contemplating the
heroic age retrospectively as something apart, utterly remote in
time. Using this word in the *Iliad*, then, Homer is looking back on
his heroes collectively from outside his poem as a vanished and
separate race. Here alone he steps outside the plot of his poem and
away from the narrator's ethos to speak from his own age of a very
distant time.[27]

The destruction of the Achaean wall, then, seems an intrusion or
at least an excursus in the epic, and its function has long been a
puzzle. The predominant ancient explanation assumed that the
whole episode of the wall's construction was a Homeric invention
(it does nicely prolong suspense and acutely symbolizes Greek
losses); but the difficulty with the invention would be that any of
Homer's audience who had traveled the Hellespont (which was a
busy trade route in the eighth century) would have seen no such
wall; accordingly, "since the poet himself assembled the wall, for
this reason he also made it disappear, thus making any opportunity of refuting him disappear at the same time."[28] But a study
by Ruth Scodel dismisses this explanation and seeks to bring the
destruction of the wall into connection with other early Greek and
ultimately Near Eastern myths in which a great destruction marks
a historic breach between god and man. In her reading, the story of
the Achaean wall depicts the Trojan War as a catastrophe that cut
off god-born heroes from later generations; such an idea can be
traced in fragments of Hesiod and the *Cypria*, and in Near Eastern
stories we see clearly how the a race of demigods may be washed
away in a cosmic deluge, marking an end of an age and the loss of
all its works. As parallels Scodel mentions, in addition to the Flood
story proper, the Nephilim who appear just before the flood in

[26]This perspective is like that in the Hesiodic *Catalogue of Women* (fr. 204.100 M-W)
conceiving of the earliest heroes as a distinct, hybrid class. See West (1978) 176–177
and 191, on *Works and Days* 160.

[27]So *hêmitheoi* is glossed in a threnody by Simonides in order explicitly to relate
the sorrows of present mourners to those of early heroes: "Not even those who
lived long ago / who were born as the sons of the lordly gods, half-gods, / not even
they spent their lives and reached old age / without toil, ruin, danger" (523 Page).

[28]Schol. *Il* 12.3; Strabo 598 (=Aristotle fr. 162 Rose [1886]). Cf. Schol. on 7.445.

Genesis, clearly analogous to the demigods of *Iliad* 12.23, and the destruction of the tower of Babel through divine anger, which marked the scattering of the "famous men."[29] On her view, these motifs have come into the monumental *Iliad* not only in its mention of "half-gods" but also in the flooding rivers that are alike a turning loose of primeval waters to destroy the achievements of the age: "The literal flood which wipes away all trace of the Achaean camp preserves its original function; the wall is destroyed less because the poet was afraid of being challenged to point to its remains than because its disappearance gives a solemn air of finality. At its very center, the poem places its events far away in a past which becomes remote and fated not only to end, but to vanish."[30]

I find the case persuasive that Near Eastern motifs cluster about this wall and that here, more strongly than elsewhere in the Homeric poems, we are presented with the utter separateness of bygone heroes and the complete loss of any trace of them. But I think the poet of the *Iliad* has stepped outside his poem to say more than that. Scodel notes that the wall's destruction involves the destruction of *kleos*, and the question of preserving fame is inextricable from the story as it appears in the *Iliad*: the wall, after all, starts out as a kind of tomb, and it is the widespread fame promised by the wall that provokes Poseidon's jealousy and Zeus's reassurances.[31] Homer is surely saying something too about the possibilities of preserving the fame of the Trojan War in physical form.

I think that in view of the epic's interest in signs as concrete devices for making fame last, the Achaean wall is relevant to the project of the epic poet, particularly one faced with the signs of writing. In this passage the poet is most "outside" the epic, and from this perspective his interest in the survival of signs cannot be wholly separate from the survival of an epic as a physical text. Indeed the Achaean wall may be taken as a figure for a written-down *Iliad*. A construction begun with Nestor's weaving (7.324), it is a massive monument that will comprehend the remains of innu-

---

[29]Gen. 6.1–4, 11.1–9; Scodel (1982) 42, 46.

[30]Scodel (1982) 48.

[31]Scodel (1982) 48 n. 1, citing Nagy (1979) 160. Poseidon's additional complaint, that it has been built without a libation, is "a commonplace, motive hunting" (Scodel [1982] 34).

merable heroes; the enormous fame of the wall will not be localized, like Hector's, but will reach "as far as dawn light is scattered." I conceive of the episode of the wall, for all its ancient elements, as formulated along with the plan to construct a monumental text of the *Iliad* of the sort we now have. As Scodel notes, its destruction is put in the "very center" of the poem, and this placement can be significant only if the general shape of the epic were already contemplated. If the episode was written or dictated by a poet who knew what final shape his poem would have, it seems to me possible that he might have thought something about the strange thing he was helping bring into the world. And at its midpoint he could have stepped out of his story for a moment and given us a heroic parable about the relation of song to text. Homer's wall is a machine for defense but also for fame, and its destruction may speak not only of the end of an age but also of the impossibility of finding any physical trace of the Trojan War, of finding any solid, tangible embodiment of such glory.

We are told that the wall was destroyed "in the tenth year . . . after the Achaeans went home" (*Il.* 12.12–16), but the preceding sentence describes its *duration* in different terms:

> As long as Hector was alive and Achilles was wrathful
> and the city of Priam was yet unsacked,
> so long the great wall of the Achaeans was fixed firmly in the
>   ground.
>
> [*Iliad* 12.10–12]

The first line is remarkable because, whether by chance or not, it is the only time in Homer that the structure of either text is precisely delineated. This line defines the action of the *Iliad*, which begins with the wrath of Achilles and ends with Hector's funeral, far more exactly than the opening of any epic poem defines its theme.[32] The next line may seem to break this parallel between wall and *Iliad*,

---

[32]Scholiast T on 12.9–12 seems to have read the passage similarly: "The poet sets forth summarily the gist of his composition. He indicates that what holds the *Iliad* together are two characters, and at the same time hints at what will happen later, because after Achilles' rage and once Hector is no longer alive the *Iliad* itself ends directly."

since it brings in the sack of Troy, something beyond the confines of this epic. Yet at *Iliad* 22.405–411 the poet equates Hector's death with the fall of Troy,[33] so that, in view of this symbolic equivalence, line 11 may taken as effectively synonymous with line 10: it need not be read as an addition, "and the wall also lasted longer (even after Achilles was assuaged and Hector died), up until the fall of Troy," but, as often in paratactic style, as cumulative: "while Achilles raged and Hector was alive, that is to say, while the fall of Troy was delayed."[34]

In this case, the wall is said to last as long as the *Iliad* lasts. The wall then is a construct very much like the proto-text of the *Iliad*: it has a fixed form and a fixed duration, encompassing a definite stretch of events that mark a great ritardando in the larger story of the sack of Troy. In this moment of objectivity the poet is able to speak accurately about the size of his work and to endow his wall with the same dimensions.

If the wall is associated with the *Iliad* as a monumental construct, its destruction demonstrates a certain vulnerability of any text of the *Iliad* from an oral poet's point of view. For all the advantages of fixity in physical form, a text is nevertheless, like Nestor's *sêma*, only a human construct. The wall is called "unbreakable" (*arrêktos*), a very strong word for a human artifact, since elsewhere it is used of divine objects or attributes, including the "unbreakable" wall that the gods made for Troy, for which the Achaean wall seems to be a rival (14.56–58, 21.446–447). But the gods are not mocked; Apollo breaches it at one point with the ease of a child knocking over a sand castle (15.362–364). In the end Poseidon and Apollo not only dismantle the wall, they obliterate any trace of it from the landscape. The role of the flood in the final destruction is significant not only because of the hovering Near Eastern myths but also because, in Greek terms, eroding rains, washing streams, and destructive torrents are the elements most inimical to the hopes of graves and tombs. In fact the watery elements of destruction, those eroders of monuments and submergers of fame, perform on this

---

[33]As Griffin (1980) 1 and others have noted.

[34]That is, I read these lines as a "Homeric simile": the framing lines "As long as . . . so long . . ." (12.10, 12.13) give the essential point of the comparison, like the "just as . . ." and "so . . ." in similes. What is in between may be expansion, divagation, or as here, repetition.

wall what James Redfield has called an "antifuneral," the symbolic opposite of commemoration.[35] Because the wall is for the gods (and perhaps too for the Ionian poet) predominantly a device for preserving fame, its destruction is the special undoing of tombs through floods and the rains of Zeus, which "diminish the works of men" (16.392).

The antifuneral is vividly depicted in book 21 when Achilles battles the rivers. Burial by water is the leitmotif of this scene: Achilles has killed Lycaon and flung him into the river, proclaiming that he will never get a funeral (21.122–125); he kills Pelegon, descended from a river god, and boasts that all waters must yield to Zeus and Zeus's descendants (21.186–199). But the river Scamander responds and attacks Achilles, uprooting, as rivers can, a great elm with which Achilles tries to brace himself (21.242–244). Achilles then fears the lowly death of drowning and would rather have died by Hector (21.279–283); the reason is the kind of burial that such a death promises in the person of Scamander:

> his splendid arms somewhere below the water
> will lie covered with mud; and his body
> I will bury in the sands, piling on a great heap of pebbles,
> numberless [murion], and the Achaeans will not know how
> to collect his bones, with so much shingle will I cover him over.
> There will his sêma be shaped, and there will be no need
> of heaping a tomb over him for his burial.
>
> [Iliad 22.317–323]

The antifuneral produces an antimonument: not solidity but mud, not structure but disintegration, not order but the unlimited. We will never be able to recover any part of Achilles or any object he held. The destruction of the Achaean wall is similar: it will be disfigured, it will lose its appearance and form:

> Break up the wall and pour it into the sea
> and cover the great shore again with sand
> in this way let the great wall of the Achaeans be disfigured.[36]
>
> [Iliad 7.461–463]

[35]Redfield (1975) 167–169, 251.

[36]The verb amaldunai in 7.463 and 12.18 32 is also used to describe Demeter, "disfiguring her form/appearance [eidos]" in the Hymn to Demeter 94.

The flood that will erode this wall-tomb, then, is also an erasing of any text of this poem and reveals another aspect of Homer's hostility to the presumptive monument. With this literally central episode, the text of the *Iliad* reaches out of the past to inform its audience about their own world and how it is to be read. Another archaic epic, the *Shield of Heracles*, uses a similar iconoclastic gesture to punctuate its conclusion. After telling the story of the death of a Thessalian hero, Cycnus, and the great funeral his father the king held for him, it adds that in the end Apollo was angry at the hero and urged a local river, the Anaurus, to "make the grave and *sêma* of Cycnus unseen [*aides*]."[37]

To acknowledge writing, to use it in making a text is one thing; to exalt it as a way of transcending the limits of time and the powers of nature is hubris. Such cautious reservations run deep in Greek literature and surface long before Plato's *Phaedrus*. Even a quite literate poet working in the fifth century, indeed, one whose epitaphs were inscribed on stone, knew the limits of writing. When Simonides read or heard the boast inscribed on a grave stele that it would bear its message "as long as water flows and tall trees grow," he retorted, "All things are less than the gods, and stone even mortal hands can shatter"; for an inscribed statue to last forever "is the expectation of a fool" (581.5–7 Page). This partly religious awe of the written word or the fixed marker is not alien to Homer, and a recent reading of the *Iliad* by Michael Lynn-George has also focused on the relations between sign, tomb, text; he says of the Achaean wall that "within the *Iliad* the contemplation of the sign of survival is also combined with a consideration of the possibility of the survival of the sign."[38]

A concern with the possible destruction of the text may seem an exclusively modern concern, and to use heroic stories for such a self-referential meditation may seem rather sophisticated. Yet the fascination with writing and its powers, dangers, and failures is

---

[37] *Shield of Heracles* 477; cf. Janko (1986) for the context of the song.

[38] Lynn-George (1988) 252. It was only after completing this chapter that I obtained this insightful, avowedly modern reading of the *Iliad* as a twentieth-century text. In my attempt to extract Homer's ideas of texts in their historical context, I find myself in agreement with many of Lynn-George's observations on the passages in this and the preceding section.

probably as old as writing itself and also appears in Near Eastern stories, for example, in the motif of the "fateful letter" at the heart of the Bellerophon story.[39] It may be that along with writing, much of this material also came from the East. Certainly, to confine ourselves to the Old Testament, we can find a number of stones and steles that behave like fixed signs and witnesses, marking sacred places. The swaddled Pythian stone placed by Zeus to be the center of his shrine is like that stone pillow Jacob erected to be a sacred pillar, which is also anointed with oils.[40] There is also an ambiguous covenant stone marking the frontier between Aram and Israel, which has different names in Aramaic and Hebrew.[41] And we find builders of monuments who are also writers of law: after the covenant at Schechem, Joshua wrote the law of God in a book and set a great stone under an oak in the sanctuary of the Lord; Moses wrote down the words of the Lord and erected an alter with twelve pillars.[42] And the death and burial of this prophet, who saw god face-to-face and whose like has not arisen in Israel since (34.9–10), have an evasiveness about them: "but no man knows the place of his burial to this day" (Deut. 34.5–6). Finally there is a tension between the stone as marking the place of God's presence and not being that presence—hence iconoclasm, the rejection of these stones by the Law and the Prophets.[43] This religious scruple has its literary counterpart in the denigration of writing down or otherwise fixing the poetry that is an epiphany of the past.

To return to Greece and the Achaean wall, the story Homer tells focuses its myth of destruction not only on the breach in history but on our loss of signs from that history. The wall may be taken as the greatest of the *Iliad*'s failed monuments and hence the failure of any monument of the Trojan War itself. The ancient explanation, that Homer razed it to account for the lack of a wall at Troy, naïve-sounding as it is, is not to be wholly rejected. The assertion of our

[39]E.g., 2 Sam. 11.14ff.

[40]Gen. 28.18—this after his ladder dream, suggestive of the ambitions of Babel.

[41]Gen. 31.44–47; cf. Gen. 31.48, 52; Jos. 22.26ff.; Is. 19.19–20.

[42]Jos. 24.26 (one thinks of Nestor's "oak or pine." Cf. Gen. 28.18; Ex. 24.4; Jg. 9.6.); Ex. 24.4

[43]See Ex. 23.34: "You will not bow down to their gods or worship them or observe their rites, but throw them down and smash their cultic stones." Cf. 34.13; Lv. 26.1; Dt. 7.5, 12.3, 16.22; and among the prophets, Ho. 3.4, 10.1; Mi. 5.12.

total separateness from that time would only be strengthened by saying that the past is not only passed but gone without a trace. If Poseidon washed the wall away, if the Greeks took Nestor's advice and brought the bones of their comrades home, and if water had scattered their armor, it would still be possible to believe in Homer's time that the relatively placid Troad had been the site of all the mayhem in the *Iliad*.

The *Iliad*, then, shows clearly the futility of writing any history on the landscape, and given the parallel between tomb building and epic making, we have read here too a refutation of the possibility of fixing any song for good. The *kleos* of Troy will not be carried in the great wall; of all the vulnerable signs that heroic men have put up, it boded to be the greatest but was assuredly the most futile. And since the wall's duration is equated with the poem's action, the destruction of the wall is the denial of any physical form of *the Iliad*. A mere text will be eroded, erased, removed from its proper place; no hero's body will be retrieved from it. I can situate such a motif only in the doubts of an oral poet confronting his own making of a text. The wall seems to provoke a jealousy in Homer as well as Poseidon, a fear that the contrivance and the mind of the gods will be overshadowed by this construct.

This Homer, then, would not have agreed with literate Horace's firm confidence in literary immortality. He knew too well that destructive waters are the enemies of texts as well as kingly tombs, that infinite, uncountable sands are irresistibly corrosive, that dissolution and unreadability encroach on any structure. Making texts will not stave off this disintegration, even if they aspire to outdo the most permanent Eastern style (*Odes* 3.30):

Exegi monumentum aere perennius
regalique situ pyramidum altius,
quod non imber edax, non Aquilo impotens
possit diruere aut innumerabilis
annorum series et fuga temporum.

I have brought to completion a monument more lasting than
   bronze
and higher than pyramids, royally built,
one that no devouring storm, no raging North wind

can dissolve into pieces, not the uncountable
succession of years or the flight of ages.

After a consideration of the signs at Troy, this doesn't sound like
the maker of the *Iliad*.

The *Odyssey* and Cenotaphs

The *Odyssey* is no less interested than the *Iliad* in reading
and making signs, and many of the signs in this more overtly self-
referring poem have been closely read as in some way expressing
the poet's work. One could develop a preliminary typology of
signs in the *Odyssey* that would be compatible with and complement those in the *Iliad*.[44] Let us, however, proceed immediately to
the use of *sêma* as a figure for the monumental epic text, the
tomblike embodiment of its hero's fame. For it is evident that the
Odyssey knows this conceit from the *Iliad* and that it develops it
quite playfully, both as aimed at earlier "monumental" texts and as
evading a final fixation for itself.

[44]Perhaps no sign has been more often read than Odysseus's scar (called a *sêma* at
21.217, 23.73), by which he is identified after being away from Ithaca for twenty
years. The scar served as the emblem for Erich Auerbach's powerful and often
resisted reading of Homeric poetry as all surface without depth (nicely discussed in
Freccero [1986]). But I will not engage here the readings that have flowed from this; I
note only that the themes I have developed from the *Iliad*, a suspicion of signs and a
praise of their oral supplements, attend this sign too. Oddly enough, this portable,
indelible sign, which is almost a name written on his body, becomes less persuasive
the closer Odysseus gets to home. When his father asks him for a "clear sign" of
who he is, Odysseus reveals the scar, but he convinces the old man only after he
recites a catalog of trees he had heard from him as a boy (24.329, 336–346). In a
similar way, Penelope is famously unpersuaded by the scar and asks Odysseus in
addition for the "secret signs" shared between them (23.110). By this she means
their bed, the quintessential artifact: an olive tree surrounded with a well-built wall
(192–194), then cut and finished with precious metals and stone (195–200). The
natural has been wholly transformed into a sign of their fidelity, and its function as
sign is immovability. Penelope suggests to Odysseus that the bed is not now where
it once was, and his amazement—"it would be hard even for a shrewd man to move
the bed, but with a god's help he might do it easily"—is what convinces her (184–
188). Signs are clearly a plaything for this poet too, and oral memory is needed here
to supplement this writing.

As we try to imagine the monumental composer of the *Odyssey*, we can agree that he must have come after the *Iliad*. The intriguing question is whether he knew the *Iliad* (and other epic poems) as a text or only as a tradition, an earlier path of the *klea andrôn* that he himself might "move along" if he liked. He certainly knows many of the traditions surrounding Troy's fall, but would the *Iliad* have been a *text* for him, a set of lines in some way fixed (by writing or memorization) so that it was a definite and definitive version of the Wrath of Achilles? There is some indication that the *Odyssey* knew the *Iliad* as a text in this strong sense in the fact—known as Monro's law—that the *Odyssey* never refers to any incident recounted in the *Iliad*. Such consistent exclusion over such a long story with so many flashbacks can be taken as evidence that the later poem is deliberately avoiding the *Iliad* as the version we have of Achilles' wrath.[45]

Other evidence has been found that may be taken to point in the same direction,[46] but let us pursue Monro's law, because there is one passage in the *Odyssey* that apparently violates it, a reference in book 24 to the burial of Patroclus, a matter well treated in the *Iliad*. To see the significance of this departure, we must consider its context. In the underworld, Agamemnon is consoling Achilles because "not even in your death did you lose your name but always / and among all men you will have a noble fame" (24.93–94). He has described the hero's funeral: Thetis and her nymphs attended the mourning, the Muses themselves sang (24.60); when they had gathered the bones,

> Your mother gave
> a golden jar, the gift of Dionysus

[45]On Monro's law, see Nagy (1979) 20–21 (who would speak only of a fixing of "traditions") and, from a different point of view, Schein (1984) 38 (who would leave open the possibility that Homer composed both poems, but in sequence). Schein also takes the allusion to Patroclus's burial in *Od.* 24 as a violation of Monro's law (44 n. 79).

[46]The implications of Pucci's study of the Sirens (1979) (extended in [1987]) are radical, for he aims to show how certain phrases of the *Iliad* can be used in the *Odyssey* as "Iliadic," that is, alluding to the former as a fixed range of expressions. In a different vein, Redfield (1973) uncovers the many ways in which the *Odyssey* seems to be aware of and reacting to the earlier great poem; similarly Griffin (1987), discussed in the next section.

she said, and the work of very famous Hephaestus.
In it lie your white bones, grand Achilles,
mixed with those of dead Patroclus,
but apart from those of Antilochus, whom you honored most
of all your comrades after dead Patroclus.
Around the bones then a great and faultless tomb
we, the sacred host of Argive spearmen, piled up
on a projecting headland beside the broad Hellespont,
so that it would be conspicuous to men far out over the sea,
to those now alive and those who will live hereafter.

[*Odyssey* 24.73–84]

Because of the often-praised economy of the *Iliad*, whereby the poem of Achilles' rage ends with Hector's funeral, the burden of burying its hero falls to the *Odyssey*. If Achilles was threatened in the *Iliad* with complete oblivion and an antifuneral, he ends up in the *Odyssey* with a superfuneral: his glory made solid in a great and faultless tomb that will reach all men, even in later times. At the heart of this memorial is a splendid artifact: it is a vessel given by the gods with the Muses heard in the background; it was wrought by Hephaestus, the master craftsman, who shares with the *Odyssey*'s bards the epithet "very famous."[47] If the *Iliad* could be thought of as a text at this time, it would be hard to distinguish it from that vessel that carries the fame of Achilles, mixed in with a description of Patroclus's funeral. And here too, an apparently otiose phrase seems to identify the *Iliad* very specifically: Achilles' bones were mixed with those of Patroclus "but apart from those of Antilochus." The death of Achilles and the death of Antilochus are of course not narrated in the *Iliad*, but both were enshrined in that part of the tradition that has come down to us as the *Aethiopis*, the sequel to the *Iliad*.[48] In explicitly leaving out Antilochus, the vessel here seems to exclude, too, any version of the *Aethiopis* and to pinpoint the *Iliad*, which describes Patroclus's funeral and binds his fate to that of Achilles. The early epics are really rather concerned

[47]For *periklutos* of bards, see *Od.* 1.325, 8.83, 367, 521. See Nagy (1979) on this passage, esp. 160.
[48]The relevant summary of the *Aethiopis* is on p. 47 of Davies' edition (32–33 K.). The *Odyssey* also confutes the *Aethiopis* tradition on the details of Achilles' final burial. See further in Nagy (1979) 208–210.

with just where the bodies are buried, even though they do not always agree among themselves.

Like the *Iliad*, this tomb not only has a quite well defined form here but is also so fully made as to have a visible solidity: it is conspicuous or "far-shining" (*têlephanês* [24.83]) so that it can be seen by those present and those to come.[49] As a marker of Achilles' fame, it resembles the *Iliad* as composed text: fixed, enduring, readable. The *Odyssey* thus appears to know the conceit of figuring the constructed text as a tomb and seems to apply it to the *Iliad* itself. One may wish to see this as a sort of tribute, though I have been persuaded by Bloom that greatly ambitious poets can rarely afford to be wholly generous to great predecessors. If the poet of the *Iliad* considered text fixation like monument making and then denied that any visible monument could be the real *Iliad*, the *Odyssey* poet may be doing him a dubious favor in laying out that text for all to see. It may be that in granting that too monumental text before him a glorious, superhuman fixity, the *Odyssey* poet hoped to retain for himself an escape from that fixation, however artful it was. Be that as it may, we can turn to the *Odyssey* and look for what monument it expects to make of itself, what stance it will in its turn take toward its own monumentality and writing. Since the poem seems to be willing to question how art makes signs and how signs mark burial and fame, we may ask of it how it expects to embody the fame of its own hero. To pursue this theme of sign as epic text, we may interrogate the *Odyssey* for its own hero's funeral marker as a way of catching Homer's reflections on how such a slippery hero could be finally fixed. After all, in one of his earlier speeches Odysseus reflects on the desirability of dying among one's peers and getting proper burial rites as against the antifuneral of a watery grave (5.306–312). If we fail to find such a marker firmly fixed, we may then look for other signs that Odysseus brought home as something solid retrieved from the past.

To speak of the death and burial of Odysseus is most antithetical

---

[49]This passage seems to underlie Pindar's elaborate figuration of song as architectural construct in his sixth Olympic ode (*Ol.* 6.2–4). He begins with the conceit that the poet will "fix fast" (*paksomen*) his poem on golden pillars, "to be gazed upon like a great hall" (*hôs hote thaêton megaron*); the Odyssean debt appears when he says its proem must be a facade that is "far-gleaming" (*têlauges*).

to the *Odyssey*, with its constant stress on deferring, delaying, and continuing voyages.[50] Yet his death appears in the text, foretold by Teiresias, and a premature burial is forestalled in the first book. We recall that Athena told Telemachus that if he found out that his father was dead he should return home and heap up a *sêma* for him and make great funeral offerings upon it (1.291–292). The cenotaph is something not found in the *Iliad*, but the *Odyssey* gives us another one: when Menelaus finds out that Agamemnon has died, he heaps up a tomb for him in Egypt "so that his *kleos* might be unquenchable" (4.584). It has been suspected that there is an Odyssean irony toward heroic burial in these empty tombs and that the poet is deliberately severing the connection between *kleos* and stone.[51] I think that the *Iliad* anticipated this skepticism, but the *Odyssey* does rather multiply ironies as we approach the underworld and the prospect of Odysseus's death.

Graveyard humor attends the first scene of the necromancy when Odysseus comes across poor Elpenor. This hapless crewman, "very young, not very / brave in war, nor sound in wit" (10.552–553), had got drunk and fallen to his death from a roof on Circe's island and as·a consequence missed a proper burial. After the famous joke when Odysseus wonders how Elpenor, on foot, beat him to the underworld, Elpenor begs Odysseus to go back to Circe's isle and heap up a *sêma* for him, "for those to come to find out about" (11.76). Elpenor instructs Odysseus on the kind of memorial he desires: "And plant an oar on my tomb / one I rowed with when I was among my companions" (11.77–78). Though an oar would not be a bad sign for a sailor, wood is hardly the stuff of which one makes monuments to endure "for those to come." Additionally, Aeaea seems a rather out-of-the-way place for such a landmark, and there is something generally droll about such scrupulous concern for the rites of this unheroic person.

Soon after, Teiresias prepares Odysseus for his return and vengeance on the suitors and enjoins on him a new voyage. No sooner than he is home and settled, he will have to take on a post-*Odyssey* odyssey: Odysseus, the man who was "very much / buffeted . . .

[50]See Pucci's recent study (1987).

[51]Redfield (1975) 230 n. 15 says that these examples show that the association has become "purely conventional"; cf. Maehler (1963) 27.

and knew the cities and mind of many men," describes this new
voyage to Penelope as to go "to the cities of very many men" (1.1–
3; 23.267). When the poem closes, then, we will know that it has
not quite been able to arrest its hero; but Odysseus's wandering
apparently is not to be endless: Teiresias says there will be a "quite
distinctive sign" that he has arrived at his destination. Odysseus is
to take with him an oar until he comes upon men who don't know
the sea; when some passerby takes the oar on his shoulder for a
winnowing fan, he is to plant it in the ground and sacrifice to
Poseidon.

Teiresias next predicts for Odysseus a quiet death in prosperous
old age among his beloved people (11.119–137), and there may be
some connection between the two extra-Odyssean episodes predicted here, between the erecting of this marker and Odysseus's
death. The oar, of course, is to mark a spot sacred in the transaction
between Odysseus and Poseidon, and possibly acts too as an etiology for inland shrines dedicated to a sea-god.[52] But it is planted in
the text about fifty lines after Elpenor had asked for an oar over his
grave, and as Teiresias goes on to speak of Odysseus's death but
not a word of his burial or later fame, in a sense this sign making
for Poseidon substitutes for any grave making or commemoration
over Odysseus. Teiresias tells a story of sign making followed by
death, a *husteron proteron* version of the standard heroic sequence
of death and remembrance; following as it does the mock monument of Elpenor, that oar will have to do instead of any splendid
tomb for Odysseus.[53] We may infer that no more than the *Iliad* will
the *Odyssey* be entombed: it will end as its hero sets out on a
voyage that is much like the one on which he had set out at its very
opening, and no one can predict for us where and whether he will
find his secure tomb. The one monument the *Odyssey* tells us that
its hero will leave behind is a very odd sign indeed: not only is it a
cenotaph of sorts, but the "sign" that it is in the right place is that a
passerby misreads it. Delighting in empty signs and wandering
signifiers, the poet subtly frustrates any desire to know where we
can see and read aright the spot where the body of the hero lies.

[52]Cf. Hansen (1977) 32, 35.

[53]Nagy (1983) 45 calls the oar "a stylized image of his own tomb" and adds that
this tomb among those who do not know the sea is "extremely removed from
Odysseus' death which comes out of the sea." Cf. now Peradotto (1990) 65–75.

Again, if it seems too sophisticated that the *Odyssey* might be referring to how it will be fixed as text or even that it might care about such a thing, consider how the Babylonian *"Odyssey"* presents its hero, Gilgamesh. This wanderer has managed to secure for his report a kind of transmission that would have been most welcome to a Ninevan scribe:

> He who saw everything [to the end]s of the land,
> [Who all thing]s experienced, [conside]red all
> [. . .] together [. . .],
> [. . .] of wisdom, who all things. [. . .]
> The [hi]dden he saw, [laid bare] the undisclosed.
> He brought forth report of before the Flood,
> Achieved a long journey, weary and [w]orn.
> All his toil he engraved on a stone stela.
> Of ramparted Uruk the wall he built,
> Of hallowed Eanna, the pure sanctuary.[54]

Like the *Iliad*, this is a message from before the flood, but it comes from an eyewitness who wrote it down. Like the *Odyssey*, this is the tale of a returning traveler, a voyager into the unknown, skilled in many things; but Odysseus writes nothing, nor does he built great walls. Gilgamesh is a writing poet and hence is also a builder of monuments, an erector of walls, and an encloser of sacred spaces. Odysseus is still an oral poet: his inscriptions, such as his bed and his scar, are secret and hidden; but he is willing to tell his tale to the Phaeacians and to tell it again to Penelope.

The *Odyssey*'s refusal to present us with a great *sêma* for its hero may then be of a piece with its refusal to present itself as text. Like the *Iliad*, it insists that there is no conspicuous sign that embodies its hero's career. In fact, the *Odyssey* includes its own version of the Achaean wall, a story of a barrier that accounts for the breach between the world narrated in the poem and the world in which the poem is heard. This is the mountain referred to in books 8 through 12, which will be in effect a wall, cutting off the Phaeacians from the outer world and cutting us off from the fairy world of the past. This "wall" is one to be erected rather than destroyed, but it

[54]Translation, Pritchard (1954) 73. For thematic comparisons with the *Odyssey*, see Gresseth (1975).

has the same purpose of severing us from direct, tangible contact with these fabulous sailors who had in the past touched the shores of Greece in their ships "swift as thought."

We first hear of it from Alcinous who recalls a prophecy as Odysseus sails off. It said that Poseidon would be angered at the Phaeacians for all their painless ferrying of men across the sea and would one day strike a ship as it was returning to port and "cover over" (*amphikalupsein*) their city with a mountain, either crushing or blockading it (8.565–569). As with the Achaean wall, the punishing god is Poseidon, and again he fears a loss of his honor (13.128–138). Again Zeus reassures him and bids him to do what he will (13.140–145). As the ship returns from its mission and approaches port, Poseidon turns it into stone and roots it to the ground (13.161–164). The sequel is in suspense: we leave the Phaeacians recalling that prophecy and preparing a sacrifice to avert the predicted mountain. Whatever the outcome, the Phaeacians will be cut off from the rest of the world, for Alcinous vows to stop ferrying mortals (13.180–181). The cutting off of Phaeacia has the same function as the destruction of the Achaean wall: both may be said to forestall objections of the simpleminded, and both put the scene of heroic action in an inaccessible place.[55] In the case of these great sailors, Homer's audience might have expected them to put in on their shores any day. (Their magic ships are the equivalent in the epic imagination of UFOs.) But now they understand that these highly civilized people will not make contact with them. In the *Odyssey*, this breaking of connection with the epic world is accompanied by the production of a great artifact: Zeus tells Poseidon to "make [the ship] stone as it approaches, / in the shape of a swift ship, so that all men may marvel at it" (13.156–157). But this god-made artifact arrests motion, and marks not the crossing over to Phaeacia but the loss of that possibility.

Like the *Iliad*, then, the *Odyssey* has no particular love for rolling up its hero under a monumental tomb and, in what I take to be a related attitude, insists on a radical break between the heroic land-

[55]The parallel is drawn in the scholia; cf. Heubeck, West, Hainsworth on *Od.* 6.8 and on 7.45, with additional parallels between the pallisaded walls of the Phaeacians and the "town wall" fortifications imposed on the Achaean wall. Also discussed by Scodel (1982) 48–50.

scape and the ground where we, the audience, live and hear the
tale. There was, however, something solid brought back from
Phaeacia; after all Odysseus came back, and not empty-handed.
Having been stripped of all he won at Troy and even what he wore
when he washed up in Phaeacia, he yet made good his loss and
came away with many gifts, the most impressive being thirteen
excellent tripods. Odysseus takes care to preserve these when he
lands in Ithaca and puts them in a magical cave of the Nymphs:

> And in it are wine bowls and two-handled jars
> made of stone, where bees deposit their honey.
> And in it are large stone looms where the Nymphs
> weave their garments, a marvel to see;
> and water ever flowing
>
> [*Odyssey* 13.105–109]

Two paths lead into this cave, one for mortals and one for the gods
(13.109–112). Such apparently gratuitous details have made this
passage a favorite target for allegorizing readers of Homer, especially Neoplatonists, who would find treated here a favorite
theme, the incarnate soul. Since their methods have been said to
approach the kind of structural analysis I have been employing in
this chapter, it may be worthwhile to distinguish my method here
from strict allegorism. In an allegory, each literal detail must be
taken as pointing to an aspect of a coherent doctrine behind the
tale. Individual details find their ultimate coherence and significance only when referred to this unexpressed doctrine. But in the
view of Homeric unity I arrived at in Chapter 2, any single and
total hidden order must be left outside of epic. Nevertheless, such
details as the poet does mention are given as parts of a world and
so can be assigned value and "meaning" in their relation to the
structure of all things in that world. In this chapter I have been
reading significance into certain objects and artifacts in the poems
not as symbolic parts to be totalized in some recondite doctrine but
simply as parts of a world that distinguishes between human and
divine artifacts and between temporary and lasting ones. I have
read each detail not only as an item in the plot but also as an item in
an inventory of all the objects there are in heaven and earth. In

trying to define writing, a thing of interest to us as readers and theorists, I have been collecting instances of human and divine signs and works as functional analogues to *sêmata*. I hope I can continue to avoid a rampantly abusive allegorism if I add the forms of art in this cave, whose significance for my theme has been made plain by the poet's careful deposition of Odysseus's material trophies there. Thus if we examine these objects both as elements of the plot and as instances of artifacts, we may see in them a special idea of artifacts, an idea that bears on the relationship of mortal works of art to the divine.

The cave of the Nymphs is by its two roads undeniably a place where the eternal meets the ephemeral, but its contents are not the elements of a Platonic soul but rather the appurtenances of civilized life, ideally immortalized. In the shapes of these stalactites and stalagmites the poet sees the the tools and trappings of festivity—wine and water, fine garments—made fixed and permanent but without loss of function. Here the instruments of art are solid as stone, and yet divinities may weave on them and bees fill them with sweetness. In this "marvelous cave" (13.363) one might lay hold of an artifact that is "made," that is stone somehow rendered functional, but is also eternal and divine. Perhaps only here, where the stream never fails, might one speak of a visible, unaging poetry playing among the festivity and skillful joining. In this place of divine art, at once solid and eternal, Odysseus deposits the goods from the Phaeacians. Yet for all his scrupulous materialism (he counts his goods up to make sure none are missing [13.218]), we do not hear that he returned to fetch them. What might have been trophies and proofs of his incredible adventures will apparently end up as dedications in a hidden shrine.

But it seems that the Greeks returned for them sometime later. Archaeology has identified a cave of the Nymphs on Ithaca.[56] It was a place of cult from the bronze age into the first century C.E. At some time Odysseus came to be honored there, for a terra-cotta mask of the second or first century B.C.E. identifies itself as a votive to Odysseus. And here too have been found thirteen (and only

---

[56]See Benton (1934–35). Perhaps this pasage conflates it with another cave near Vathy; see Frank H. Stubbings, "Ithaca," in Wace and Stubbings (1962) 416, 418–419.

thirteen) bronze tripod cauldrons whose design suggests a date of the ninth or eighth century B.C.E. The thirteen is certainly suggestive of the tithe of tripods that Alcinous exacted from his twelve princes, to which he added his own (*Od.* 8.387ff., 13.13). It may be that Homer was touting a local antiquity here or that some entrepreneurs after Homer contrived an attraction for the large audience of the *Odyssey*. In either case the trophies of Odysseus, buried along with these stone devices, attests to the thirst to find a hard trace of the magic of the past and an instinct that the poet will direct us to it.

Like the *Iliad* then, the *Odyssey* lets its audience know that they can expect no unmediated contact with the heroic world through any physical thing. In place of Odysseus's grave we are given the ambiguous oar, a wandering signifier, never at home until it is misread; the imaginary realm of Phaeacia, land of the supreme travelers, is blockaded; we cannot reach it except through the tales of the wanderer, though some may claim to have found traces of it in a cave full of stone cups and looms we cannot use. The *Odyssey* prefers the telling of tales to the reading of history in objects; it prefers keeping its hero in constant motion to incorporating him into a chef d'oeuvre. Its hero's *kleos* will not be carried in any tomb, however splendid, but is already reaching heaven as its hero lives and moves and extends it himself; his fame resides in performance and action, not inscription.

Each poem avoids closure, the fixing of fame by mortal means, once and for all, though each does so in a different way: if the *Iliad* wreaks destruction on the presumptive sign, the *Odyssey* casts off possible final signs lightly, always deferring its hero's coming to rest under a clear and stable mark of his fame. Odysseus is a great signified, his name written in his flesh, who must journey far and be stripped of all before he comes back to his rightful name and identity. Along the way we hear that tombs may be cenotaphs, empty signs of glory, and unheroic Elpenor has more of a grave than the hero. The *Iliad* warns us that signs can be destroyed and moved from their proper place and that no sign satisfactorily embodies *kleos*; it erases any possible concrete sign, whereas the *Odyssey* declines to show us a final sign.

As in my investigation of the different strategies by which the

two poets achieved vividness, the *Odyssey* assumes the problematic of the *Iliad* and exacerbates it to find a new freedom.
Whereas the *Iliad* had denied that it was a later song, the *Odyssey*
won a different kind of earliness by insisting on its own lateness, or
the priority of song to deed. A similar victory is won from near
defeat in evading fixity, limitation, and unchangingness: the *Iliad*
denies the powers of fixity; the *Odyssey* fixes the *Iliad* and entombs
Achilles but refuses to bury its own. In this refusal is a kind of
freedom that the *Iliad* does not have. The almost irresponsible
wildness of the *Odyssey* in regard to truth and tale-fixing monuments may make the *Iliad* seem slow and awkward as it almost
trips over the objects in the ground and has to battle them; they
seem to resist it as it makes its own world appear. The *Odyssey*,
delighting in fictions, throws up too many signs of Odysseus and
points out that there can be signs with nothing beneath. The resourcefulness of the *Odyssey* is impressive, though it may seem a
resourcefulness imposed on it by the achievement of its too, too
solid predecessor. Without adjudicating between the poems on
this point we may at least say that *Odyssey* succeeds on its own
terms, to make the newest song that rings in men's ears. Its leap
beyond any possibility of leaving written texts behind is a great
cast, like Odysseus's discus throw on Phaeacia: "Even a blind man
might distinguish your *sêma* / just by touching it, since it is not
mixed in with the throng of the others" (8.195–196).

The Poet and the Work of Art

Before concluding, I should note that my reading has been
directly contrary to one sympathetic view of Homeric poetry which
sees the poet as extolling his artistry in his poems and celebrating
his craftsmanlike powers of making. On such a view, mastering
and fixing the variable oral form is the poet's triumph, not his fear,
and a more appropriate symbol in the *Iliad* of its own making
would be the great shield that Hephaestus forges for Achilles, so
lovingly described in book 18.[57] Indeed, one must agree that the

[57]E.g., Reinhardt (1961) 401–411, who concludes: "Since poetry is a craft, we
expect craftsmanship of the poet, corresponding to his profession" ("Da nun

artisanal conception of making is idealized in this shield, on which Hephaestus *"made* many curious designs with his knowing ingenuity" (18.482). But I have noted in Chapter 1 that the epic poets eschew the artisanal vocabulary for their own practices, and it is far from clear that that this artifact would have been an adequate analogue of the singer's art.

It is beyond doubt that the shield of Achilles is an ideal, even magical artifact, but it also precisely transcends the limits of any mortal construction in the same way that Hephaestus's mechanical handmaids transcend statuary. And it is true that Hephaestus uses his art to represent much of the same world as the *Iliad* does, but like the Sirens, he also includes much more. If the immense *Iliad* spans only the time that Hector lived and Achilles raged, what text could ever hope to be so vast as the shield, depicting both war and peace, encompassing the earth, sea, and stars, circumscribed only by Ocean? This is finally an uncanny making that the poet cannot hope for. The shield transcends even the limits of its plastic form: the engraved scenes incorporate motion, process, and sound: the furrows on a plowed field "turn to black, / although they were gold, such an exceptional marvel this was" (18.548–549); when a boy sings a harvest song, the engraving somehow communicates that it is "on a clear lyre, charmingly, with a delicate voice" (18.569–571). The verdict of Achilles is definitive: "My mother, the god has given such arms as are fitting / to be the work of immortals, and not for a mortal man to have accomplished" (19.21–22). The shield is so splendid that the mere sight of it stirs fear not only in the Trojans but in Achilles' own men as well, who cannot bear to look at it directly and avert their eyes, trembling (20.44–46, 19.14–15). No less powerful is its effect on the goddess's son: when he sees it anger rises in him and an answering gleam flashes out from his own eyes (19.15–19). The shield is perhaps a paean to the metalworker, not the singer, and not to the beauty of his work but to its superhuman limits.

A measure of the unapproachable also surrounds an artful im-

Dichten Handwerk ist, so wird vom Dichter Handwerkliches, seinem Beruf Êntsprechendes erwartet" [410]); Marg, using an earlier form of Reinhardt's chapter, carries the idea to allegorical extremes (1957) 21–37; see too Schadewaldt (1965) 352–374.

plement in the *Odyssey* that Jasper Griffin has suggested may stand for the *Iliad* as text: it is the golden baldric of Heracles, wrought with scenes of war. The object seems to dismay Odysseus. When he encounters it in the underworld, he cries, "May the one who fashioned it never fashion another one, / the one that laid up that baldric in his art [*technê*]" (*Od.* 11.613–614). Griffin richly suggests that Odysseus's just-preceding encounter with Achilles was symbolically a brush with his poem, so that his comment implies a judgment that the *Iliad* was "a marvelous creation . . . yet grim and terrifying, immoderate, never to be repeated."[58] Perhaps I am too literal here, but I take this artifact to refer not to the *Iliad* but to some saga of Heracles, a hero even earlier and more savage than Achilles; accordingly, his baldric is golden, not silver like that on the later hero's shield (*Il.* 18.480). In any case, if these admirable artifacts are in some ways like ideal poems, they are decidedly beyond human making and even endurance. An apocryphal story from the "Roman" *Life of Homer*, which seems to derive from the description of the shield, reads it well: Homer went to Achilles' tomb and prayed for the hero to appear to him in his splendid armor; when Achilles appeared, Homer was blinded by the gleam of the arms, and Thetis and the Muses compensated him with the gift of poetry.[59] It is only after turning away from such marvelous fabrications that singers become singers.

In this chapter I have sought in the texts moments of self-reflection on the part of those still-capable poets through whom they came to be written. I have found that, though writing is generally banished from the heroic world, each poem has a great deal to say about signs and in particular about their limitations as a way of preserving fame. In view of the fact that in its one reference to writing the *Iliad* calls it "signs," I have read the stories of heroic signs as insisting on the superiority of singing to making, an attitude that seems consonant with the presentation of the poem as song rather than text. Even if the passages that I have suggested refer to the poems as monumental texts be regarded as implausibly self-conscious, there remains through both poems a recurrent

[58]Griffin (1987) 101–102.
[59]Wilamowitz-Mollendorff (1903) 31. Cf. Burkert (1985) 207, who refers to a story reported by Herodotus (6.117) in which a man is blinded by the epiphany of a hero.

theme of the failure or loss of physical artifacts and a suspicion of the hope of fixing things for good.

I do not deny that we may think of those who finally made the *Iliad* and *Odyssey* as artists, or that they might have eagerly acceded to the new technology and created or helped create these texts. But whatever the original purposes of the texts—to be aids in performance, memoranda, or precious objects—they could not have immediately usurped the older conception of poetry as singing, not making. The poet of the *Iliad* and the *Odyssey*, when greeted with a pen or face-to-face with his amanuensis, certainly acceded to this new sign making, but not without misgiving, or rather, not without reserving for his oral art a separate place that could not be usurped by the scribe. As those texts were made they incorporated a warning that no mortal making could produce a complete and adequate embodiment of this art as it had been and continued to be practiced. Even this public art—apparently so open, declaring itself flatly and without hidden meanings to its people—retains reservations about being completely appropriated. These are the reservations of an art that exists and is "made" only when it is being given to its audience, one that is unwilling to be reduced to other arts, especially to monumental makings. In recent times critics have been able to locate a form of literary resistance similar to this, a resistance on the part of texts ever to yield up a final meaning, whether because of the ungovernability of writing or the aporias of criticism. In Homer we may see an early form of this reserve of meaning in the singer's resistance to the stone carver and inciser, even as his special presentation of the past undergoes a passage into inscribed lines. Nietzsche's apothegm may well be profoundly right: "How Classicists torment themselves with the question whether Homer could write without grasping the much more important principle that Greek art exhibited a long inward hostility to writing and did not want to be read."[60]

[60]Translation by W. Arrowsmith, "Nietzsche: Notes for 'We Philologists,'" *Arion* n.s. 1 (1973): 328. In the edition of Nietzsche edited by Giorgio Colli and Mazzino Montinari, *Werke: Kritische Gesamtausgabe*, 30 vols. (Berlin: Walter de Gruyter, 1967–1978), "Wir Philologen" is in 4.1.87–88.

CHAPTER 5

POETRY
The Voice of Song

Voice

The stories about the destruction or elusiveness of mortal signs treated in the previous chapter suggest that the traditional oral art would have found it undesirable to idealize the physical fixing of fame in the way writing offered. What, then, was the poet reserving from the scribe? In practical terms, it may have been the license to sing "wherever his heart moved him," the ability to follow the situation and not any pre-fixed plan, however well-wrought. I think what the poet would have said he was preserving from textualization was his voice, the sound of ongoing, changeable song. For the word for what the singer did, "singing," suggests that the "voice" of song was its soul. Homer's "singing," *aoidê*, appears to be etymologically related to a particular word for the voice, *audê*. This ancient etymological connection, though obscure in points of detail, is still preserved in Homer and Hesiod. In addition, the traditional epithet, *thespis*, something like "divine," also indicates a close and ancient connection between singing and this voicing, for the epic language has restricted *thespis* almost completely to the words "voice," "singer," and "song" (*audê*, *aoidos*, and *aoidê*).

The poet's claim to a special kind of singing, then, is a claim to a special kind of voice. As a way of approaching a general statement of what poetry was for Homer, I examine in this chapter Homer's word for the poet's voice, along with its distinctive epithets. But that voice must be defined in Homer's terms. "Voice" has been a common metaphor in recent criticism, very often as a figure for the individual or intimate aspect of a poet's poetry. Such a romantic trope (one thinks of phrases like "finding a voice" or a "voice of one's own") is rather vulnerable to being deconstructed and in any case is not what I think Homer had in mind in speaking of the voice of song. The poet's *audê* was, as we will see, specifically a human voice, but it was not an individual's recognizable voice, nor was it voice as the expression of a personality. It was a voice we can understand but also the voice as the physical medium of singing. For Homer and Hesiod use the word in such a way as to explore the special material qualities of poetry, in particular its fluidity and its lasting continuity.

In this privileging of speech over writing, the poet as intoner rather than maker, we will recognize a fundamental literary ploy that was reenacted with great acuity by Plato in his *Phaedrus* and deconstructed in our time by Jacques Derrida. It would be easy now to reverse this Homeric opposition and to say that "singing" or voicing is not necessarily a more "natural" or intimate form of expression than writing, and to point out that Homer's words naming this unartful, spontaneous poetry are themselves tropes, that is, already the product of revision and rhetorical strategy. Like Plato, Homer could be shown to be feigning a central value of his art in pretending that his fluid voice is closer to the truth than mere scratches on stone. But for my purposes it will be less useful to give the dialectic yet another twist than to give full credence to the poet's unapologetic phonocentrism. I want to accept the claim that poetry is a voicing and to press on to ask what kind of voice it was that the poet insisted on retaining. We have to do with a rather complex idea here, for if *audê* is normally the human voice, *thespis audê*, "divine human voice" approaches oxymoron. I want to locate *audê* in relation to other words for "voice" and then to examine the epithet that connects Homer's "voice" and "singing." Uncovering the full meaning of the poet's "divine voice," *thespis audê*, will help us understand more deeply his special art of "divine singing," *thespis aoidê* and lead to conclusions on the general question of what singing was for the epic poet. In essence, this voicing was the freedom not to become one thing, even a great thing, an unbreakable voice and iron heart. This freedom is figured in the poems as a liquidity of voice, against which is set the fixity and solidity of things made. However massive and well constructed a text might be, the poet as oral performer needed to keep something of his performance unwritten, to keep his beginnings attached to the Muse's total song and to end only when it was time for sleep. We will come as close as we can to the poets' idea of their poetry if we can name this last thing that they withheld from their texts.

Audê: Human Voice

Homer says of both Phemius and Demodocus that they are "like gods in their *audê*" (*Od.* 1.371, 9.4), and he says this of no one else. When the Muses teach Hesiod "singing" (*aoidê*), they "breathe" an *audê* into him.[1] Indeed the very name Hesiod may incorporate this same root, so that he names himself in his proem as "the one who sends forth the *audê*."[2] But *audê* is only one among several Greek words for the voice; in selecting this word, Homer has allied singing with the human voice as we use it to communicate with each other.[3] *Audê* is essentially the voice producing human speech, and so it remains even when the gods assume it to communicate with men.[4]

---

[1]*Theog.* 22, 31–32. Because of the intimate association of *aoidê* and *audê* it is not uncommon for the manuscripts to confuse them: see West (1966) on *Theog.* 32.

[2]So Frisk (1960–70) s.v. See further in Nagy (1979) 296–297.

[3]Fournier (1946) 229 defines the word: "the human voice seen as the ability to emit a sound that is harmonious, powerful, and above all endowed with meaning" ("la voix humaine, envisagée comme une faculté d'émettre un son harmonieux, puissant et surtout doué de sens"). Similarly, Chantraine (1977) and Frisk (1960–70). For a fuller treatment and references to previous discussions see Clay (1974) 131–134.

[4]Clay (1974) establishes this central point, the neglect of which vitiates the definitions of *audê* in *LfrgE*.

Homer's vocabulary for the sounds produced by animate beings is very rich and includes a consideration of voice in its aspect as sound as well as an instrument of expression.[5] In addition, the voices that are heard in epic can be arranged on a scale that extends from those attributed only to the gods to those of mortals and those of animals. At the top of the scale, we must allow for the speech of the gods and demigods. For just as the gods differ from us in their food and drink, so it seems that they have a separate language of their own.[6] How this may sound to them we do not know, but when their speech is heard on earth special words for voice may mark its provenience. Such is *omphê* (related to our "song"): in Homer it is a divine voice that gods use when they speak to mortals in dreams or when they appear beside them but without assuming physical human form.[7]

Somewhat less consistently divine but still a bit beyond human speech is *ossa* (derived from a root whence come *epos* and our "voice"). Homer only uses it in the phrase "the *ossa* of Zeus," which is rumor, a dynamic voice that seems to circulate among men on its own power.[8] In Hesiod, it several times names the voice of the Muses who "send forth" (*hieisai*) an *ossa* that is "very beautiful," "immortal," "lovely," or "charming" (*Theog.* 10, 43, 65, 67). It has been suggested that *ossa* has something of the divine in it.[9] Hence, in these instances, all for the ears of other immortals, *ossa* would seem to name the Olympian ring of that voice (*audê*) that Hesiod "sends forth" on earth. So the poet of the *Hymn to Hermes* seems to use *ossa* as an Olympian equivalent to his own "divine song": when Hermes first performs on his lyre for his brother, Apollo names this new thing twice, calling it "divine singing" (*thespin aoidên*) and glossing it: "for this newly spoken *ossa* I hear is marvelous [*thaumasiên*]" (442–443). But when an *ossa* appears on earth, it may take the form of awe-inspiring sounds, not only voice: the monster Typho utters "the *ossa* of a bull" (*Theog.* 832) and the

---

[5]*LfrgE* s.v. *audê* 1541.28–51 briefly resumes the difference of many of these words from *audê* through a consideration of their epithets.

[6]See West (1966) 387–388 and Clay (1972).

[7]*Il.* 2.41 (of Dream as "Nestor" to Agamemnon), 20.129 (of a god standing beside Achilles), *Od.* 3.215 = 16.96. Cf. *LfrgE* s.v. *audê* 1541.44–49 and Leaf on *Il.* 2.41.

[8]*Od.* 1.282, 2.216; *Il.* 2.93–94.

[9]Fournier (1946) 227–228.

great conflagration of the Titanomachy produces an amazing "sight for the eyes and *ossa* for the ears" (*Theog.* 701).[10] *Ossa*, then, is a superhuman or unearthly sound that may be marvelous or beautiful in the songs of the gods but is terrible or uncontrollable on earth.

If *ossa* is the dynamic and powerful sound of voice, a quality that only divine singing can control as beautiful song, another word, known as *opa*, names the pleasing or affecting qualities of voice. When Muses "sing with a beautiful *opa*" (*Il.* 1.604; *Theog.* 68), we should think primarily of the "music" of their song, as when it names the "beautiful *opa*" the Sirens "send forth," and the singing of Calypso or Circe.[11] For *opa* is basically a distinctive vocal sound; it may name voices that convey intelligence or thought, but these are the especially emotional or stirring voices, such as of the anguished Hecuba, Penelope, or Cassandra.[12] It is not a particularly "signifying" voice when Odysseus speaks and "cast[s] forth from his chest a great voice [*opa*] / and words [*epea*] like winter snows," for he stuns rather than persuades the Trojan court (*Il.* 3.221–222; cf. 224). Hence it may be used of bleating lambs (in a simile describing the polyglot Trojans marshaling [*Il.* 4.435], or of cicadas "sending forth their lilylike voice" (*Il.* 3.152). In these cases it is clearly sound apart from sense, and so it must be when the Muses' "lilylike voice" disperses throughout the halls of Zeus (*Theog.* 41). Typho, who uses all voices, as we will see, "sends forth" an *opa* as well. (*Theog.* 830).

The *opa* of a singer, then, is especially the musical sound or tone of his voice. But this voice can also be heard as a *phthongos*: Almost always used of human voice, *phthongos* (or *phthongê*) names the distinctive voice of an individual. If the Sirens, like the Muses, sing "with a beautiful voice [*opa*]," the performance also has a dis-

---

[10]On the basis of the latter passage it has been said that in Hesiod this word means nothing more specific than "sound": West (1966) on *Theog.* 701. Yet no human being or "normal" animal utters an *ossa* in epic.

[11]*Od.* 12.192, 5.61, 10.221. Hesiod too may have spoken of the Sirens' "clear *opa*" according to West's restoration of fr. 150.33 M–W.

[12]*Il.* 22.451; *Od.* 20.42, 11.421. Fournier (1946) 228 and Clay (1974) 135. Cf. *LfrgE* s.v. *audê* 1541.41–44.

tinctive, identifying sound, and as Odysseus approaches them he strains to "hear their *phthongos* or singing [*aoidê*]" (*Od.* 12.198). The Cyclops has a "heavy *phthongos*," which frightens Odysseus and his men.[13] *Phthongos* names the voice of the charioteer which his horses recognize (*Il.* 5.234) and the voice of an individual which a god assumes in order to impersonate him (*Il.* 2.791).

Last, to name the voice most essentially as mere sound, as "noise," there is *phônê*. *Phônê* is most frequently used of mortals, often when they shout, but it is also the sound of animals (*Od.* 10.239) and may even be extended to the sound of a trumpet (*Il.* 18.219).[14] The language of barbarian races may be called *phônê*, for even if they are intelligible to each other, to the Greek ear their speech is mere phonic "babbling."[15]

Within this spectrum of vocalization, *audê* is properly used only of humanly intelligible speech. When *audê* is attributed to animals in epic, it is figurative, reinterpreting their noise as intelligible sound.[16] Properly, animals have *phônê* but not *audê*: when Circe changes Odysseus's men into swine, they keep their human intelligence (*noos*), but because they have taken on the heads of ani-

---

[13]*Od.* 9.257; cf. 9.167 of animals. Chantraine (1977) s.v. defines the verb *phthengomai*: "to emit a sound, a noise, make oneself heard"; cf. Fournier (1946) 231.

[14]For *phônê*, see Fournier (1946) 230–231.

[15]Cf. *Il.* 2.867; *Od.* 1.183, 8.924. The Greek word "barbarian" seems to be an onomatopoeic word, like "babbling," which defines other races by their senseless language. In an interesting passage Herodotus 2.55.2–2.57.2 recounts a legendary founding of an oracle in which doves flew to a tree and first spoke in a *phônê*, then, transformed into priestesses, began to "utter a human speech" (*exaudan*). His rationalistic explanation is that the "doves" must have been barbarians.

[16]Cf. Chantraine (1977) s.v. *audê* and *LfrgE* 1541.12–16. That animals have *audê* only by metaphorical extension can be seen from comparing a series of epic cicadas: Homer uses *opa* appropriately when he compares the Trojan elders to cicadas "sitting in a tree and sending forth their lilylike voice [*opa*]" (*Il.* 3.152). But Hesiod speaks metaphorically when he describes a cicada sitting in the same tree (Homer's line-opening formula is slightly varied) which "pours down its clear song [*aoidê*]" (*Works and Days* 583). Here, significance is bestowed on the animal's voice because it announces summer to mortal men. Similarly, the *Shield of Heracles* grants *audê* to its cicada, "sitting on a branch, it pours forth its *audê* all day long" (396, cf. 283). In this light we should understand a famous simile in the *Odyssey* (21.404–411) in which a plucked bowstring "sings like a swallow in its *audê*." The extended use of both "singing" and *audê* here were prepared for when Odysseus strung the bow "like a man skilled in the lyre and singing [*aoidê*]."

mals, they can only cry to their leader with the *phônê* (10.239).[17]
Hence, *audê*, the "voice intelligible to humans," also means "the
voice characteristic of mortals": when Odysseus is awakened by
inarticulate female shouting on Phaeacia, he wonders at first if he
has heard mountain Nymphs or "human beings [*anthrôpôn*] of
human voice [*audêentôn*]" (*Od.* 6.125).[18]

When *audê* is used of the gods it is because they can share in or
temporarily assume the speech of mortals. Minor goddesses such
as Calypso and Circe, who live on earth and have intercourse with
mortals, can speak to them; they are called *audêessa*, "speaking
with the human voice,"[19] as is the sea goddess Ino, who had pre-
viously been a "mortal with the voice of mortals [*brotos audêessa*]."[20]
When the Olympians descend to earth in bodily form and communicate with men, they often take on "human form and human
voice [*demas kai audên*]." Jenny Strauss Clay has studied these expressions and notes that when *audê* is used in this formula it sig-
nifies that the gods "modulate their voices in some way" in order
to communicate with men.[21]

The gods can assume the language we use and understand, and
they can also bestow it where it does not naturally belong. For a
brief moment Hera makes Achilles' horse "speak with the *audê*
used by mortals," and he uses the gift appropriately to lament his
master's mortality (*Il.* 19.407). But this is a temporary crossing of
orders, and the fates soon silence him (19.418). Equally extraordinary are the robotic handmaidens Hephaestus creates for himself
with "voice, strength, and intelligence" (*audê, sthenos, noos* [*Il.*

---

[17]Conversely, when an eagle speaks to Penelope in a dream it uses "mortal"
(*broteiê*) *phônê* (*Od.* 19.545); the adjective would be redundant with *audê*.

[18]Cf. *Theog.* 142b which speaks of the cyclops as "born from the gods, but mortals
[*thnêtoi*], with human voice [*audêentes*]" (see West [1966] on *Theog.* 142). This use as
an epithet characteristic of mortals is problematic for *LfrgE* s.v. *audêeis* B because it
assumes that the gods have *audê* too; but they have it only when they assume it to
communicate to mortals.

[19]*Od.* 10.136, 11.8, etc. Note too that both Circe and Calypso also sing (*aeidein* [*Od.*
10.136, 12.449]).

[20]*Od.* 5.334. This locution gave trouble to Aristotle, who emended (fr. 171 Rose
[1886]), but not to Schol. HPQ, Aristophanes on *Od.* 5.334: these goddesses "speak
audêessa, that is, taking a share in human *phônê*."

[21]Clay (1974) 131.

17.419]). Inasmuch as these creatures are counterfeit human beings rather than gods, the voice they are given is human.[22]

The inspired poet is obviously another case in which divinity bestows a special ability to speak intelligibly on earth. Poetry is heard as a human voice—one that we use and can understand—but at the same time divine. Poets speak what is meaningful to mortals but as no other human might speak. We probably should not try to specify in rhetorical terms how the poet's "divine *audê*" differs from other forms of eloquence. The special quality of this song is not likely to be located in its form rather than content; we can simply observe that the Muses seem to raise the power of human speech to a higher order. Yet it remains to ask in the poets' terms in what respect the poet's song is divine. One way gods may augment the voice is simply to make it louder, but volume would seem to be an aspect of *phônê:* so heralds have a voice (*phônê*) like the gods (*Il.* 19.250; cf. *Il.* 5.786). Though sheer vocal power and a pleasant timbre are undoubtedly aids to an oral poet, they hardly seem to be all a poet needs, and such heralds are not said to have *thespis audê.* Nor is the bestowing of this voice on poets a kind of ventriloquism. When the Muses "breathe divine *audê*" into Hesiod to make him a poet, it is not a matter of his mouthing their words any more than it is in the case of the horse Xanthus. (Hera gives him the ability to speak, but does not put the sentiments and words in his mouth.) Clay concludes of poets and heralds that when they are said to be "like the gods in their voice" this "does not suggest that they possess divine speech, but rather that their voices are of superhuman excellence or power."[23] The clues to further defining this superhuman or excellent singing will be found in its epithet *thespis.*

---

[22]In Hesiod's Pandora story Hephaestus gives her "a human's voice and strength" (*anthrôpou . . . audên kai sthenos,* [*Works and Days* 61–62]). When Hermes adds *phônê* a few lines later (77–80), Hesiod is either inattentively repetitious (see West [1978] on 79) or is pairing *phônê* with *logoi* to suggest the ability to make audible her "lies and deceitful tales." Cf. *LfrgE* s.v. *audê* 4a. Related creations by Hephaestus are animated dogs (*Odyssey* 7.91ff.) and the crown for Pandora, which has on it all the monsters of the land and sea (582) "like living things with voice [*phônessin*]" (*Theog.* 584).

[23]Clay (1974) 131.

Thespis: Divine Speaking

The mysterious modulation of the human voice in the direction of the divine that is poetry is summed up in the epithet *thespis.* I have noted that Homer and Hesiod restrict *thespis* to describing the "singer" (*aoidos*), his "song" (*aoidê*), and his "voice" (*audê*).[24] In Homer it occurs only in a formula with the word for singing, the line-ending *thespin aoidên* (*Od.* 1.328, 8.498; *H. Herm.* 442) and in a related form in a generic description of the singer (17.385). Hesiod uses these terms only of the "voice" (*audên / thespin*) that the Muses breathe into him (*Theog.* 32) and in a generic description of the man whom the Muses make "divinely voiced" (*thespion audêenta* [fr. 310.2 M-W]).

The complex idea of a "divine *audê*" is a special mark of the singer. Just as, in all of hexametric poetry, only professional bards are properly called "singers" (*aoidoi*) and only to such singers is given the gift of "singing" (*aoidê*), so too, singers alone are said to be "like the gods in their voice [*audê*]" or to have a "divine *audê*." The restrictiveness of this phrase helps us distinguish singing from other forms of eloquence, for no other figure in epic has quite the same gift. The *audê* of eloquent Nestor "flows sweeter than honey from his tongue" (*Il.* 1.249), but inasmuch as he is not inspired, it is not called "divine." Hesiod can say that the Muses bestow a beneficent kind of speech on the good king, but it is words (*epea*) that "flow honeyed from his mouth" (*Theog.* 84); the Muse-given *audê* that "flows sweet from the mouth" is reserved for singers (*Theog.* 97; cf. Hymn 25.5.). The phrase that serves Homer for poetry, *thespis aoidê,* "divine song," is a specific "divine" kind of voice, *thespis audê.*

It is clear that *thespis* is a traditional epithet for poetry and evidently expressed something abiding in the nature of poetry. Etymologically, it is apparently composed of a root that underlies the Greek for "god" (as in "theology") and a word for speaking; its original meaning, then, seems to be something like "pronounced

---

[24]For the exceptional phrase *thespis aella,* used in a Homeric hymn, see note 49 herein.

or spoken by a god."[25] But since epic uses the epithet so re-strictively, the phrase *thespis aoidê* is almost a cipher, and it is not clear in what respect the poet, his song, and his voice are "divine" or "divinely spoken." Obviously, some aspect of the Muses' spon-sorship of singing is indicated here, but it is only later that forms of this word were reinterpreted in the sense of "prophetic" or "prophesy."[26] A better sense of the meaning of *thespis* can be got from its fuller form, *thespesios*. This word too is used of "singing" (that of Thamyris and the Sirens),[27] but it is also applied more widely in epic. Indeed, it is so widely used that sometimes the etymological meaning, "spoken by a god," seems to have been lost, and it is applied to things like a fire or a gleam of light that have nothing to do with speaking or the gods. But the the dictio-naries may be too quick to say that *thespesios* has lost its original sense and only means "marvelous" or extraordinary in epic.[28] For it can be seen that in almost all cases the "marvelous" objects denoted by *thespesios* are such as confound cognition and articula-tion: they are multitudes, mixtures, immensities in the literal sense. I think this word and *thespis* belong in a semantic field that preserves the concept of the unutterably large or the indescribably great. the related words I will look at are *thesphatos*, "pronounced by a god," "fated"; *athesphatos*, "beyond the god's pronounce-ments"; and *aspetos*, "unsayable," "ineffable."

It has been suggested that originally these words were a magical, apotropaic defense against naming "unspeakable" abominations, lest they be inadvertently summoned.[29] With the passing of such beliefs, the words would have remained in the poetic language but

[25]So *LfrgE* s.v. *thespesios* B and s.v. *thespis* B.

[26]For post-Homeric uses of *thespis* and *thespizein* as "prophetic" and "prophesy" (1950) in poetry, see Fraenkel (1950) on *Agamemnon* 1154. Koller (1965) would reduce the Homeric meaning to an original "prophetic," but this a too-narrow sense of prophecy, one aiming solely at the future.

[27]*Il.* 2.600; *Od.* 12.158. Cf. Pindar's reference to the "god-spoken words" (*thespe-siôn epeôn*) of Homer's poetry (*Isth.* 4.39).

[28]Respectively the glosses of LSJ and Chantraine (1977) s.v. *thespesios*.

[29]Such seems to be the case for *ouk onomastos*, "not to be named," used of the hundred-handed monsters, and "accursed Troy" (*Theog.* 148; *Od.* 19.260); so too *ou (ti) phateios*, "not to be mentioned," of Cerberus and the Gorgons (*Theog.* 310; *Shield* 230). See West on *Theog.* 148 and *LfrgE* s.v. *aspetos* B.

reduced to strong intensives (like English "unspeakable"). Hence we may see in the poetry that in some formulas *thespis* is apparently replaced by the more neutral *theios*, "godlike"; and *aspetos*, "unspeakably many or much," by *asbestos*, "unquenchable." Nevertheless, sometimes their root meanings are quite apparent, and though the etymological connections of these words with speech in many cases seems to have been effaced, the contexts in which they are used testify to a persistent idea that the "marvelous" exceeds human speech or may be spoken only by a god. In Homeric and Hesiodic poetry they congregate around experiences of the "marvelous" that are daunting or disconcerting, and the objects they modify are very numerous, manifold, or so shapeless as to defy description. Collectively, they suggest a class of objects and phenomena that are sublime in the sense that I describe in Chapter 2: they refer to great multitudes or powers that overwhelm human speech. A further look at these associated words suggests that the Muses make the poet's voice different from that of others in its ability to transcend such limitations.

Thesphatos is made of the same root as in *thespis* for "god" and a different root for "utter" or "pronounce" (as in "phatic," "infant," and "fate"). Its general sense is fairly clear: *thesphatos* refers to things that are "uttered by a god" in the sense of being "decreed" or "fated," since it is often used of portentous or destined events, that is, those that have been ordained or predicted in divine speech. Zeus in particular is the god who can pronounce or know what is *thesphatos* (e.g., *Il.* 8.477; Hesiod fr. 193.8 M-W), whereas mortals, of course, do not normally know what has been "decreed by god" (*Il.* 5.64). But other gods may "learn" the fates from the *omphê* of Zeus (*H. Herm.* 472; cf. 534), and demigods and prophets may communicate them to mortals—as does Circe to Odysseus (*Od.* 12.155) or Proteus to Menelaus (*Od.* 4.561).[30]

In *athesphatos* we have the same word with what seems to be the the privative prefix *a-*.[31] But *athesphatos* appears not to mean simply

---

[30]On the use of *thesphatos* in *Od.* 7.143, see note 40 herein.

[31]*LfrgE* s.v. *athesphatos*. Chantraine (1977) s.v. takes the *a-* as intensive, and sees the word as a synonym of *thesphatos*, but reducing the two terms to synonyms would not account for the latter word's distinctive association with fate and destiny. Benveniste (1969) 413–415.

"what has not been decreed by the gods," for we see it used of such unfated things as the wine that gets Elpenor drunk (*Od.* 11.61) or of longer winter nights (*Od.* 11.373, 15.392). Accordingly, some interpret *athesphatos* as "monstrous," that is, what goes beyond the gods' decrees or the dooms of "fate."[32] But it is better to follow Hermann Fränkel, who argues that *athesphatos* is a cognitive rather than a moral term, closer to "unlimited" than "unfitting." He takes it as the negation of *thesphatos* in the sense of "defined by the gods"; hence, *athesphatos* refers to things not subject to definite limitation or which go beyond their proper bounds.[33] But what goes beyond the gods' cosmic articulations also has a cognitive dimension for mortals: thus, the word makes sense as applied to a "great [*polus*] storm of hail or snow" (*Il.* 10.6), a raging sea, also called "boundless" (*Od.* 7.273), or great amounts of corn, oxen, or wine (*Od.* 13.244, 20.211, 11.61). *Athesphatos*, then, though it has evolved away from meaning literally "not pronounced by a god," is still connected to speech because it refers to things that are beyond mortal articulation or exhaustive definition.

The idea that some things might go beyond the powers of mortals to tell is at the root of *aspetos*, literally, "not to be spoken" or "ineffable." Frequently it is used of multitudinous things—royal flocks (*Il.* 11.704), gifts (*Od.* 20.342), money (*Od.* 14.297), or abundant meat (*Od.* 9.162).[34] If the word is applied to such phenomena as flame, air, "broad" earth, or ocean, so that its etymological meaning seems to have degenerated into a general "immense,"[35] such objects have in common with the *athesphatos* group the fact that they are, as a scholiast puts it, "very great, numerous and not

[32]Leaf (1900–1902) on *Il.* 3.4.

[33]Fränkel (1923) 281–282. Similarly, Benveniste (1969) 414–415 defines *athesphatos* as "that to which no limit has been set by divine pronouncement": as opposed to what is *thesphatos*, "with fixed limits" decreed or uttered by the all-knowing god.

[34]Further passages in *LfrgE* s.v. 1ab.

[35]Chantraine (1977) s.v.: "'infinite, immense,' though the original sense is likely 'unsayable'" ("'infini, immense' mais le sens originel doit bien être 'indicible'"). *LfrgE* s.v. E reports that the *a-* may be intensive, but see s.v. B: "originally, probably in connection with sensations that exceed the power of speech (or representation) . . . later, generally emphatic, for what is extraordinary or of abnormal dimensions" ("urspr. wohl in bezug auf Eindrücke, die das Sprach- (u. Vorstellungs-) Vermögen übersteigen . . . dann überhaupt emphatisch von Aussergewöhnlichem, über das normale Mass Hinausgehendem").

to be taken in at a single glance."[36] *Aspetos* is always used of things that are beyond precise measurement and so not to be fully comprehended in speech.[37]

Within this cognitive sublime I would put *thespesios* and *thespis,* "spoken by a god." Sometimes *thespesios* retains its etymological connection with speech in Homer,[38] but it may also describe objects that are "divine" simply by virtue of belonging to or being connected with a god: such are the threshold of Zeus (*Il.* 1.591), the fleece of Polyphemus's prize ram (*Od.* 9.434), or the aroma of the wine of Maron, Apollo's priest (*Od.* 9.211).[39] Yet, when the word has no immediate connection with a particular divinity, *thespesios* remains attached to "marvelous" objects that are extraordinary in a particular way: they are multitudes, mixtures, immensities in the literal sense. In such contexts the word might be rendered as "unearthly," but with the connotation that such things are what (only) a god might say because they confound human cognition and articulation: they are by nature so borderless or unarticulated that they defy expression or boggle the mind. In Homer such divine gifts are often said to be "poured down" on their recipients, as when Athena "pours down" an "unearthly" grace over a favorite to make him more beautiful or to render him invisible (*Od.* 2.12 = 17.63, 8.19, 7.42).[40] Similarly inarticulable, streaming, and befuddling are the "unearthly" mists and clouds that gods "pour down upon" or dispel from armies (*Il.* 15.669, 23.342). "Divine" is not a strong enough gloss here, for *thespesios* suggests a special kind of copi-

[36]Commenting on *Il.* 16.300. The scholiast's term (*asunoptos*) nicely opposes the Aristotelian prescription that ideal plots be not too large but "easily taken in in a single view" (*eusunoptos* [*Poetics* 1451a4; cf. 1459a33]). Frisk (1960–70) s.v. glosses *aspetos* "unendlich, unermesslich" ("endless, immeasurable").

[37]Cf. *LSJ* s.v. "*unspeakable, unutterable;* mostly in sense of *unspeakably great . . .;* less freq. of number, *countless.*" *LfrgE* (s.v. *B*) divides the uses of epic *aspetos* under two heads: (1) "'unsayable,' i.e., 'vast, many,' of great quantity" ("*unsagbar,* [*gross, viel*] von grosser Quantität"), and (2) a single example of an "adverbial" use—*Il.* 2.367, discussed in note 43 herein.

[38]E.g., an adverbial form clearly means "by divine decree" in *Il.* 2.367.

[39]So too it is used of the "unearthly" cave of the Nymphs in *Od.* 13.363 (cf. 24.6 of an eerie cave in a simile).

[40]In this vein I would explain the use of *thesphatos* for the mist Athena "pours" over Odysseus (*Od.* 7.143), a mist that is also called *thespesios* (7.42).

ousness, even unwieldiness, like the "unearthly wealth" that Zeus "pours down" on a king (*Il.* 2.670).[41]

Though the specific literal meaning at root of *thespesios* and *thespis* may have been eroded in some uses, they both belong to a semantic field that preserves the concept of the unutterably large. Something bestowed by the gods may originally have been called *thespesios* because it was such a thing as only god could tell or describe. The "divine" aspect of the poet's voice, *thespis audê*, then may be its ability to encompass and master the sublime infinity of the past. In connection with speech, these words carry the suggestion that the most ambitious forms of language must face the ineffable immensities of the world. The capacious voice of the *thespis aoidos* again allies him with prophets like Teiresias and Melampus, who can "catalog" or "tell all" the manifold dooms of fate (*thesphata* [*Od.* 11.151,297]). I think it is significant too that when *athesphatos* is twice used for unusually long nights (*Od.* 11.373, 15.392), these are nights to be filled with stories.

Thespis aoidê, then, defines the poetry whose object, the infinite past, is such a vast thing, as may be seen in a passage that is paradoxically taken to indicate the word's development into a general intensive meaning "great." In *Iliad* 15.637 it seems as if the instrumental *thespesiêi* should be translated as "greatly": "All the Achaeans / were routed 'greatly' by Hector and Zeus."[42] But this line describes a confused scattering of heroes, emphasized in two preceding similes of the sublime: a ship capsizing in waves and foam (15.623–628) and a lion attacking a "myriad" herd (15.630–636). In context, the word suggests that the Achaean army was scattered "in a way [so confused] that only a god could describe [it]." Note too that immediately thereafter the poet begins to name Hector's victims in catalog style (15.638ff.), so that this single word, inserted before a catalog and after a pair of sublime similes, is the functional equivalent of the *recusatio* in 12.175–178 discussed in Chapter 2.[43]

---

[41]The scholiast rightly explains "many and in a heap"; in telling the same story of Tlepolemus (*Ol.* 7.50), Pindar puts it that Zeus "rained down *much* gold."
[42]So *LfrgE* s.v. *thespesios* B.
[43]So I would explain the sole example *LfrgE* s.v. 2 gives of the presumed "weak-

Thespis audê approaches a paradox or oxymoron: it is a *human* voice, but one that can include all the incidents of the divinely speakable numerous to give us a full vision of the great unseen history of the world.[44] But if it is a sublime of sense and meaning, a sublime of the intelligible voice cataloging, it is also one of sheer power. The objects and phenomena described by these words are also so great or overwhelming as to provoke wonder (*thauma*) in men and a sense of the dynamic sublime in readers: so when Telemachus gazes upon the the splendid palace of Nestor, he speaks of "ineffably many" (*aspetos*) metals that make it up and compares it to the hall of Zeus (*Od.* 4.74–75). Similarly, when *aspetos* is applied to "woods," it suggests many, many trees; but it often turns out that this wood is about to be consumed in an awesome conflagration.[45] Hence we find it adding height to similes of the natural sublime:

> Like a fire that blazes in an *aspetos* wood
> on mountain peaks, and the gleam appears from far off,
> So, as they went, from their bronze unearthly [*thespesiê*]
> a ray, shining in all directions, went through the air to heaven.
>
> [*Iliad* 2.455–458]

The association of *thespesios* with a terrifying, dynamic sublime is clearest when it is used of aspects of nature. Like "ineffable" (*aspetos*), *thespesios* describes awesome natural phenomena, especially as composing many particulars—a storm, snow, hail. Again, sometimes these might be thought of as "divine" in the simple sense of "god-sent," such as the tempestuous wind Zeus raises (*Od.* 9.68 = 12.314), but this wind happens also to be part of a storm that hides

---

ened sense" of *aspetos:* when Apollo says to Aeneas "you (Trojans) tremble in an *aspetos* way and do not fight" (*Iliad* 17.332), the unique use of this word as an adverb may mean more than "very much"; it may refer to their indescribable confusion and disorganized din.

[44]Hence later developments of *audê* to mean oracle: Euripides *Iphigeneia in Tauris* 976; cf. Sophocles *Oedipus the King* 392.

[45]*Aspetos* is used of the wood gathered for Patroclus's "great" pyre (*Il.* 23.127) and for Hector's, gathered over nine days (24.784). Cf. Hesiod *Works and Days* 511: *nêritos hulê*, an "uncountable wood." (In Hymn 26.10 it is used of a living wood that is filled with the noise (*bromos*) of Dionysus reveling with his Nymphs.)

heaven and earth, and the astonishing, disorienting qualities of such objects are more often the point of emphasis. In particular *thespesios* may describe natural phenomena that are accompanied by great noise and destruction: the word is applied to the sound of the west and north winds as they rise up, driving a storm (*Il.* 23.213); to the unearthly din of the east and south winds smashing together trees in a "deep wood" (*Il.* 16.769, in a simile); to the "unearthly uproar" of a gust of winds that strike the sea while many waves roil about (*Il.* 13.797, in a simile).

This dynamic sublime I think tries to capture the sheer phonetic power of the poet's *thespis audê*. The brute material power that a sublime voicing requires is suggested by phrases referring to the "unearthly din" of nature—its great, clashing, startling sounds (*êkhêi thespesiêi*). Often indeed sent by a god, such sounds are also typically the din, hubbub, and confused uproar that comes from such crowds as routed armies or from contending natural forces. The "unearthly din" is usually disconcerting and often transcendent, "reaching through the ether to heaven." So, for example, the "unearthly din" of battle goes up to heaven and reaches the rays of Zeus (*Il.* 13.834, 837; cf. 15.355); it is heard when Hector and his men "pour" missiles upon the Greeks (*Il.* 8.159) or when they attack, spurred on by Zeus, who stirs up a dust storm to "bewitch the mind of the Achaeans" (*Il.* 12.252, 255). Similar terrifying sounds often accompany routs, as when Patroclus scatters the Trojans with "an unearthly uproar" (*homados* [*Il.* 16.295]), or the Achaeans are oppressed by Hector and his "unearthly shouting" (*alalêtos* [*Il.* 18.149]).[46] These sounds are not individuated or intelligible; they typically come from a shower of weapons, a mass of men, or a single man shouting. And they can cause fear: the echo from the mourning of Thetis and the Nereids for Achilles causes an "unearthly trembling" among the Achaeans (*Od.* 24.49).[47] Hence fear or personified Panic is also *thespesios* (*Il.* 17.118, 15.637), not simply because it is often "divine(ly sent)," but because such routs

---

[46]The same words are used when Heracles and Cycnus, two divine offspring, close in single combat (*Shield of Heracles* 383).

[47]Cf. Sappho 44.26–27 Voigt: the sound of a maiden's chorus reaches heaven through the air. Similar is *Od.* 11.43.

are also typically either occasioned by a sublime epiphany or accompanied by a disordered and noisy confusion.

The poet's epithet *thespis*, then, belongs to a semantic field in which great multitudes are expressed as beyond mortal articulation, as ineffable or what gods might speak, and also as of a superhuman, almost unendurable force. Though the range of objects to which these words are applied extends slightly beyond the strictly "speakable," all are the kinds of phenomena that cannot be reduced to an exact enumeration of details and that at the same time provoke wonder, as one of the most sublime of Homeric similes illustrates. At the end of book 8 of the *Iliad* (554–559) the Trojan campfires on the plain are compared to stars in the *aspetos* ether; it is just a few lines later (*Il.* 9.2) that an "unearthly panic" (*thespesios*) seizes the Greeks. This panic is not, at least not directly, god-sent, and the scholiast seems thus to have rightly sensed that the word is used to indicate that it was a "great" (*pollê*) fear; for immediately there follows a simile comparing the feeling in the hearts of the Achaeans to a sea that is heaped up in masses (*amudis*) by two winds. This vocabulary and the sublime similes combine to dramatize the multitudes and immensities that threaten intellection and stun the beholder. In Hesiod too we can observe these words used to signal the sublime, and in a context where the content of the Homeric similes appears as narrated fact. In a climactic moment in the *Theogony*, Zeus takes up his thunderbolts against the Titans: throwing them in heaps (*amudis* [689]), he made the *aspetos* wood crackle loudly and "an *aspetos* flame reached the bright ether" (*Theog.* 694, 698).[48] This blinded the Titans, "mighty though they were," and an "unearthly" (*thespesios*) heat seized Chaos. This passage manages to evoke in narrated cosmogony the sublime of Homeric similes, and it uses similar diction to do so. With such language the poet creates a scene that, "to see with one's eyes or hear with one's ears, was as if earth and wide heaven came together" (700–703).[49]

---

[48]See West (1966) for the reading of 698.

[49]In this context it is possible to understand the sole epic use of *thespis* outside the context of poetry. In a line-ending formula (*thespis aella*, apparently modeled on the formula *thespin aoidên*) it modifies the Zeus-sent gale that snatched Ganymede up to Olympus. Perhaps it is called "divine" because it was sent by Zeus or, more simply,

We have, then, a set of words that originally had related meanings suggesting that the language of the gods excels human language both in its power to express everything in the world and in its sheer material force. And the voice that poets borrow from them shares in both these sublimes. That the heart of the poet's song is found in the sound as well as the sense of his voice appears in two unique epithets for song in epic.

Thespis Audê: Unwearying Voice, Unbreakable Sound

The sublime and threatening power of song that *thespis* names can also be observed in a final set of words, a peculiar triad of predicates for "singing" or voice in Homer and Hesiod: *athesphatos humnos,* "song without limits"; *akamatos audê,* "weariless voice"; and *phônê arrêktos,* "unbreakable sound or voice." Beyond such immediately intelligible epithets for song, such as "sweet," "charming," "holy," "fair," "clear" or "sorrowful,"[50] these phrases suggest, like *thespis,* a transcendence in the poet's voice and song, but one that is reducible to the bare force of voicing, a material sublime of song.

We begin with a word from the sublime semantic group, which is used once of song in Hesiod. The passage (*Works and Days* 646–662) is a transitional proem in which Hesiod promises to teach Perses about sailing the seas, even though he himself is hardly knowledgeable about such matters. But he is in a position to reveal such things because the Muses have taught him to sing the *athesphaton humnon* (662). *Athesphatos* is not a good word merely to indicate the "divine" inspiration that puts the poet in touch with matters beyond his direct experience. Fränkel would take it as meaning that the poet is "free," to sing "wherever I will" because no limits have

---

because it is a strong wind. Yet too it is a bewildering wind for Ganymede's father, who "did not know / in what direction the *thespis* gale had snatched his son" (*H. Aphr.* 207–208). This gale is similar in effect to a wind (*aella*) in a Homeric battle simile, which Zeus drives with his thunderbolts in an "unearthly uproar" (*Il.* 13.795, 797).

[50]See *LfrgE* s.v. *aoidê* G for references.

been set to his song.[51] But I think the song is *athesphatos* because it reveals what is in the "mind of Zeus" (661); all-knowing, all-seeing Zeus is the one who truly knows the "measures of the much-murmuring sea" (648). Hesiod's "unlimited" hymn enables the poet to speak of something so measureless as the sea, which is typically imagined as infinitely wide, without any fixed points of reference in it.[52] Hence I think Emile Benveniste is right in taking Hesiod to say that the Muses have taught him "a song which has no limits."[53] Only a song from the Muses could measure the sublime enormity of the sea.

This idea of poetry as a sublime voicing is matched by a counterimage in the description of one of Hesiod's most awesome monsters, Typho. The last of Earth's children, Typho mounts the final and most nearly successful challenge to Zeus before he can take up his orderly reign on Olympus (*Theog.* 820–880). Marcel Detienne and Jean-Pierre Vernant see Typho as "a power of confusion and disorder, an agent of chaos," and an antagonist to Zeus's "measure."[54] In form this prodigious monster (*pelôrê* [821]) appears to resemble a dragon,[55] but among the dreadful features typically found in dragons the poet emphasizes especially Typho's din of voices: sometimes he speaks with the language of the gods,[56] but he roars, hisses, bellows, and barks as well. In a brief but dense passage nearly all the words for voice are attributed to Typho: *phônê* (829), *opa* (830) *phthengesthai* (831), and in a moment of categorical transgression, the *ossa* of a bull (831–832).[57] As Detienne and Vernant put it, Typho's voices transfer to the auditory level the traditional polymorphous nature of the beast.[58] He is a "marvel to

---

[51]Fränkel (1923) 281.

[52]The sea (*thalassa*) is itself called *athesphatos* (*Od.* 7.272; *Hymn* 15.4), and "uncontrollable" (*amaimaketos* [*Shield* 207]), and (as *pontos*) is especially qualified by epithets that mean "without borders"; cf. *LfrgE* s.v. *apeirôn* B 1ab and *apeiritos* B 1a.

[53]Benveniste (1969) 414.

[54]Detienne and Vernant (1974) 115, 116.

[55]Cf. *Il.* 5.741; *Od.* 11.634. For studies of Typho, see West's discussion and bibliography (1966) 379–383 and Detienne and Vernant (1974) 114–120.

[56]For this reading of *Theog.* 831, see Snell (1924) 43.

[57]If this use of *ossa* is not deliberately confusing, it may be a case of what West says are the awkwardnesses and difficulties "one would expect of a poet like Hesiod writing on a theme like the Typhonomachy" (1966) 382.

[58]Detienne and Vernant (1974) 116.

hear" (834) in a transfixing sense, for he is fearful, paralyzing.[59]
This is the voice of a creature who with his hundred snaky heads
(825) reminds us of Homer's Gorgons.[60]

In part, then, Hesiod's Typho is a mind-boggling image of un-
controlled and undifferentiated voice: "In each of his dreadful
heads were voice-boxes [*phônai*] / each sending forth a voice, of
every kind and unlimited in number [*pantoiên op' hieisai athesphaton*]" (*Theog.* 829–830).[61] Typho's voices and sounds are not
wholly intelligible, which distinguishes his *opa athesphaton* from the
athesphaton humnon taught by the Muses.[62] The diction "sending
forth" a voice that is "of every kind and unlimited in number"
suggests that the *opa* this beast utters is a superhuman but infernal
counterpart to the "immortal" (or "lovely," etc.) *ossa* that the Muses
"send forth."[63] It is a super- and subhuman version of the orderly,
Olympian-sanctioned singing of Hesiod—"he who sends forth the
audê."

The special difference between divine voicing and this inhuman
cacophony may be expressed in another striking word used of the
Muses' voice in Hesiod—"unwearying." When they sing the past,

[59]In Homer, Typho occurs only parenthetically, but significantly, as the focus of
the final simile magnifying the marshaled Greek host (*Il.* 2.780–783).
[60]The face of the Gorgon is terrifying in *Il.* 8.349 and 11.36, and there are snaky,
"unapproachable, unspeakable" Gorgons in the *Shield of Heracles* 223–237. Hesiod
says the Gorgons live with the "clear-voiced Hesperides" a trio of lovely singers,
like the Sirens (*Theog.* 274–281); but the Hesperides are no threat to men, perhaps
because they sing only to themselves in their distant paradise, see West (1966) on
Theog. 275.
[61]This last phrase and interpretation are taken from Benveniste (1969) 414, who
compares the *athesphaton humnon* given to Hesiod by the Muses. One might also
compare the gifts of Poseidon to Periclymenus in the *Catalogue*, "gifts of all kinds,
not to be named" (*dôra pantoia, ouk onomasta*)—i.e., the ability to change into various
animal shapes (Fr. 33a17–18 M-W).
[62]Pindar (*Pythian* 1.1–27) also evokes Typho as an awe-inspiring noise contrasted
with the "golden lyre" of the Olympians. The lyre brings us ordered dance and
quenches even Zeus's "thunderbolt of ever-streaming fire" (5–6). But when the
disordered creatures of the world (those "whom Zeus loves not") hear the sound
(*boan*) of the Muses, it astonishes (*atuzontai*) them, on land and over the "uncontrollable" sea ([13–14] *amaimaketos* is used by Homer of the Chimaera [*Il.* 6.179, 16.329;
Theog. 319]). Such is Typho, whose volcanic eruptions are "a marvelous prodigy to
see, a marvel even to hear of from those who have been there" (26).
[63]One can compare also *Hymn* 27.18, where the chorus of the Muses and Graces
celebrate Artemis by "sending forth their immortal *opa* / in a hymn to Leto" (*hai d'
ambrosien op' ieisai / humneusin Letô*).

present, and future, their *"audê* flows unwearyingly [*akamatos*] from their mouths" (*Theog.* 39–40; cf. 44). An unwearying stream of voice appears to be the supreme eloquence, for we have seen that what an *audê* does at its best is flow (*Theog.* 84, 97; *Il.* 1.249). But for Hesiod to say that the Muses' voice flows "unwearyingly" may be more than a synonym for natural enough expressions such as calling their voice "immortal" (*Theog.* 43, 69; cf. Hymn 27.18). In Hesiod the adjective *akamatos* is used of the fire Zeus denies to mortals (*Theog.* 563, 566) and to characterize attributes of demigods: Atlas's hands (*Theog.* 519, 747), Typho's feet (824), and the strength that permits Argus never to sleep (fr. 188.3). In Homer it is applied only to fire, and in the *Iliad* it is usually an extraordinary or god-sent fire, such as the "weariless" and "unquenchable" fire that the Trojans put to the Greek ships, or the magic flares that blaze from a rampaging hero's helmet.[64] We gather from these uses that *akamatos* describes again a sublime force or fire, often destructive or terrifying and always unspent.[65] This unwearying stream of song seems to be the Muses' special grace: whenever they appear in epic they are singing, and the word evokes the awesomely enduring but beneficent voice of the Muse, "ever the singer," as Alcman calls her (14a Page).

Such a gift belongs to the gods, and may be destructive in mortals, as can be seen in the case of Tithonus. In the Homeric *Hymn to Aphrodite*, Tithonus wins from the gods the gift of immortality but not eternal youth; as he aged unendingly and lost his physical strength, Aphrodite confined him in a chamber, where "his voice [*phonê*] flows ceaselessly [*aspetos*]" (5.237).[66] This is one human

[64]*Il.* 16.122–123; 15.598, 731; 5.4; 18.225. Cf. 21.341 (a fire sent by Hephaestus to help Achilles against Xanthus) and 23.52 (on Patroclus's pyre). *Akamatos* is also used of a fire in a simile in 21.13. On the use of *akamatos* in the *Odyssey*, see the next note.

[65]The *Odyssey* would seem to disrupt the pattern and to be playfully reducing the epithet (as it sometimes will), for it uses *akamatos* of hearth fires that are kindled by slave women or even Melanthus (*Od.* 20.123, 21.181). But the first is explicitly the sacred hearth fire, never to be allowed to die away, and these lowly characters only "stoke it" (*anakaiô*).

[66]"Ceaselessly" is from Allen, Halliday, and Sikes (1936). The line seems related to *Il.* 18.402–403: Hephaestus worked as a smith for nine years in the cave of the sea Nymphs "and around there the stream of Ocean / flowed ceaselessly [*aspetos*]." The poet of the hymn puts the flourishing youth of Tithonus "by the streams of Ocean at the ends of the earth" (227). Cf. *LfrgE* s.v. *aspetos* 1c for discussion and references.

voice that can, by divine intervention, flow in an unbroken stream; yet Tithonus pays a price: though the tale of his transformation into a cicada seems not to be known to the author of the hymn, his ever-diminishing voice is called a *phônê*, not an *audê*, perhaps because its articulations are becoming ever fainter. Poets by contrast are allowed a divine *audê*, flowing and sweet (*Theog.* 97). Through the Muses' favor, the poet of the past partakes of their unwearying stream of voice and survives to give us at least a part of their unending singing.

If Homer were to speak of his "unwearying" voice we might understand it as another negation of the reduction of poetry to shapable matter, for in Homer "wearying" has to do with craft, as in the formula "he wearied himself out working," or "wrought with toil" (*kame teukhôn*), used of Hephaestus and human artisans fashioning a variety of objects.[67] But we do not find his version of this word (*akamas*) used of voice. Yet Hesiod's use of this adjective helps us better understand the one time that Homer mentions his poet's voice, at *Il* 2.490, where he says that he could not sing all who came to Troy even if he had an "unbreakable *phônê* and a breast of bronze within." Homer rejects as inadequate not the "unwearying voice" of Hesiod's Muses but a voice that is more solid and yet "unbreakable" (*arrêktos*). Calling this voice "unbreakable," is, as I noted in Chapter 4, suggestive of the impiety in such a wish; for the word is elsewhere, with the pointed exception of the Achaean wall, a quality of divine attributes. The poet desires not a voice that is "unbreakable" matter but a sound that might, through all its stops and starts, at least echo the perpetual song of Muses.

The poet here forgoes a material enduringness or strength of voice, as is also suggested in his refusal of a brazen breast.[68] Bronze is often called "unerodable" (*ateirês*).[69] It may be a metaphor of

---

[67]Hephaestus "wrought with much toil" Pleops's scepter, (*Il* 2.101), Diomedes' corselet, (8.195), Achilles' shield (19.368); Tukhios, the shield of Ajax (7.220). Cf. Ritoók (1989) 345.

[68]West on *Theog.* 764 notes that in *Il.* 2.490 we do not expect this phrase, usually meaning "pitiless," when "enduring" is wanted.

[69]*LfrgE* s.v. Poseidon takes on the unerodable *phônê* to impersonate Chalcas (13.45), Athena to imitate Phoenix (17.558) and Deiphobus (22.227).

enduringness and power, but when it is used of the voice (*phônê*) in Homer, it suggests a loud and penetrating sound, not the meaningful *audê*. Stentorian heralds have a voice (*phônê*) like the gods (*Il.* 19.250), and when Hera impersonates one with a voice of bronze (*khalkeophônos*), she "shouts with the voice of fifty men" (*Il.* 5.786). When gods in the *Iliad* assume the "form and voice" of mortals, they may take on a "form and unerodable voice [*ateirês phônê*]."[70]

These brazen voices are unusually strong, but essentially in their massy solidity; the metaphor of a bronze voice evokes the dynamic sublime of sheer power rather than the mathematical sublime of totality: Cerberus, Typho's offspring, also has a bronze voice (*Theog.* 311). One final example of a brazen voice combines the dynamic sublimes of the terrific sound and the blinding gleam: before he is to get his dazzling armor, Achilles leaps to the battlements and panics the Trojans with a shout of pure sound: "His voice [*phônê*] was as clear as the blare of a trumpet" (18.221). This shout is but half of the awesome epiphany: Athena sends a radiant blaze of fire shining from a gold cloud round his head and stands beside him, lending the power of her voice (*phthengksat'* [218]). This double sublime—the Trojans heard his "bronze voice" (*opa khalkeon* [*Il.* 18.222]) and saw the "unwearying fire" around his head (*akamaton pur* [18.225])—"stirred up unspeakable [*aspeton*] confusion among the Trojans" (18.218).

We may say in structural terms that Homer and Hesiod give us an anatomy of sublime voices across the categories of monster, mortal, and god. The dynamic sublime of sheer volume is instantiated by Cerberus, Stentor, and Hera, respectively. Similarly, Typho, the poet, and the Muses represent the mathematical sublime of the infinite in these same classes. The poet's "divine human voice" does not hubristically aspire to Tithonus's immortality or to the unlimited power of Typho. Yet his *thespis audê* gives us more than the most powerful *phônê* can. If the mind of the Muses is capable of subsuming all the facts of the world and their order, their "wearyless human voice" (*akamatos audê*) is capable of uttering

---

[70]All in scenes of great contention. In 13.45 Poseidon becomes like Calchas, rallying the hard-pressed Greeks; in 17.555 Athena as Phoenix addresses (*prosêuda*) Menelaus to rouse him to seize Patroclus's body. In 22.227 Athena as Deiphobus stands beside Hector being pursued by Achilles.

them in a continuous stream. When this speech descends to earth, albeit in the reduced form of *thespis audê,* it retains the ability, if not to say all, at least to say each thing in its particularity, to present the detailed, circumspect account of the past without breaking down or leaving gaps. Human speech may attain this sublime, which is one of content and form at once; it may be *thespis aoidê.*

Thespis aoidê, then, is our access to a past in which every detail has the right, by the mere fact of having existed, to be mentioned, to be heard again on earth. The poetry of the past, to be adequate to that enormous past, must be a fluent, continuous voicing that goes beyond the speech of any other powerful speaker. The poet's "divine human voice" is not an oxymoron or ventriloquism but an epiphany: divine knowledge appears in sound and presents to human senses a world not otherwise apparent. This sound, the body of the poet's voice, is the substance of the heroic world in all its presence; in it the human account of the past and the divine perspective upon it, as far as they can, appear together on earth.

No material device can embody or substitute for the divine afflatus: if his heart were bronze and he had ten mouths and the voice were unbreakable within him, the poet would still need the Muse and her special voice. This is the fiction at the heart of song which the poet will not let the pen or any toiling art approach. The singer, as vehicle of this fluid, ever-renewed voice, does not want to be mistaken for an artisan, nor does he want his singing to be identified with any visible thing, any text. Such song is a voice, the sound of poetry is its soul. It is not to be wrought or sought, and it is never to be confused with the still, silent letters on a page.

Poetry for Homer, then, was singing, not as an abstraction but as a voicing. It was making the names of heroes sound again on earth. This fiction is perhaps the one most alien to our conceptions of literature, for on its most basic level, poetry thereby becomes not an art of storytelling, but an act of mentioning: merely sounding a name, recalling an exploit or repeating a story gives life to fame and on each occasion restores the shade loitering in Hades to heroic vitality.

There is something of the catalog heritage of epic poetry in this sense of a dispassionate inventory, a placid listing of who did and said what. Of course, the poet speaks not just inventories but stories. These stories are named and defined structures of action in which the choices of heroes and their consequences ramify and reach certain resolutions. Of course, these patterns are always referred to a larger complex—the will of Zeus or fate—but to view Homer as the fashioner or shaper of his world is to invoke metaphors of the artist that are more common in a fifth-century Democritus or Pindar.

This flat *audê* is also the voice one hears as heroes speak, for speeches make up nearly half of the epics, and many follow Aristotle in making Homer the father of drama. Yet the poet becomes the speaking hero only within the world of mentioning; in the organization of epic, narration follows invocation, and reported speech follows narration. Homer's speeches appear in the poems in the first instance as part of an exact account of what was done. Although his speeches are rightly praised for their dramatic force and their subtle characterizations, and though rhapsodes could later seize on them for intensely dramatic effects, sawing the air and moving their audience to tears, the simple fact that a speech that is repeated in the story may be reiterated word for word in the text points to their basic justification in this account: a complete rendering of what happened to the heroes ideally involves repeating word by word what they said on each occasion. Speeches, no less than the exact pronunciation of a name or a deed, are finally part of that full epiphany that the poet's voice makes possible.

Modest as such a project may be, it suggests a great role for heroic song. In some sense epic reanimates the heroes, restoring them to action and speech, for the poet's voicing retains some magical power, even as it retains some of its magical taboos: naming was invocatory and not naming was apotropaic. From this point of view, each utterance is of equal value, for the opposition at work here is simply saying against not saying, naming or refusing to name. The briefest mention of the death of the most marginal character evokes that fact and preserves its fame to the same degree as the fullest and most poignant account of the fall of a Hector or a Patroclus; the cordoned bedstead, the smooth tholepin are retrieved from oblivion by poetry no less than the shield of Achilles or the palace of Menelaus. The poet's picture of song is very different from that constructed by the critic. A reader who selects "central" themes or episodes from the whole neglects the power inherent in each thing. An inventory of every third item, or only of gold-plated items, will be a totally different kind of inventory. To transform the song into an artistic structure is a distortion of this aspect of its nature. It is not a poem to be read into, not a coded message to be deciphered, not an artifact to be appreciated in aesthetic contemplation. As a form of *audê*, singing was, finally, sound and not the stored-up structure of a song.

CONCLUSION

What have I assembled here? Before characterizing the view of poetry in Homer, I want to recall the limits of this study, for every book about Homer is to some extent also about his poetics. I began by invoking Curtius's distinction of the history of the theory of poetry from the practice of poets since I have not tried to demonstrate the unconscious theory that governed his composition. The "views" of poetry that I have found in these texts can only be fictions spoken by a poetic persona or attributed to fictitious characters; they are part of the poet's larger fiction and binding neither on him nor on his audience. Hence we cannot expect to divine from the texts Homer's true and final opinions about art, and far less to use such views as authoritative rules for how to read him. It is, then, a representation of poetry I have sought; but such a representation is more than a "theme" running through the epic as it reflects on itself, although such themes have been part of my evidence. Taken as a whole, the references to poetry that I have assembled do not come together to form a leitmotif or counterpoint to the narrative, for they were found in various registers of the texts: the formalities with which the poet introduces himself and his song to his audience; the terms that tradition has left him for naming poetry, kinds of poetry, and its parts; the stories he tells about poets, perhaps idealized and archaized, within his stories.

Other stories too been consulted, especially the myths and tales that bear on the nature of language, its powers, shapes, and kinds. In reading the Homeric poems for their own representation of poetry I have tried to catch the poet not as allegorist of himself or as theorist manqué, but as a singer thinking as he sings. I have hoped to extend our awareness of Homer's poetry beyond its systems, categories, and classification and to take note of poetic choice and will animating them. In concluding these deliberations, I have no wish to extract a theory of poetry from the poems, but I want to look over what has developed to ask how far Homer has satisfied us and what we expect of poetry.

I began by trying to show how such a poetry might classify and define itself. The definitions I sought were of a poetry without texts, fixed only in the sight of the Muses. Though it may have been highly regulated by social custom and religious practice, it was still an ephemeral poetry that came and went with divine condescension. Such a poetic prescribed a singer's behavior before it prescribed a song's form, and it answered few of the demands of formalist criticism. Though highly elaborated in many of its aspects, it did not separate form from content or speak of "how" a tale is told apart from what tale is told. It sustained a view of singing in which the themes, though demonstrably variable to a tape recorder, were the only stable elements, and these it figured as paths across a celestial field.

Yet some of the lines it drew in the air, such as that encompassing the *klea andrôn*, enabled the poets to define themselves and to mark themselves off from other tellers of tales. This most important and most elusive line demarcated the realm of divine singing itself. Divinity bestowed on this special discourse about the past a near-immediate closeness to the event, approaching the closeness of seeing. The Muses not only provided knowledge of things that were gone but also superintended them, so that all the notable actions ever done remained in place under their gaze. In their eyes there is no past: to know is at once to have seen and to have in memory all the events of history in a timeless order. Homeric epic was a poetry of the invisible past, visiting an unseen realm that holds these actions as they were in life. I settled on a definition of epic as the poetry of the past in the sense that it alone claimed to make the past appear before our minds' eye. Its "art" was to be the site of an epiphany through the voice, speaking of the past beyond the limits of mortal perception and articulating it "truly," as if seeing it in all its complexity and detail. In rhetorical terms, Homer suggests that poetry achieves this effect by its very full telling, by presenting to us the actions in all their particulars as they looked to the gods at that time. But its real status was phenomenological. Making the past present, a "god-spoken song" transports us out of our present place and time and makes the past appear to us more clearly than any other version can. It knows and has seen all: the heroes, the gods—even when the heroes themselves could not see them—and makes them vivid for us.

Epic pretends that its art is not one of selection but of mentioning. But of course, the poet cuts down his story again and again, so that epic is always a human voicing that cannot embrace "all that happened." But in its crises of selection epic manages to evoke that all, and we approach a comprehension of the immeasurable past. At such moments, this nearly insubstantial, never fully apparent tradition could take on weight, even weightiness for a poet. The human epic is driven to its exclusion, and it scapegoats what cannot belong. Because performance is a speech borrowed from the Muses' vision, it becomes necessary in beginning each performance to negotiate the distance between ephemeral occasion and the perfect, unchanging song that belongs to no individual. The desire to connect this tale to a larger lineage of tales is stronger than the desire to make an autonomous whole without such a support.

If we follow Aristotle and assign epic to the long-enduring and many-formed tradition of praise poetry (noting, in addition, that such a genre is of Indo-European antiquity), we must note that it has fundamentally changed its purpose, for it no longer makes overt obeisance to king or court. It celebrates the noble ancestors of the race, all the while refusing to speak directly to those present. Its hearers too are represented as silently enchanted, pleased and inactive. If they come to know more than they knew before hearing it, they are not morally instructed or even addressed in the way that exhortation demanded.

Yet in the dynamics of performance it must always have happened that the deliberate flatness of the poet's ethos and the consistent austerity of his self-presentation were enlivened: the context of performance could excite dormant tensions in the poetry of the past in the way a magnetic current excites a field of electrons. To tell the deeds of the great men impersonally, to present them without pointing, without moralizing, was an enormous trope when facing an audience of Ionian Greeks. To be speaking at one moment as a named and known poet and then, a few lines later, as Agamemnon or Athena, was a performative tour de force that the poetry and its poetic developed and exploited fully. Here we are, centuries removed, profoundly cut off from the heroic age, and a form of song dares to claim it can present that reality simply and let us hear what the heroes said directly. In the performative context of epic poetry a great irony necessarily arises, and the poet delights in playing the past and present together. In this way the crucial relationship the poet establishes among himself, his audience, and other poets can be reinforced and figuratively represented by the relations that the poets in his songs have with their heroes and the gods.

The poet will not distract us with claims of originality, of authorship, of his own contributions; he does not want to pose as master craftsman, cunning maker, original deployer of old materials; he forgoes for the moment his own zeal to declare himself above his peers and even to set himself up for posterity. And the refusal of settling on a text is only the last of many refusals needed to purify this voice. The poet is an undeconstructed phonocentrist or, better, "audocentrist," but I have noted less how his fiction is a fiction than the many self-effacements needed to sustain it. Looking at the "voice" inside of "song" we saw that singing had to be human to be meaningful but more than human to make the past present and apparent in speech, and that speech or voice was simultaneously the poet's intelligible, perceptible, and fluent medium. Its truth was the truth of particulars, of the accumulation of details vividly seen; its substance was its ephemeral sound, finer and more lasting than bronze.

If we reflect that behind this figure of the voice was an avid and excellent Greek poet who made a living from his art, no doubt we will judge these disclaimers to be disingenuous. And much that

the poet gives up in this theory of poetry might have been re-
claimed outside the path of singing: in proem and epilogue he
might well have been able to give us that portrait of the artist we
look for, the artful, readable artist of the kind that a Pindar weaves
inextricably into his songs. But these postures would have been
asides, necessarily excluded from a song too great to bear his or
any name.

There have indeed been many refusals needed to bring before us
a poetry that is only a voice that, in its unalloyed form, flows
constantly on Olympus. Homer's poetry was not only conceived
within a world very different from our own but was also given a
very different relationship to that world. For us, the most trou-
blesome refusal may be that this oral poetry invited no reading, no
interpretation. It pretended not even to need a human audience,
since, whether or not it was heard on earth, song existed completely and timelessly in the Muses' performance. Of course, as
readers we will interpret; but in doing so we may remember that
we are listening not to that original and indifferent choir or even to
its first echoes in early Ionia, but to a book, a format for storing
singing that in some ways changed singing forever. As we try to
sound out our text, we may remember that the early form of singing lurking behind its letters presents its own idea of what poetry
may be. It was not a text, an icon, a well-shaped artifact. It was not
moral exhortation or history or the pleasurable play of subtle language. Conceived in terms shared with magic, religion, and mythology, it was nothing very much like what we are accustomed to
think of as poetry or literature or art—except, of course, insofar as
it was a poetry of the imagination.

BIBLIOGRAPHY

Periodicals are generally abbreviated as in *L'Année philologique* (with some fuller abbreviations). Abbreviations used in the notes are listed alphabetically.

Abrams, M. H. 1989. *Doing Things with Texts.* New York: Norton.
Adkins, A. W. H. 1972. "Truth, *KOSMOS*, and *ARETE* in the Homeric Poems." *CQ* 22: 5–18.
Alexiou, M. 1974. *The Ritual Lament in Greek Tradition.* Cambridge: Cambridge University Press.
Allen, T. W. 1924. *Homer: The Origins and Transmission.* Oxford: Clarendon Press.
——, ed. 1946. *Homeri opera.* 5 vols. Corr. rpt. of 1912 ed. Oxford: Clarendon Press.
Allen, T. W., W. R. Halliday, and E. E. Sikes, eds. 1936. *The Homeric Hymns.* Oxford: Clarendon Press (rpt. Amsterdam, 1983).
Aly, W. 1914. "*Rapsôidos.*" *RE*[2] 1.A: 244–249.
Austin, N. 1975. *Archery at the Dark of the Moon: Poetic Problems in Homer's "Odyssey."* Berkeley: University of California Press.
Bakhtin, M. M. 1981. *The Dialogic Imagination: Three Essays.* Ed. M. Holquist. Trans. C. Emerson and M. Holquist. Austin: University of Texas Press.
Barron, J. P. 1969. "Ibycus: To Polycrates." *BICS* 16: 119–149.
Becker, O. 1937. *Das Bild des Weges. Hermes* Einzelschriften 4. Berlin: Weidmann.
Bellamy, R. 1989. "Bellerophon's Tablet." *CJ* 84: 289–307.
Bentley, R. 1938. *Collected Works.* Ed. A. Dyce. London: MacPherson.

Benton, S. 1934–35. "Excavations in Ithaca, III: The Cave at Polis, I." *ABSA* 35: 45–73.

Benveniste, E. 1969. *Indo-European Language and Society.* Trans. E. Palmer. London: Faber and Faber.

Bernabé, A. 1988. *Poetae epici Graeci: Testimonia et fragmenta.* Leipzig: Teubner.

Bing, P. 1988. *The Well-Read Muse.* Göttingen: Vandenhoeck and Ruprecht.

Bloom, H. 1973. *The Anxiety of Influence: A Theory of Poetry.* London: Oxford University Press.

Böhme, R. 1937. *Das Prooimion.* Buhl: Baden.

Bowie, E. L. 1986. "Early Greek Elegy, Symposia, and Public Festivals." *JHS* 106: 13–35.

Bowra, C. M. 1952. *Heroic Poetry.* London: Macmillan.

Boyancé, P. 1937. *Le culte des Muses chez les philosophes grecs.* Paris: E. de Boccard.

Bremer, J. M., I. J. F. De Jong, and J. Kalff, eds. 1987. *Homer beyond Oral Poetry: Recent Trends in Homeric Interpretation.* Amsterdam: B. R. Grüner.

Bruneau, R. 1970. *Recherches sur les cultes de Délos à l'époque hellénistique et à l'époque impériale.* Paris: E. de Boccard.

Bundy, E. L. 1972. "The 'Quarrel between Kallimachos and Apollonios,' Part I: The Epilogue of Kallimachos' *Hymn to Apollo.*" *CSCA* 5: 39–94.

———. 1986. *Studia Pindarica.* Berkeley: University of California Press.

Burkert, W. 1972a. "Die Leistung eines Kreophylos: Kreophyleer, Homeriden und die archaische Heraklesepik." *Mus. Hel.* 29: 74–85.

———. 1972b. *Lore and Science in Ancient Pythagoreanism.* Cambridge: Harvard University Press. Rev. by the author and trans. by E. L. Miner, Jr., from *Weisheit und Wissenschaft.* Nürnburg: Hans Carl, 1962.

———. 1976. "Das Hunderttorige Theben und die Datierung der Ilias." *WSt.* 10: 5–21.

———. 1979. "Kynaithos, Polycrates, and the Homeric Hymn to Apollo." Pp. 53–62 in *Arktouros: Hellenic Studies Presented to Bernard M. W. Knox,* ed. G. W. Bowersock, W. Burkert, and M. C. J. Putnam. Berlin: Walter de Gruyter.

———. 1983a. "Itinerant Diviners and Magicians: A Neglected Element in Cultural Contacts." Pp. 115–119 in Hägg 1983.

———. 1983b. "Oriental Myth and Literature in the *Iliad.*" Pp. 51–56 in Hägg 1983.

———. 1984. *Die orientalisierende Epoche in der griechischen Religion und Literatur.* Heidelberg: C. Winter.

———. 1985. *Greek Religion.* Trans. J. Raffan. Cambridge: Harvard University Press.

———. 1987. "The Making of Homer in the Sixth Century B.C.: Rhapsodes versus Stesichoros." Pp. 43–62 in *Papers on the Amasis Painter and His World.* Malibu: Getty Museum.

Bury, J. B. 1965. *The Nemean Odes of Pindar.* Amsterdam: Hakkert.

Buschor, E. 1944. *Die Musen des Jenseits*. Munich: F. Bruckmann.

Bynum, D. E. 1969. "The Generic Nature of Oral Epic Poetry." *Genre* 3: 236–258.

Bywater, I. 1909. *Aristotle on the Art of Poetry*. Oxford: Clarendon Press.

Calame, C. 1977. *Les choeur des jeunes filles en Grèce archaïque*. 2 vols. Rome: Ateneo and Bizzarri.

Calhoun, G. M. 1938. "*Odyssey* VIII.499." *CP* 33: 205–206.

Càssola, F. 1975. *Inni omerici*. Milan: Fondazione Lorenzo Valla.

Chadwick, H. M., and N. K. Chadwick. 1940. *The Growth of Literature*. Cambridge: Cambridge University Press.

Chadwick, N. K. 1942. *Poetry and Prophecy*. Cambridge: Cambridge University Press.

Chantraine, P. 1977. 1968. *Dictionnaire étymologique de la langue grec*. 2 vols. Paris: Klincksieck.

Clay, J. S. 1972. "The Planktai and Moly: Divine Naming and Knowing in Homer." *Hermes* 100: 127–131.

——. 1974. "Demas and Aude: The Nature of Divine Transformation in Homer." *Hermes* 102: 129–136.

——. 1983. *The Wrath of Athena: Gods and Men in the Odyssey*. Princeton: Princeton University Press.

Coldstream, J. N. 1976. "Hero-Cults in the Age of Homer." *JHS* 96: 8–17.

——. 1977. *Geometric Greece*. London: Ernest Benn.

Cole, A. T. 1983. "Archaic Truth." *QUCC* n.s. 13: 7–28.

Cornford, F. M. 1952. *Principium Sapientiae: A Study of the Origins of Greek Philosophic Thought*. Cambridge: Cambridge University Press.

Cowgill, W. 1978. "*Agôn:Ageirô*, a New R/N Alternation." Pp. 29–32 in *Literary and Linguistic Studies in Honor of Archibald A. Hill*, ed. M. A. Jazayery et al. The Hague: Hain.

Cunliffe, R. J. 1986. *A Lexicon of the Homeric Dialect*. Norman: University of Oklahoma Press.

Curtius, E. R. 1953. *European Literature and the Latin Middle Ages*. Trans. Willard R. Trask. Princeton: Princeton University Press.

D = Davies 1988.

Davies, M. 1986. "Prolegomena and Paralegomena to a New Edition (with Commentary) of the Fragments of Early Greek Epic." *NGG* 2: 91–111.

——. 1988. *Epicorum Graecorum fragmenta*. Göttingen: Vandenhoeck and Ruprecht.

——. 1989. "The Date of the Epic Cycle." *Glotta* 67: 89–100.

Davison, J. A. 1955. "Peisistratus and Homer." *TAPA* 86: 1–21.

——. 1962. "The Transmission of the Text." Pp. 215–233 in Wace and Stubbings 1962.

De Martino, F. 1982. *Omero agonista in Delo*. Antichitá classica e cristiana 22. Brescia: Paideia Editrice.

Detienne, M. 1967. *Les maîtres de vérité dans la Grèce archaïque*. Paris: François Maspéro.

——, ed. 1988. *Les savoirs de l'écriture en Grèce ancienne.* Cahiers de Philologie 14. Lille: Presses Universitaires de Lille.

Detienne, M., and J.-P. Vernant. 1974. *Les ruses d'intelligence: La métis des grecs.* Flammarion: Paris. English translation by J. Lloyd, *Cunning Intelligence in Greek Culture and Society.* Brighton: Harvester Press; Atlantic Highlands, N.J.: Humanities Press, 1978.

Devereux, G. 1987. "Thamyris and the Muses." *AJP* 108: 199–201.

Diehl, E. 1940. "Fuerunt ante Homerum poetae." *Rh. Mus.* 89: 81–114.

Diels, H., and W. Kranz. 1952. *Die Fragmente der Vorsokratiker.* 6th ed. 3 vols. Berlin: Weidmann.

Dimock, G. E. 1963. "From Homer to Novi Pazaar and Back." *Arion* 2: 40–57.

——. 1989. *The Unity of the Odyssey.* Amherst: University of Massachusetts Press.

D-K = Diels and Kranz 1952.

Dodds, E. R. 1957. *The Greeks and the Irrational.* Berkeley: University of California Press.

Dunkel, G. 1979. "Fighting Words: Alcman Partheneion *Makhomai.*" *Journal of Indo-European Studies* 7: 249–272.

Durante, M. 1957. "Il nome di Omero." *Rend. Acc. Lincei.* 12: 94–113 (= Durante 1976: 185–204).

——. 1958. "Epea pteroenta: La parole come 'cammino' in immagini greche e vediche." *Rend. Acc. Linc.* 13: 3–14 (= Durante 1976: 123–134).

——. 1960. "Ricerche sulla preistoria della lingua poetica greca: La terminologia relativa alla creazione poetica." *Rend. Acc. Linc.* 15: 231–249 (= Durante 1976: 167–184).

——. 1971. *Sulla preistoria della tradizione poetica greca, parte prima: Continuità della tradizione poetica dall' età Micenea ai primi documenti.* Incunabula graeca 50. Roma: d'Ateneo.

——. 1976. *Sulla preistoria della tradizione poetica greca, parte seconda: Risultanze della comparazione indoeuropea.* Incunabula graeca 64. Roma: d'Ateneo.

Eagleton, T. 1990. *The Ideology of the Aesthetic.* Oxford: Blackwell.

Edwards, A. T. 1985. *Achilles in the "Odyssey."* Königstein/Ts.: Anton Hain.

Edwards, M. 1987. *Homer: Poet of the "Iliad."* Baltimore: Johns Hopkins University Press.

Egger, E. 1886. *Essai sur l'histoire de la critique chez les Grecs.* Paris: Pedone.

Else, G. F. 1967. *Aristotle's "Poetics": The Argument.* Cambridge: Harvard University Press.

Ernesti, J. C. T. 1962. *Lexicon technologiae Graecorum rhetoricae.* Rpt. Hildesheim: Georg Olms.

Fälter, O. 1934. *Der Dichter und sein Gott beui den Griechen und Römern.* Diss. Würtzberg.

Finley, M. I. 1965. *The World of Odysseus.* Rev. ed. New York: Viking Press.

——. 1975. *The Use and Abuse of History.* London: Chatto and Windus.

Finnegan, R. 1977. *Oral Poetry: Its Nature, Significance, and Social Context.* Cambridge: Cambridge University Press.

Foley, J. M., ed. 1981. *Oral Traditional Literature: A Festschrift for Albert Bates Lord.* Columbus, Ohio: Slavica.

Ford, A. 1985. "The Seal of Theognis: The Politics of Authorship in Archaic Greece." Pp. 82–95 in *Theognis of Megara: Poetry and the Polis,* ed. T. J. Figueira and G. Nagy. Baltimore: Johns Hopkins University Press.

———. 1988. "The Classical Definition of *RHAPSOIDIA.*" *CP* 83: 300–307.

Förstel, K. 1979. *Untersuchungen zum Homerischen "Apollonhymnos."* Bochum: Brockmeyer.

Fournier, H. 1946. *Les verbes "dire" en grec ancien.* Paris: Klincksieck.

Fraenkel, E., ed. 1950. *Aeschylus: "Agamemnon."* 3 vols. Rpt. 1980. Oxford: Clarendon Press.

Fränkel, H. 1923. "Homerische Wörter." Pp. 274–282 in *ANTIDORON: Festschrift Jacob Wackernagel.* Göttingen: Vandenhoeck and Ruprecht.

———. 1925. "Griechische Wörter. *Glotta* 14: 3–6.

———. 1960. *Wege und Formen frügriechischen Denkens.* 2d ed. Munich: C. H. Beck.

———. 1973. *Early Greek Poetry and Philosophy.* New York: Harcourt Brace Jovanovich. Trans. Moses Hadas and J. Willis from *Dichtung und Philosophie des frühen Griechentums.* 2d ed. Munich: C. H. Beck, 1962.

———. 1974. "Xenophanes' Empiricism and His Critique of Knowledge." Pp. 118–134 in *The Presocratics: A Collection of Critical Essays,* ed. A. P. Mourelatos. New York: Anchor Books.

Freccero, J. 1986. *Dante: The Poetics of Conversion.* Cambridge: Harvard University Press.

Frei, J. 1900. *De certaminibus thumelicis.* Diss. Basel.

Friedlander, P. 1914. "Das Proömium von Hesiods *Theogonie.*" *Hermes* 49: 1–16.

Friis Johansen, K. 1967. *The "Iliad" in Early Greek Art.* Copenhagen: Munksgaard.

Frisk, H. 1960–70. *Griechisches etymologisches Wörterbuch.* 2 vols. Heidelberg: Carl Winter.

Frontisi-Ducroux, F. 1986. *La cithare d'Achille: Essai sur la poétique de l'"Iliade."* Rome.

Gentile, B. 1984. 1988. *Poetry and Its Public in Ancient Greece: From Homer to the Fifth Century.* Trans. and intro. A. T. Cole. Baltimore: Johns Hopkins University Press.

Gernet, L. 1981. *The Anthropology of Ancient Greece.* Trans. J. Hamilton, S. J. Nagy, and B. Nagy. Baltimore: Johns Hopkins University Press.

Gnoli, G., and J.-P. Vernant, eds. 1982. *La mort: Les morts dans les sociétés anciennes.* Cambridge: Cambridge University Press.

Goody, J., and I. Watt. 1968. "The Consequences of Literacy." Pp. 27–68 in *Literacy in Traditional Societies,* ed. J. Goody. Cambridge: Cambridge University Press.

Görgemanns, G. 1976. "Rhetorik und Poetik im Homerischen *Hermeschymnus.*" Pp. 113–128 in Görgemanns and Schmidt 1976.

Görgemanns, G., and E. A. Schmidt, eds. 1976. *Studien zum antike Epos.* Meisenheim am Glan: Anton Hain.

Gow, A. S. F., ed. and trans. 1965. *Theorcritus.* 2 vols. Cambridge: Cambridge University Press.

Greindl, M. 1938. *KLEOS, KUDOS, EUCHOS, TIME, PHATIS, DOXA: Eine bedeutungsgeschichtliche Untersuchung des epischen und lyrischen Sprachgebrauches* Diss. Erlangen: Lengerich.

Gresseth, G. K. 1975. "The Gilgamesh Epic and Homer." *CJ* 70: 1–18.

Griffin, J. 1977. "The Epic Cycle and the Uniqueness of Homer." *JHS* 97: 39–53.

———. 1980. *Homer on Life and Death.* Oxford: Clarendon Press.

———. 1987. "Homer and Excess." Pp. 85–104 in Bremer et al. 1987.

Griffith, M. 1983. "Personality in Hesiod." *CA* 2: 37–65.

Grube, G. M. A. 1965. *The Greek and Roman Critics.* Toronto: University of Toronto Press.

Gudeman, A. 1934. *Aristotles: PERI POIHTIKHS.* Berlin: De Gruyter.

Hägg, R., ed. 1983. *The Greek Renaissance of the Eighth Century B.C.: Tradition and Innovation.* Proceedings of the Second International Symposium at the Swedish Institute in Athens, 1–5 June 1981. Stockholm: Åströms.

Hainsworth, J. B. 1969. *Homer.* Greece and Rome: New Surveys in the Classics 3. Oxford: Clarendon Press.

———. 1970. "The Criticism of an Oral Homer." *JHS* 90: 90–98.

Halliwell, S. 1986. *Aristotle's Poetics.* Chapel Hill: University of North Carolina Press.

Hansen, W. F. 1977. "Odysseus' Last Journey." *QUCC* 24: 27–50.

Harriott, R. 1969. *Poetry and Criticism before Plato.* London: Methuen.

Harris, W. V. 1989. *Ancient Literacy.* Cambridge: Harvard University Press.

Hartog, F. 1988. *The Mirror of Herodotus.* Berkeley: University of California Press. Trans. by J. Lloyd from *Le miroir d'Hérodote: Essai sur la représentation de l'autre.* Paris: NRF, 1980.

Harvey, A. E. 1955. "The Classification of Greek Lyric Poetry." *CQ* 49: 157–175.

Havelock, E. A. 1963. *Preface to Pato.* Cambridge: Harvard University Press.

Heath, M. 1985. "Hesiod's Didactic Poetry." *CQ* 35: 245–263.

Hédelin, François, abbé d'Aubignac. 1715. *Conjectures académiques; ou, Dissertation sur l'"Iliad."* Paris: Rpt., ed. V. Magnien, Paris: Hachette 1925.

Heldmann, K. 1982. *Die Niederlage Homers im Dichterwettstreit mit Hesiod.* Hypomnemata 75. Göttingen: Vandenhoeck and Ruprecht.

Herington, J. 1985. *Poetry into Drama: Early Tragedy and the Greek Poetic Tradition.* Berkeley: University of California Press.

Heubeck, A. 1966. "Thukydides III 104." *WS* 79: 148–157.

——. 1979. *Schrift*. Archaeologia Homerica 3.10. Göttingen: Vandenhoeck and Ruprecht.

——. 1982. "Zur neueren Homerforshung." *Gymnasium* 89: 385–447.

Heubeck, A., S. West, and J. B. Hainsworth. 1981. *Omero: "Odissea."* 6 vols. Milan: Fondazione Lorenzo Valla. Vols. 1 and 2 trans. as *A Commentary on Homer's "Odyssey."* Oxford: Clarendon Press, 1988–89.

Hiller, S. 1983. "Possible Historical Reasons for the Rediscovery of the Mycenean Past in the Age of Homer." Pp. 63–68 in Hägg 1983.

Hubbard, T. K. 1985. *The Pindaric Mind: A Study of Logical Structure in Early Greek Poetry.* Leiden: E. J. Brill.

Hutton, J. 1982. *Aristotle's Poetics.* New York: Norton.

Huxley, G. L. 1969. *Greek Epic Poetry.* Cambridge: Harvard University Press.

IEG = West 1971.

Janko, R. 1981. "The Structure of the Homeric Hymns: A Study in Genre." *Hermes* 109: 9–24.

——. 1982. *Homer, Hesiod, and the Hymns: Diachronic Development in Epic Diction.* Cambridge: Cambridge University Press.

——. 1986. "The *Shield of Heracles* and the Legend of Cycnus." *CQ* 36: 38–59.

Jeffery, L. H. 1962. *The Local Scripts of Archaic Greece.* Oxford: Clarendon Press.

——. 1976. *Archaic Greece: The City-States, c. 700–500 B.C.* London: Ernest Benn.

Jensen, M. S. 1980. *The Homeric Question and the Oral-Formulaic Theory.* Copenhagen: Museum Tusculanum.

——. 1986. "Storia e verità nei poemi omerici," *QUCC* 51: 21–38.

K = Kinkel 1877.

Kambylis, A. 1965. *Die Dichterweihe und ihre Symbolik.* Heidelberg: C. Winter.

Kannicht, R. 1988. *The Ancient Quarrel between Philosophy and Poetry: Aspects of the Greek Conception of Literature.* Canterbury: University of Canterbury.

Kant, I. 1973. *Critique of Judgement.* Trans. J. C. Meredith. New York: Oxford University Press.

Kassell, R., ed. 1976. *Aristotelis: "Ars Rhetorica."* Berlin: De Gruyter.

Kearns, E. 1982. "The Return of Odysseus: A Homeric Theoxeny." *CQ* 32: 2–8.

Kennedy, G., ed. 1989. *The Cambridge History of Literary Criticism,* vol. 1: *Classical Criticism.* Cambridge: Cambridge University Press.

Kinkel, G. 1877. *Epicorum Graecorum fragmenta.* Leipzig: Teubner.

Kirk, G. S. 1962. *The Songs of Homer.* Cambridge: Cambridge University Press.

——. 1985. *The "Iliad": A Commentary.* Vol. 1. Cambridge: Cambridge University Press.

Koller, H. 1956. "Das kitharodische Prooimion." *Phil.* 100: 159–206.

———. 1965. "*Thespis aoidos.*" *Glotta* 43: 277–285.

———. 1972. "*Epos.*" *Glotta* 50: 16–24.

Koster, S. 1970. *Antike Epostheorien.* Palingenesia 5. Wiesbaden: F. Steiner.

Kranz, W. 1924. "Das Verhältnis des Schöpfers zu seinem Werk in der althellenischen Literatur." *Neue Jahrbb.* 53: 65–86 (= Kranz 1967: 7–26).

———. 1961. "Sphragis: Ichform und Namensiegel als Eingangs und Schlussmotiv antiker Dichtung." *Rh. Mus.* 104: 3–46, 97–124 (= Kranz 1967: 27–78).

———. 1967. *Sphragis: Studien zur antike Literatur.* Heidelberg: C. Winter.

Kraus, W. 1955. "Die Auffassung des Dichtersberufes im frühen Griechentum." *W. St.* 68: 65–87.

Krischer, T. 1965a. "*Etumos* und *Alethes.*" *Phil.* 109: 161–174.

———. 1965b. "Die Entschuldigung des Sängers." *Rh. Mus.* 108: 1–11.

———. 1971. *Formale Konventionen der Homerischen Epik.* Zetemata 56. Munich: Beck.

Kristeller, P. O. 1951–52. "The Modern System of the Arts: A Study in the History of Aesthetics." *JHI* 12: 496–527 and 13: 17–46.

Kube, J. 1969. *TEXNH und APETH: Sophistisches und Platonisches Tugendwissen.* Berlin: De Gruyter.

Kullman, W. 1960. *Die Quellen der "Ilias."* *Hermes* Einzelschriften 14. Wiesbaden: F. Steiner.

Lamberton, R. 1983. *Porphyry: On the Cave of the Nymphs.* Barrytown, N.Y.: Station Hill.

Lanata, G. 1963. *Poetica preplatonica.* Florence: La Nuova Italia.

Latacz, J. 1985. *Homer.* Artemis Einfürungen 20. Munich: Artemis.

Latte, K. 1946. "Hesiod's Dichterweihe." *Ant. u. Abend.* 2: 152–63.

Lattimore, R., trans. 1951. *The "Iliad" of Homer.* Chicago: University of Chicago Press.

Leaf, W. 1900–1902. *The Iliad.* 2d ed. 2 vols. London: Rpt. Amsterdam: Adolf M. Hakkert, 1971.

Lefkowitz, M. K. 1984. "The Poet as Athlete." *SIFC* 77: 5–12.

Lenz, A. 1980. *Das Proöm des frühen greichischen Epos: Ein Beitrag am poetischen Selbstverständnis.* Bonn: Rudolf Habelt.

Le Roy, C. 1973. "La naissance d' Apollon." *Etudes Deliennes, BCH* Suppl. 1. Paris.

Lesky, A. 1957. *Geschichte der griechischen Literatur.* Bern: Francke.

LfrgE. = *Lexicon des frügriechischen Epos.* Ed. B. Snell et al. Göttingen: Vandenhoeck and Ruprecht, 1979–.

Ll-J–P = Lloyd-Jones and Parsons 1983.

Lloyd-Jones, H., and P. Parsons. 1983. *Supplementum Hellenisticum.* Berlin: De Gruyter.

Lord, A. B., ed. 1954. *Serbocroatian Heroic Songs.* Vol. 1. Cambridge: Harvard University Press.

———. 1960. *The Singer of Tales.* Cambridge: Harvard University Press.

——. 1962. "Homer and Other Epic Poetry." Pp. 179–214 in Wace and Stubbings 1962.

——. 1981. "Memory, Fixity, and Genre in Oral Traditional Poetics." Pp. 451–461 in Foley 1981.

LSJ = Liddell, H. G., R. Scott, and H. S. Jones, eds. 1940. *A Greek English Lexicon.* 9th ed. Oxford: Clarendon Press.

Lucas, D. W. 1968. *Aristotle: "Poetics."* Oxford: Clarendon Press.

Luther, W. 1935. *Warheit und Lüge im ältesten Griechentum.* Borna Leipzig: Robert Noske.

Lynn-George, M. 1988. *Epos: Word Narrative and the "Iliad."* London: Macmillan.

Macleod, C. 1983. "Homer on Poetry and the Poetry of Homer." Pp. 1–15 in *Collected Essays.* Oxford: Clarendon Press.

Maehler, H. 1963. *Die Auffassung des Dichterberufs im frühen Griechentum bis zur Zeit Pindars.* Hypomnemata 3. Göttingen: Vandenhoeck and Ruprecht.

——. 1982. *Die Lieder des Bakchylides*, pt. 1: *Die Siegeslieder.* Leiden.

Marg, W. 1957. *Homer über die Dichtung.* Orbis antiquus 11. Rpt. 1968. Münster: Aschendorff.

Martin, R. P. M. 1984. "Hesiod, Odysseus, and the Instruction of Princes." *TAPA* 114: 29–48.

——. 1989. *The Language of Heroes.* Ithaca: Cornell University Press.

Merkelbach, R., and M. L. West. 1967. *Fragmenta Hesiodea.* Oxford: Clarendon Press.

Meuli, K. 1938. "Scythica." *Hermes* 70: 121–176.

Meyer, E. 1918. "Die Rhapsoden und die Homerischen Epen." *Hermes* 53:330–336.

Meyer, H. 1933. *Hymnische Stilelemente in der frügriechischen Dichtung* Diss. Köln. Würtzburg: Konrad Triltsch.

Miller, A. M. 1983. "N. 4. 33–34 and the Defense of Digressive Leisure." *CJ* 78: 202–220.

——. 1986. *From Delos to Delphi: A Literary Study of the Homeric "Hymn to Apollo."* Mnemosune Sup. 93. Leiden: E. J. Brill.

Miller, D. G. 1982. *Improvisation, Typology, Culture, and "the New Orthodoxy": How Oral Is Homer?* Washington, D.C.: University Press of America.

Minton, W. W. 1960. "Homer's Invocations to the Muses: Traditional Patterns." *TAPA* 91: 292–309.

Moran, W. S. 1975. "*Mimnêskomai* and 'Remembering' Epic Stories in Homer and the Hymns." *QUCC* 20: 195–211.

Morris, I. 1988. "Tomb Cult and the 'Greek Renaissance': The Past in the Present in the 8th Century B.C." *Antiquity* 62: 750–61.

Moulton, C. 1977. *Similes in the Homeric Poems.* Hypomnemata 49. Göttingen: Vandenhoeck and Ruprecht.

Muellner, L. 1976. *The Meaning of Homeric EUXOMAI through Its Formulas.* Innsbruck: Innsbrucker Beiträge zur Sprachwissenschaft.

Murnagham, S. 1987. *Disguise and Recognition in the "Odyssey."* Princeton: Princeton University Press.

Murray, G. 1934. *The Rise of the Greek Epic.* 4th ed. Oxford: Oxford University Press.

Murray, P. 1981. "Poetic Inspiration in Early Greece." *JHS* 101: 87–100.

M-W = Merkelbach and West 1967.

Nagy, G. 1974. *Comparative Studies in Greek and Indic Meter.* Cambridge: Harvard University Press.

——. 1976. "Formula and Meter." Pp. 239–260 in Stolz and Shannon 1976.

——. 1979. *The Best of the Achaeans.* Baltimore: Johns Hopkins University Press.

——. 1982. "Hesiod." Pp. 43–74 in *Ancient Writers,* ed. T. J. Luce. New York: Scribner's.

——. 1983. "Sêma and Noêsis: Some Illustrations." *Arethusa* 16: 35–55.

Nannini, S. 1982. "Lirica greca arcaica e *recusatio* augustea." *QUCC* n.s. 39: 71–78.

Niles, J. D. 1983. *"Beowulf": The Poem and Its Tradition.* Cambridge: Harvard University Press.

Norden, E. 1913. *Agnostos Theos: Untersuchungen zur Formengeschichte religiöser Rede.* Leipzig: Teubner.

Norwood, G. 1945. *Pindar.* Berkeley: University of California Press.

Notopolous, J. A. 1938. "*Mnemosune* in Oral Literature." *TAPA* 69: 465–493.

——. 1949. "Parataxis in Homer." *TAPA* 80: 1–23.

——. 1951. "Continuity and Interconnection in Homeric Oral Composition." *TAPA* 82: 81–101.

——. 1964. "Studies in Early Greek Oral Poetry." *HSCP* 68: 1–77.

Ong, W. J., S. J. 1977. *Interfaces of the Word: Studies in the Evolution of Consciousness and Culture.* Ithaca: Cornell University Press.

——. 1982. *Orality and Literacy.* London: Methuen.

Page = Page 1962.

Page, D., ed. 1962. *Poetae melici Graeci.* Oxford: Clarendon Press.

——. 1974. *Supplementum lyricis Graecis: Poetarum lyricorum Graecorum fragmenta quae recens innotuerunt.* Oxford: Clarendon Press.

Pagliaro, A. 1951. "La terminologia poetica di Omero" *Ricerche linguistiche* 2: 1–46.

——. 1956. "Il proemio dell' *Iliade.*" Pp. 3–46 in *Nuovi saggi di critica semantica.* 2d ed. Messina: G. d'Anna.

Parry, A. 1966. "Have We Homer's *Iliad?*" *YCS* 20: 175–216.

Parry, M. 1970. 1932 "Studies in the Epic Technique of Oral Verse-Making II." *HSCP* 43: 1–50 (= M. Parry 1971: 325–364).

——. 1971. *The Making of Homeric Verse: The Collected Papers of Milman Parry,* ed. A. Parry. Oxford: Oxford University Press.

Patey, D. L. 1988. "The Eighteenth Century Invents the Canon." *Modern Language Studies* 18: 17–37.

Pavese, C. O. 1967. "Alcmane, il 'Partenio' del Louvre." *QUCC* 4: 113–133.

Peradotto, J. 1990. *Man in the Middle Voice: Name and Narrative in the "Odyssey."* Princeton: Princeton University Press.

Perry, B. E. 1937. "The Early Greek Capacity for Seeing Things Separately." *TAPA* 68: 403–427.

Pfeiffer, R., ed. 1949–1953. *Callimachus.* 2 vols. Oxford: Clarendon Press.

———. 1968. *History of Classical Scholarship: From the Beginnings to the End of the Hellenistic Age.* Oxford: Clarendon Press.

Pfister, F. 1933. Review of G. Herzog-Hauser, *Soter: Die Vorstellung des Retters im altgriechischen Epos.* (Vienna) *Philol. Woch.* 53: 936–943.

Polignac, F. de. 1984. *La naissance de la cité grecque.* Paris: Editions de la Découverte.

Pritchard, J. B. 1954. *Ancient Near Eastern Texts relating to the Old Testament.* Princeton: Princeton University Press.

Pucci, P. 1977. *Hesiod and the Language of Poetry.* Baltimore: Johns Hopkins University Press.

———. 1979. "The Song of the Sirens." *Arethusa* 12: 121–132.

———. 1980. "The Language of the Muses." Pp. 163–186 in *Classical Mythology in Twentieth Century Thought and Literature,* ed. W. M. Aycock and T. M. Klein. Lubbock: Texas Tech Press.

———. 1982. "The Proem of the *Odyssey.*" *Arethusa* 15: 39–62.

———. 1987. *Odysseus Polutropos: Intertextual Readings in the "Odyssey" and the "Iliad."* Ithaca: Cornell University Press.

Redfield, J. 1973. "The Making of the *Odyssey.*" Pp. 141–154 in *Parnassus Revisited: Modern Critical Essays on the Epic Tradition,* ed. A. C. Yu. Chicago: American Library Association. Also pp. 1–17 in *Essays in Western Civilization in Honor of Christian W. Mackauer,* ed. L. Botstein and E. Karnofsky. Chicago: College of the University of Chicago, 1967.

———. 1975. *Nature and Culture in the "Iliad."* Chicago: University of Chicago Press.

———. 1979. "The Proem of the *Iliad*: Homer's Art." *CP* 74: 95–110.

Reinhardt, K. 1916. *Parmenides und die Geschichte der griechischen Philosophie.* Bonn: Friedrich Cohen.

———. 1961. *Die "Ilias" und ihr Dichter,* ed. U. Hölscher. Göttingen: Vandenhoeck and Ruprecht.

Renehan, R. 1976. *Studies in Greek Texts.* Hypomnemata 43. Göttingen: Vandenhoeck and Ruprecht.

Richardson, N. J. 1974. *The Homeric "Hymn to Demeter."* Oxford: Clarendon Press.

———. 1985. "Pindar and Later Literary Criticism in Antiquity." *Papers of the Liverpool Latin Seminar* 5: 383–401.

Risch, E. 1974. *Wortbildung der Homerischen Sprache.* Berlin: Walter de Gruyter.

Ritoók, Zs. 1989. "The Views of Early Greek Epic on Poetry and Art." *Mnem.* 42: 331–348.

Romer, F. E. 1982. "The *Aisumneteia:* A Problem in Aristotle's Historical Method." *AJP* 103: 25–46.

Rose, V., ed. 1886. *Aristotelis qui ferebantur librorum fragmenta.* 3d ed. Leipzig: Teubner.

Rösler, W. 1980. "Die Entdeckung der Fiktionalität in der Antike." *Poetica* 12: 283–319.

———. 1985. "Alte und neue Mündlichkeit: Über kulturellen Wandel im antiken Griechenland und heute." *Der altsprachliche Unterricht* 28: 4–26.

Russo, J., and B. Simon. 1968. "Homeric Psychology and the Oral Epic Tradition." *Journal for the History of Ideas* 29: 483–498.

Rüter, K. 1969. *Odysseeinterpretationen: Untersuchungunen zum ersten Buch und zur Phaiakis.* Hypomnemata 19. Göttingen: Vandenhoeck and Ruprecht.

Said, E. 1975. *Beginnings.* New York: Basic Books.

Schadewaldt, W. 1965. *Von Homers Welt und Werk.* 4th rev. ed. Stuttgart: K. F. Koehler.

———. 1973. "Der Umfang des Begriffs der Literatur in der Antike." Pp. 12–25 in *Literatur und Dichtung,* ed. H. Rüdiger. Stuttgart: K. F. Koehler.

Schein, S. L. 1984. *The Mortal Hero: An Introduction to Homer's "Iliad."* Berkeley: University of California Press.

Schmid, W., and O. Stählin. 1929. *Geschichte der griechischen Literatur.* Vol. 1. Munich: C. H. Beck.

Schmitt, R. 1967. *Dichtung und Dichtersprache in indogermanischer Zeit.* Wiesbaden: Harassowitz.

Schwartz, E. 1940. "Der Name Homeros." *Hermes* 75: 1–9.

Scodel, R. 1982. "The Achaean Wall and the Myth of Destruction." *HSCP* 82: 33–50.

Segal, C. P. 1983. "*Kleos* and Its Ironies in the *Odyssey.*" *Ant. Class.* 52: 22–47.

Setti, A. 1958. "La memoria e il canto: Saggio di poetica arcaica greca." *SIFC* 30: 129–171.

Sinos, D. 1980. *Achilles, Patroclus, and the Meaning of Philos.* Innsbruck: Innsbrucker Beiträge zur Sprachwissenschaft.

Snell, B. 1924. *Die Ausdrücke für den Begriff des Wissens in der vorplatonischen Philosophie.* Philologische Untersuchungen 29. Berlin: Weidmann.

———. 1953. *The Discovery of the Mind.* Trans. from the 2d ed. (Hamburg: Claasen and Goverts) by T. G. Rosenmeyer. Cambridge: Harvard University Press.

———. 1964. "Mnemosune in der frühgriechischen Dichtung." *Arch. für Begriff.* 9: 19–21.

Snodgrass, A. 1971. *The Dark Age of Greece: An Archaeological Survey of the Eleventh to the Eighth Centuries.* Edinburgh: Edinburgh University Press.

———. 1980. *Archaic Greece: The Age of Experiment.* London: Dent.

———. 1982. "Les origines du culte des héros dans la Grèce antique." Pp. 107–120 in Gnoli and Vernant 1982.

——. 1987. *An Archaeology of Greece*. Berkeley: University of California Press.

Solmsen, F. 1961. *Aristotle's System of the Physical World*. Ithaca: Cornell University Press.

Sowa, C. A. 1984. *Traditional Themes and the Homeric Hymns*. Chicago: Bolchazy-Carducci.

Sperdutti, A. 1950. "The Divine Nature of Poetry in Antiquity." *TAPA* 81: 209–240.

Stanford, W. B. 1974. *The "Odyssey" of Homer*. 2d rev. ed. London: Macmillan.

Stevens, W. 1942. *The Necessary Angel: Essays on Reality and the Imagination*. New York: Knopf.

Stolz, B. A., and R. S. Shannon, eds. 1976. *Oral Literature and the Formula*. Ann Arbor: University of Michigan.

Svenbro, J. 1976. *La parole et le marbre: Aux origines de la poétique grecque*. Lund: Studentlitteratur.

Thalmann, W. G. 1984. *Conventions of Form and Thought in Early Greek Poetry*. Baltimore: Johns Hopkins University Press.

——. 1988. "Thersites: Comedy, Scapegoats, and Heroic Ideology in the *Iliad*." *TAPA* 118: 1–28.

Thomas, R. 1989. *Oral Tradition and Written Record in Classical Athens*. Cambridge: Cambridge University Press.

Tigerstedt, E. N. 1970. "*Furor Poeticus*: Poetic Inspiration in Greek Literature before Democritus and Plato." *JHI* 31: 163–178.

Van der Valk, M. H. 1963–64. *Researches on the Text and Scholia of the "Iliad."* 2 vols. Leiden: Brill.

Van Groningen, B. A. 1946. "The Proems of the *Iliad* and the *Odyssey*." *Mededelingen der Koninklijke Nederlandsche Akademie van Wetenschappen, Afd. Letterkunde* n.s. 9.8: 279–294.

——. 1958. *La composition littéraire archaïque grecque*. Amsterdam: North Holland.

Vernant, J.-P. 1959. "Aspects mythiques de la mémoire en Grèce." *Journal de psychologie* 56: 1–29 (= Vernant 1965: 51–94).

——. 1965. *Mythe et pensée chez les grecs*. Paris: François Maspéro.

——. 1982. "La belle mort et le cadavre outragé." Pp. 45–76 in Gnoli and Vernant 1982.

Vidal-Naquet, P. 1981. "Land and Sacrifice in the *Odyssey*." Pp. 80–94 in *Myth, Religion, and Sacrifice*, ed. R. S. Gordon. Cambridge: Cambridge University Press.

Voigt, E.-M., ed. 1971. *Sappho et Alcaeus*. Amsterdam: Polak and Van Gennep.

Wace, A. J. B., and F. H. Stubbings, eds. 1962. *A Companion to Homer*. New York: Macmillan.

Wade-Gery, H. T. 1952. *The Poet of the "Iliad."* Cambridge: Cambridge University Press.

Walsh, G. B. 1984. *The Varieties of Enchantment: Early Greek Views of the Nature and Function of Poetry.* Chapel Hill: University of North Carolina Press.

Weber, L. 1934. *"ALLE AOIDE." Phil. Woch.* 445–448.

Webster, T. B. L. 1939. "Greek Theories of Art and Literature Down to 400 B.C." *CQ* 33: 166–179.

———. 1964. *From Mycenae to Homer.* New York: Norton.

Wegner, M. 1968. *Music und Tanz.* Archaeologia Homerica U 3. Göttingen: Vandenhoeck and Ruprecht.

Weiler, I. 1974. *Der Agon im Mythos: Zur Einstellung der Griechen zum Wettkampf.* Darmstadt: Wissenschaftliche Buchgesellschaft.

West, M. L., ed. 1966. *Hesiod: "Theogony."* Oxford: Clarendon Press.

———, ed. 1971. *Iambi et elegi Graeci.* 2 vols. Oxford: Clarendon Press.

———. 1973. "Greek Poetry, 2000–700 B.C." *CQ* 23: 179–192.

———. 1974. *Studies in Greek Elegy and Iambus.* Berlin: Walter de Gruyter.

———, ed. 1978. *Hesiod: "Works and Days."* Oxford: Clarendon Press.

———. 1981. "The Singing of Homer" *JHS* 101: 113–129.

———. 1985. *The Hesiodic "Catalogue of Women."* Oxford: Clarendon Press.

———. 1988. "The Rise of the Greek Epic." *JHS* 108: 151–172.

Whitley, J. 1988. "Early States and Hero Cults: A Re-appraisal." *JHS* 108: 173–182.

Whitman, C. 1958. *Homer and the Heroic Tradition.* Cambridge: Harvard University Press.

Wilamowitz-Moellendorff, U. von. 1903. *Timotheos: "Die Perser."* Leipzig: J. C. Hinrichs.

———. 1916. *Die "Ilias" und Homer.* Berlin: Weidmann.

———, ed. 1929. *Vitae Homeri et Hesiodi.* Berlin: de Gruyter.

Williams, F. 1978. *Callimachus: "Hymn to Apollo": A Commentary.* Oxford: Clarendon Press.

Windekins, A. J., van 1986. *Dictionnaire étymologique complémentaire de la langue grecque.* Paris: Peeters.

Wolf, F. A. 1963. *Prolegomena ad Homerum.* Rpt. of 1795 Hall ed. Hildesheim: Georg Olms. English trans. by A. Grafton, G. W. Most, and J. G. Zetzel, *Prolegomena to Homer.* Princeton: Princeton University Press, 1985.

Wünsch, R. 1914. "Hymnos." *RE* 9: 140–183.

Yates, F. 1966. *The Art of Memory.* London: Routledge and Kegan Paul.

Young, D. C. 1983. "Pindar, Aristotle, and Homer: A Study in Ancient Criticism." *CA* 2: 156–170.

Zanker, G. 1981. "Enargeia in the Ancient Criticism of Poetry." *Rh. Mus.* 124: 297–311.

INDEX LOCORUM

GENERAL INDEX

Achilles: and Aeneas, 64–67; arms of, 168–169, 194; funeral of, 158–159; sings *klea andrôn*, 16, 60, 123; tomb of, 143–144, 170
aeidein, 16, 178n
Aethiopis, 83, 159
agôn, 116
akamatos, 191–193
alêtheia. See Truth
Allegorical interpretation, 165, 169n
amaimaketos, 190n, 191n
Anachronistic interpretation, 17, 49, 51, 72, 136
Animal voices, 16n, 176–178, 190
aoidê, 15, 36–39, 47, 112n, 180
aoidos, 13, 16, 32, 47, 180
Argonauts, song of, 128
arkhomai + genitive, 27, 46, 112
arrêktos, 152, 193
Artisanal metaphors for poetry, 35–39, 168–170, 193. *See also* Making; Weaving
aspetos, 183–184
ateirês, 193–194
athesphatos, 182–183, 189–190
audê, 174, 177–179
Audience: of epic, 7, 14–15, 20–23, 89–92, 109, 126–127; within epic, 28, 30–31, 51–56
Authorship, 14, 34, 68–69, 135–136
autodidaktos, 33, 34, 42, 95

Beginnings, 18–19, 77, 82. *See also arkhomai* + *genitive*
Beowulf, 36
Bird Divination, 30, 44n

Calchas, 48, 55, 87–88
Calypso, 106, 110, 176, 178
Catalog poetry: 45, 75–80, 185, 195–196; of women, 30, 45, 46, 76
Cave of the Nymphs, 165–167, 184n
Cenotaphs, 161
Cerberus, 181n, 194
Competition among poets, 94–117, 118–120
Cypria, 149

Delos, 119–120
dêmiourgos, 36–37

Echenous, 60
Elegiac poetry, 29–30
Empedocles, 30
enargês, 54. *See also* Vividness
Enchantment, 51n, 52, 83–84
Endings, 44–45, 83. *See also lêgô*
Epic, definition of, 30–31, 46–47
Epic distance, 30–31, 126n, 148–149. *See also* History
Epic objectivity, 23, 53
epos, 29, 35, 65

Library of Congress Cataloging-in-Publication Data

Ford, Andrew Laughlin
    Homer : the poetry of the past / Andrew Ford.
       p.   cm.
    Includes bibliographical references and indexes.
    ISBN 0-8014-2700-2 (alk. paper)
    1. Homer—Criticism and interpretation.   2. Epic poetry, Greek—History and
criticism.   I. Title.
    PA4037.F56   1992   91-55543
    883'.01—dc20